The Road to
St Helena

The Road to St Helena

NAPOLEON AFTER WATERLOO

J. DAVID MARKHAM

Pen & Sword
MILITARY

To my nephew, Adam David Kent, who, like Napoleon,
inspires pride in all who know him.

First published in Great Britain in 2008 by
Pen & Sword Military
An imprint of
Pen & Sword Books Ltd
47 Church Street
Barnsley
South Yorkshire
S70 2AS

ISBN 978-1-84415-751-8

Printed and bound in England
By Biddles Ltd, King's Lynn, Norfolk

Pen & Sword Books Ltd incorporates the imprints of Pen & Sword Aviation,
Pen & Sword Maritime, Pen & Sword Military, Wharncliffe Local History,
Pen & Sword Select, Pen & Sword Military Classics and Leo Cooper.

For a complete list of Pen & Sword titles please contact
PEN & SWORD BOOKS LIMITED
47 Church Street, Barnsley, South Yorkshire, S70 2AS, England
E-mail: enquiries@pen-and-sword.co.uk
Website: www.pen-and-sword.co.uk

Contents

Illustrations

All illustrations are from the David Markham Collection

Engraving showing Napoleon as he looked in exile on Elba

Gilt snuffbox, dated 1815, showing Napoleon, Marie Louise and their son, the King of Rome

Early nineteenth-century engraving showing Napoleon's triumphal return to the Tuileries Palace

Nineteenth-century engraving of Marshal Emmanuel Grouchy

Marshal Ney, in a rare nineteenth-century engraving by Martinet

Nineteenth-century engraving after the painting by Steuben, showing Napoleon as he leaves the field of Waterloo

Mid-nineteenth-century porcelain statue showing the Marquis de La Fayette

Marshal Joachim Murat, one of Napoleon's greatest soldiers

King Louis XVIII, in a period engraving

Francis II, Napoleon's father-in-law, in an 1815 engraving

Nineteenth-century engraving of Field Marshal Blücher

Snuffbox showing the Duke of Wellington

Joseph Fouché, in a nineteenth-century engraving

Nineteenth-century engraving of Marshal Louis Nicolas Davout, one of Napoleon's best marshals

Nineteenth-century engraving of Charles Maurice de Talleyrand-Périgord

Period painting on ivory showing Count Molé, whose memoirs are key to understanding this period

Period miniature on ivory of Mlle George, a beautiful and gifted actress, whose charms Napoleon enjoyed during the Hundred Days

Nineteenth-century engraving of Armand-Augustin-Louis Caulaincourt, Duke of Vicence

Period miniature on ivory of General Henri Gratien Bertrand, one of Napoleon's most loyal companions

Nineteenth-century engraving of Napoleon's stepdaughter, Queen Hortense

Napoleon's home on the Île d'Aix

The commemorative plaque on the monument

Napoleon's brother Joseph, in a rare period engraving

Period engraving (detail) showing Baron General Charles Lallemand

Count Emmanuel Las Cases, in an 1824 engraving

Count Charles Montholon who followed Napoleon to St Helena

1825 engraving showing Napoleon leaving French soil for the last time

Captain Frederick Maitland, who received Napoleon aboard his ship

Large period engraving showing Napoleon returning as Caesar, accompanied by Winged Victory and happy cherubs

Preface and Acknowledgements

Few people in all of human history command as much interest as Napoleon Bonaparte. His rise from virtual obscurity to become one of history's most towering figures has inspired countless books, articles, documentaries, podcasts and works of art. His abilities as a reforming ruler and a conquering emperor are the stuff of legend.

Yet, ironically, it is the end of his career, from the Battle of Waterloo in June 1815 to his death in exile in St Helena on 5 May 1821 that often seems to inspire the most interest. Perhaps it is because, like Caesar two thousand years earlier, Napoleon was throwing the dice one last time in an all-or-nothing bid for power. Perhaps it is the story of what might have been, or the tales of treachery and deceit that capture the imagination. Certainly the pathos of a fallen emperor, his options running out, unsure where to turn and finally turning to the British who, for his efforts, condemned him to lonely exile on a desolate rock in the South Atlantic, is guaranteed to enthrall all but the most jaded reader.

This, then, is the story that I shall tell here. To tell it, I have consulted every memoir that has been translated into English and that covers this period. Some of them are quite rare and I have felt free to include some lengthy quotes to give the reader a real flavor of how people who were there felt about what happened. I have also read and consulted a number of secondary sources. Finally, I have had the complete set of the laws of the Hundred Days translated, as well as a number of other documents important to this story. All but the accounts of Napoleon at Rochefort and Aix that were published in periodicals are in my private library, and all of the images used in this book are from my collection. Any quotes have remained untouched save for occasional modernization of punctuation and correction of minor spelling errors.

As always, any number of people deserve to be thanked for their help. This is my second book for Pen & Sword, and one of the real benefits of that relationship has been the opportunity to work with Rupert Harding. His encouragement and ideas are invaluable. Indeed, this book was actually his idea. Special thanks also to Susan Milligan, who served as copy-editor for this book, as she did for my *Napoleon and Dr Verling on St Helena* (Pen & Sword, 2005). Her friendly professionalism is greatly appreciated. As has always been the case, all of the major translation work has been done by my friend and native French-speaker Bernadette Workman. Without her help, much of the material would have been left out of this story.

I have obtained a rather large collection of the *Bulletin des Lois* from this and other periods in Napoleon's career, and I am indebted to my friend, David Fayon, for his help in obtaining them and his guidance in selecting them. Another friend, Xavier Pénicaut, has been most helpful in obtaining some excellent engravings for this and other books. Both of these French gentlemen are experts and excellent sources. Betje Klier and Jonathan North were also most helpful in obtaining some important primary source material, and to them I extend my sincere gratitude.

Thanks also to my dear friend and colleague John G. 'Jerry' Gallaher for helping find some important sources and, as always, giving much needed advice and encouragement.

Of course, the greatest praise is reserved for my wife, Barbara. Without her help and encouragement this project, like all others I undertake, would have been far more difficult and far less successful. She encourages me to 'get back to work' when I lag, edits my work and doesn't hold back any suggestions for improvement. Together we have followed Napoleon throughout Europe. For this book, in 2005 we joined a good friend, Tom Morgan, on a visit to Rochefort and the Île d'Aix, places that are the centerpiece to the last phase of this story. To stand where Napoleon last stood on French soil was one of my most memorable moments.

As always, any success this book may achieve must be shared with these and others who have encouraged my work. Any errors or omissions are mine alone.

J. David Markham
www.NapoleonicHistory.com
Olympia, Washington, 2007

Cast of Characters

Bathurst, Earl Henry (1762–1834). Lord Bathurst had a long and somewhat distinguished political career. His duties included service as Master of the Mint, Foreign Secretary, President of the Board of Trade and Secretary for War and the Colonies. He gave Wellington necessary support during the Peninsular campaign and was involved in deciding Napoleon's fate after Waterloo, having the unhappy task of telling the Emperor that he was going to St Helena as a general.

Beauharnais, Hortense de (1783–1837). Hortense was Josephine's daughter with her first husband, General Beauharnais, who was executed during the Terror. Her brother Eugène was a loyal supporter of Napoleon, and Hortense matched his love for and loyalty to their stepfather. Napoleon ordered her to be married to his brother Louis, and the couple eventually served as king and queen of Holland. Louis was neither a great king nor husband, and the two separated. After Napoleon's fall, Hortense lived at Malmaison and provided much support for Napoleon after Waterloo. Her memoirs, while sometimes suspect, are an important look at Napoleon from a very personal point of view.

Beker, Lieutenant General Nicolas-Léonard Bagert, Count of Mons (1770–1840). A cavalry general who rose during the French Revolution (he was wounded at the Battle of Valmy), Beker served under Ney in 1797 and later was sent to Santo Domingo. He was taken prisoner in Italy in 1799 but soon exchanged. Other major actions include Austerlitz, Pultusk and Essling, where his actions disgraced him in the eyes of Napoleon. Elected a member of the Chamber of Peers in 1815, Beker was put in charge of the defense of Paris and subsequently assigned to accompany Napoleon to Rochefort.

Bertrand, Henri Gratien, General, Comte de (1778–1844). An able general and loyal companion, Bertrand served Napoleon in numerous campaigns. But he is most known for his service on Elba and, especially, during the Hundred Days and the St Helena exile. Loyal to the end, Bertrand was with Napoleon when he died, having served as Grand Marshal of the Palace on both Elba and St Helena. After a stint as Commandant of the École Polytechnique, Bertrand was selected to accompany Napoleon's body back to Paris from his burial plot on St Helena.

Blücher, Field Marshal Gebhard Leberecht von, Prince of Wahlstadt (1742–1819). Blücher started his military career in the Swedish army but after being a prisoner of war he switched to the Prussians in 1760. He had success against the French forces during the French Revolutionary Wars and developed an almost pathological hatred of all things French. After the Prussian defeat in 1806, Blücher had little to do until 1813, when he took up the cause against the French. His great success at the Battle of Leipzig led to his promotion by King Frederick William III to Field Marshal. The Campaign of France in 1814 brought him more success. Napoleon's return in 1815 brought him into action one more time. He was defeated at Ligny and almost captured or killed by the French, but survived to link up with Wellington at Waterloo, which was the primary reason for the Allied victory in that battle. Blücher would have shot Napoleon on the spot had he captured him during the move to Paris, but he just missed catching him at Malmaison. Blücher was one of the best, and certainly one of the most colorful, of all the Allied commanders.

Bonaparte, Joseph, King of Naples, King of Spain (1768–1844). Joseph was Napoleon's older brother but always understood that Napoleon was head of the family. Loyal to his brother, Joseph served in numerous positions, including as a member of the Council of Five Hundred, as ambassador to Parma and Rome, and as Napoleon's representative in the negotiation for the treaties of Luneville and Amiens. Joseph served as King of Naples, but Napoleon later coerced him into taking the title of King of Spain, a role for which he was ill suited. His liberal reforms met with strong resistance from the Spanish peasants and he was eventually driven out of the country. He was accused of leaving Paris prematurely in 1814, but rallied to the cause in 1815. Unlike Napoleon, Joseph made good his escape to the United States and lived in Philadelphia for most of his remaining years.

Bonaparte, Lucien (1775–1849). Lucien was an important supporter of his brother Napoleon in the early years, using his Jacobin connections to rally support to Napoleon's cause. He was President of the Council of Five Hundred when Napoleon took power, and used that position to stave off a crisis brought on by Napoleon's unexpected fumbling at the critical moment. After that, however, Lucien had little to do with his brother or the Empire, though he did rally to Napoleon during the Hundred Days. After Napoleon's exile, Lucien moved to Italy where he spent most of the rest of his life.

Bunbury, Lieutenant General Sir Henry Edward (1778–1860). After an education befitting his privileged station in life, Bunbury served in the British army from 1795 until 1809. Though his career was not especially distinguished (save for action at the Battle of Maida in Italy in 1806), Bunbury was appointed Under-Secretary of State for War and the Colonies in 1809, a post he held until 1816. It was in this capacity that he was given the task of telling Napoleon that he would be sent to St Helena rather than to England.

Carnot, Count Lazare (1753–1823). Carnot was an engineer officer who was active in the French Revolution, eventually serving as head of the War Section for the Committee on Public Safety. He worked to reorganize the army and was instrumental in its success in both the Revolution and the Empire. He served Napoleon as Minister of War during the early days of the Consulate, but his Revolutionary ideals put him at cross-purposes with Napoleon, especially during the Empire. Napoleon recognized that a man with his republican reputation would be very useful during the Hundred Days and brought him into the government as Minister of the Interior. This gave Napoleon the support of the liberals who might otherwise have opposed his return, but Waterloo and Fouché crushed that coalition.

Caulaincourt, Armand-Augustin-Louis, Marquis de, Duke of Vicence (1773–1827). Caulaincourt first came to Napoleon's attention in 1801 with a mission to Russia, and over time he became one of Napoleon's most loyal supporters. He played several roles, including ambassador to Russia, controller of the imperial household and, in 1813, Foreign Minister. He accompanied Napoleon to Russia in 1812 (an invasion taken over his objections), and rallied to the cause in 1815, again as Foreign Minister. He served as a member of the Provisional Government, but was unable to overcome Fouché's work to force Napoleon from power.

Davout, Marshal Louis Nicolas, Duke of Auerstädt, Prince of Eckmühl (1770–1823). Davout was one of the best and most loyal of all the marshals and served Napoleon from the Egyptian campaign to the Hundred Days. His major battles include Austerlitz, Auerstädt, Eylau and Wagram. He performed well in Russia, and rallied to Napoleon in the Hundred Days, where he served as Minister of War and Military Governor of Paris. He remained loyal to Napoleon until he felt that his loyalty to the army required him to work to preserve it rather than Napoleon's imperial title. His efforts gained him exile and demotion from all his titles, but everything was restored a few years later.

Decrès, Admiral Duke Denis, Minister of Marine (1761–1820). Decrès joined the navy at a very early age and rose rapidly through the officer ranks. After service in India he became a rear admiral in 1797. He blew up his ship rather than let it be captured at Aboukir in 1800, and for that Napoleon gave him a Sabre of Honor in 1804. He served as Minister of Marine from 1801–14, but switched to the Bourbon cause during the First Restoration. He was assassinated by his valet in 1820.

Flahaut, General Count Charles-Auguste-Joseph (1785–1870). Flahaut had the dubious distinction of being a son of Talleyrand, the result of an affair with Flahaut's mother. He distinguished himself at the Battle of Marengo and was soon an aide-de-camp to Marshal Murat. His affair with Countess Potocki, Anna Poniatowski while serving in Warsaw gave him unwanted attention, but he served with distinction in Spain and Russia, becoming in 1812 a general of division. Old habits die hard and many believe he was Hortense's lover, fathering the Duke of Morny. During the Hundred Days, Napoleon sent him on an unsuccessful mission to Vienna to bring Marie Louise to Paris. Though he was loyal to Napoleon to the end, Talleyrand protected him after Napoleon's fall, and he retired to England where he married Admiral George Keith Elphinstone's daughter.

Fleury de Chaboulon, Baron Pierre Alexandre Édouard (1799–1835). A skilled administrator, Fleury de Chaboulon (whose name appears in different forms) served as an auditor in the council of state and then as a sub-prefect. During the difficult years of 1813 and 1814, de Chaboulon was noted for his excellent administrative service as well as courage when France was invaded. Marshal Ney thought highly of him and Napoleon gave him important duties in organizing resistance in Reims in 1814. De Chaboulon twice visited Napoleon on Elba and met the Emperor in Lyons when he returned for the Hundred Days. Napoleon made him his Fourth Secretary and sent him on a mission to Basel in early May. After Waterloo, de Chaboulon was allowed to retire to England, where in 1819 he published his memoirs. Napoleon was highly critical of this work and said so in an extensively annotated copy of the two-volume work. Even so, de Chaboulon's memoirs continue to serve as a significant source of basic information on this period, and his inclusion of various letters and other documents is invaluable.

Fouché, Joseph, Duke of Otranto (1759–1820). After beginning studies for the priesthood, Fouché turned to politics during the French Revolution. He took his work seriously, and became a strong supporter of Robespierre and the Terror. He was known for his brutal revenge against counter-revolutionary forces and voted for the death of Louis XVI. The ultimate survivor, Fouché avoided Robespierre's fate and played a role in the Directory. Fouché was always able to anticipate events, and declared his support for Napoleon before the coup that put him in power. He soon came into his own with his appointment as Minister of Police. His secret police were feared by all, including perhaps Napoleon himself. Fouché had an on-again, off-again relationship with Napoleon, serving as Minister of Police from 1800–2 and then from 1804–10.

Loyalty, however, was not his strong point, and Napoleon broke with him in 1810 due to strong suspicion that Fouché was plotting with royalists. In 1814 he ingratiated himself with Louis XVIII while staying in touch with Napoleon in exile on Elba.

Napoleon appointed him Minister of Police for the Hundred Days, but his lack of loyalty doomed the restored Emperor to yet another exile. To the dismay of many in his court, Louis XVIII gave him a role in the new government, but ultimately gave in to the extreme members of his government and exiled Fouché to Trieste, where he lived the rest of his life.

Gourgaud, General Gaspard, Baron de (1783–1852). An artillery officer who served in several campaigns and also as one of Napoleon's personal staff officers. Like Bertrand, Gourgaud is most known for his service during Napoleon's decline. He served as Napoleon's Master of the Horse on St Helena and took extensive dictation from Napoleon. Gourgaud accompanied Napoleon's remains back to Paris in 1840 and had the honor of placing Napoleon's hat on the Emperor's coffin in ceremonies before King Louis-Philippe.

Grouchy, Marshal Emmanuel (1766–1847). A noble by birth, Grouchy fought during the Revolutionary Wars and became a premier cavalry officer. A divisional commander of some note, his battles included Ülm, Eylau, Friedland, Wagram and Borodino. It was Grouchy who subdued the uprising in Madrid in 1808, and he served under Eugène de Beauharnais in the 1812 Russian campaign. Grouchy was the last marshal appointed by Napoleon, receiving his baton on 15 April 1815. Shortly thereafter, Napoleon made him commander of his right wing. He did a mediocre job at Quatre Bras and failed to properly pursue the Prussians after Ligny, which led directly to Field Marshal Blücher's ability to turn French victory into defeat at Waterloo. He was able to return his forces to Paris in good order, but by then it was too late for Napoleon. Louis XVIII exiled Grouchy to America, where he lived until 1821, when he was allowed to return to France.

Hotham, Vice Admiral Sir Henry (1777–1833). Hotham spent most of his early years in the navy in the Mediterranean, and then moved on to service in the Atlantic. He was put in charge of the naval blockade of France designed to keep Napoleon from escaping to Europe, and in this he gained success and a reputation. He later became a lord and a vice admiral.

Keith, Admiral Viscount George (1746–1823). A Scottish naval officer, Keith rose quickly and was a rear admiral by 1795. His appointment in 1800 as commander in the Mediterranean upset Lord Nelson, and the two men maintained a feud for years. He served well at Alexandria in 1801, becoming a full admiral in the process. His next claim to fame was in July 1815, when he played a major role in Napoleon's surrender to the British and ultimate exile to St Helena.

La Bédoyère, General Charles de (1786–1815). La Bédoyère had a distinguished military service that included time under Lannes and Eugène de Beauharnais. His valor in Russia and afterwards earned him promotion to brigadier general. During the First Restoration, Bédoyère remained devoutly loyal to Napoleon's cause, spending a great deal of time with Queen Hortense and her followers. One of Napoleon's aides-de-camp for the Hundred Days, he is most noted for his actions in support of Napoleon in the Waterloo campaign. A firebrand who urged Napoleon to ignore the legislature and claim power outright, he was in great disfavor with the Bourbons and was shot upon their return to power in 1815.

La Fayette, Marie Joseph Paul de Motier, Marquis de (1757–1834). As a fabulously wealthy French nobleman, La Fayette supported the American War of Independence and became very close to George Washington. A very liberal noble, La Fayette served in the National Assembly of 1789 and formed the National Guard that same year. He fell out with the increasingly radical government and eventually surrendered to the Austrians who, rather than treating him as a defecting hero, threw him into prison. Napoleon Bonaparte was instrumental in obtaining his release in 1797. Not one to show gratitude, La Fayette stayed in Germany until 1814, when he returned to France to support the King. During the Hundred Days he served in the Chamber of Deputies and, after Waterloo, led the movement to demand that Napoleon abdicate a second time. In 1824 he had a triumphal tour of the United States, and in 1830 he once again became commander of the National Guard during the revolution of that year.

Lallemand, Baron General François-Antoine Charles (1774–1839). A cavalry officer, Lallemand served well throughout the Napoleonic epoch, with service in Egypt, Italy, Santo Domingo, Austria, Prussia, Poland and France. Louis XVIII imprisoned him for disloyalty, but when Napoleon returned he was released. He served under Napoleon and was wounded at Waterloo. Lallemand accompanied Napoleon to Rochefort and hoped to go with him into exile. Instead he was sent to Malta. Though he had been condemned to death by France, he was not repatriated and soon thereafter managed to escape. He and his brother are perhaps best known for their unsuccessful attempt to establish a colony in Texas for veterans of Napoleon's army to settle. Lallemand became a US citizen and lived in New York until 1830. He then returned to France and at the end of his life was serving as the military governor of Corsica.

Las Cases, Count Emmanuel Auguste Dieudonné (1766–1842). As a nobleman, Las Cases fled France during the Terror but returned when Napoleon took command. He was useful in repelling the British in the 1809 Walcheren action, and Napoleon gave him increasingly important assignments thereafter. He rallied to Napoleon for the Hundred Days and accompanied the Emperor to Rochefort and from there to St Helena. Sir Hudson Lowe expelled him from the island in 1816, but Las Cases had the last laugh when he published his *Mémorial de Sainte Hélène*, one of the most important memoirs from that stage of Napoleon's life. He was well treated by King Louis-Philippe and served in the Chamber of Deputies during his reign.

Louis XVIII, King of France (1755–1824). Brother to executed King Louis XVI, the future Louis XVIII first fled east, ending up in Warsaw, and then found sanctuary in Britain, where he was allowed to live peacefully in luxury (a courtesy the British would not extend to Napoleon years later). Talleyrand had paved the way for his return in 1814, and he was initially well received by a people anxious for peace. But he suffered from a poor image (he was extremely fat) and a general fear that many of his radical émigré supporters would demand return of church property and other anti-revolutionary actions.

Napoleon's return chased him to Ghent in Belgium. After Napoleon's abdication, 'Louis the Inevitable', as he was sometimes called, returned to a somewhat skeptical France. While he initially used the services of the ever-conspiring Talleyrand and Fouché, he eventually removed them from their posts and tried to rule as a moderate king. The ultra-royalists engaged in an orgy of bloodletting known as the White Terror (led by the King's brother, the Compte d'Artois), but after that Louis was able to keep things on a generally even keel.

Maitland, Captain Sir Frederick Lewis (1777–1839). After a bit of a rocky beginning, Maitland by 1799 had command of a ship and two years later accompanied General Sir Ralph Abercromby to Egypt. His service there was distinguished and he was subsequently given a succession of commands. In 1815 he was prepared to sail to the United States of America, but Napoleon's escape caused his orders to be changed. He was given command of the *Bellerophon* and sent to help prevent Napoleon's presumed effort to escape to the United States. It was to him that

Napoleon ultimately surrendered, and there is some controversy as to whether or not Maitland misled Napoleon and his followers into believing that they would be allowed to retire to England. Maitland continued service in the navy, dying at sea in 1839.

Marchand, Louis (1791–1876). Marchand became a domestic servant to Napoleon's household in 1811 and served Napoleon in increasingly important positions. In 1814, when so many valets and other domestics were fleeing Napoleon, Marchand stayed loyal and accompanied Napoleon to Elba. Marchand was with Napoleon at Rochefort and accompanied him to St Helena. A faithful valet and executor of Napoleon's will, Marchand was with Napoleon throughout his exile and present at the exhumation of his body in 1840. His account of his years with Napoleon is one of the most important sources available today.

Maret, Hughes-Bernard, Duke of Bassano (1763–1839). A lawyer by training, Maret gained fame as an editor of newspapers, most notably the *Moniteur Universel*, the official government mouthpiece under Napoleon. He supported Napoleon's coup in 1799, becoming first secretary-general to the Consulate and then head of Napoleon's office operations as First Consul. He continued to produce material for Napoleon's propaganda effort (including material for the *Moniteur*), and in 1809 undertook a two-year stint as Foreign Minister. He remained loyal to Napoleon until the end and was exiled by Louis XVIII for his efforts.

Masséna, Marshal André (1758–1817). Often considered as perhaps Napoleon's finest marshal, Masséna started his career as an enlisted man but became an officer during the Revolution. Now a general, he was with Napoleon at Toulon and in the first Italian campaign. One of the first group of marshals appointed in 1804, Masséna earned a well-deserved reputation as an outstanding commander with a willingness to help himself to his share of the available loot. He met with little success in the Peninsular War, and had minor assignments afterwards. He declared for Napoleon during the Hundred Days but played a relatively limited role, and happily retired to his home with the Restoration.

Metternich-Winneburg, Prince Clemens Lothar Wenzel, Fürst von (1773–1859). An Austrian diplomat of extraordinary ability, Metternich represented the Austrian court in Dresden, Berlin and Paris. He negotiated treaties with France and the marriage of Napoleon and the Austrian Princess Marie Louise. After 1812, however, Metternich deserted his French alliance and contributed to Napoleon's fall in 1814, notwithstanding the fact that his Emperor was Napoleon's father-in-law. At the Congress of Vienna he represented Austria's interests with vigor and after Napoleon's second exile became the most powerful person in Austria. His belief in an absolute monarchy ill served him during the revolutions of 1848 and he was forced to retire from public life.

Montholon, Charles Tristan, Comte de (1783–1853). Montholon served as an aide-de-camp to Berthier and others, as well as being an Imperial Chamberlain. Though never really close to Napoleon, Montholon and his wife Albine followed Napoleon after his abdication and accompanied him to St Helena. Napoleon seemed to trust him, but some feel he may have poisoned Napoleon. After Napoleon's death, he wrote his memoirs, which, while important, must be read with caution. In 1840 he participated in Louis Napoleon's attempted coup and later served as a deputy in the National Assembly.

Murat, Marshal Joachim (1767–1815). Murat was famously the son of an innkeeper from Gascony and one of the most colorful of all of Napoleon's supporters. At his peak he was probably the finest cavalry commander of his century, and his flamboyance made him the most recognizable of all of Napoleon's commanders. First Consul Napoleon Bonaparte made him commander of the Consular Guard and shortly thereafter he married Napoleon's sister, Caroline. In 1804 he became one of the first marshals, and a year later was made Prince of the Empire. He had great success at Ülm and Austerlitz, but his flamboyance and tendency to overreach his abilities sometimes got him into trouble. Nevertheless, Napoleon made him the Grand Duke of Berg and Cleves in 1806, and his successes at Jena, Heilsberg and Eylau justified Napoleon's confidence. Murat was initially given control of Spain, but Napoleon replaced him with Joseph, Murat getting the job as King of Naples instead. He joined Napoleon for the 1812 campaign in Russia, serving with his usual flair, but without his usual success.

Caroline's loyalty to her brother Napoleon was not her strong suit, and she had made overtures to the Allies to secure her husband's throne. When Murat returned from Russia, he accepted his wife's treachery and in 1813 declared against Napoleon and attacked French interests in northern Italy. The disgusted Allies declined to promise him his throne when they met at the Congress of Vienna.

When Napoleon returned for the Hundred Days, Murat switched sides again and attempted to drive the Austrians out of Italy. This only served to convince the Allies that Napoleon could not be trusted, and Napoleon was understandably livid with his brother-in-law. When Murat arrived in France and offered his services to Napoleon, the Emperor ignored him. This may have been a fatal mistake, as he would have been a far better cavalry commander than Grouchy. After Waterloo, Murat attempted to replicate Napoleon's return by landing in Italy, but he was captured and executed on the spot.

Ney, Marshal Michel, Duke of Elchingen (1769–1815). Like Murat, Ney had a reputation as a flamboyant, dashing and brave commander. Indeed, the two of them are often thought of together. They were both somewhat limited in intelligence but made up for it in other ways. The two men also engaged in a sometimes bitter feud throughout their career. Joining the military as an enlisted man, Ney was a general by 1796. He served under Bernadotte and Masséna, and was one of the original marshals in 1804. He served well in 1806 and 1807, most notably at Friedland. In 1808 Napoleon made him the Duke of Elchingen, and Ney fought in the Peninsular War with limited success. His reputation was restored, however, by his sterling performance in Russia. He fought well at Smolensk and Borodino, and was most famous for being in command of the rearguard. It is said he was the last Frenchman to leave Russia, and Napoleon dubbed him 'the bravest of the brave' for his efforts. The next year he was given the title 'Prince of the Moscowa'.

Ney served in the defense of France in 1814, but was ineffective and ultimately led an effort with some other marshals to urge Napoleon to abdicate. He declared loyalty to King Louis XVIII, but returned to Napoleon's side for the Hundred Days. His repeated cavalry attacks without infantry support were one of the premier causes of Napoleon's defeat at Waterloo. Ney returned to France after Waterloo and was urged to leave the country. He stayed too long, however, and was tried for treason and executed in December 1815.

O'Meara, Barry Edward (1782–1836). O'Meara was an Irishman serving in the British navy. He was serving as surgeon on the *Bellerophon* when Napoleon surrendered to the British, and he made a favorable impression on the Emperor. When Napoleon's French doctor declined the honor of accompanying the Emperor to St Helena, O'Meara accepted the position, though with some fears regarding the obvious difficulty of the situation. O'Meara soon ran into difficulty trying to be both a good doctor to Napoleon and a good British soldier, and in 1818 the governor of St Helena, Sir Hudson Lowe, sent him back to Britain, where he was soon kicked out of the military. His recollections of Napoleon in exile are of the utmost importance.

Savary, Anne Jean Marie René, Duke of Rovigo (1774–1833). Like many officers of the period, Savary joined the military as an enlisted man but was soon promoted to high rank as an officer. Savary served in Egypt under General Desaix, whom he followed to Italy. When Desaix was killed at the Battle of Marengo, Savary was put on Napoleon's staff. There he served in a variety of capacities, often as Napoleon's eyes and ears. Made general of division in 1805, he fought at Austerlitz, Jena, Friedland and other actions for several years. In time, Savary replaced Fouché as Minister of Police, serving in that office from 1810 to 1814. Savary retired from public life after Napoleon left for Elba, but returned to his benefactor's side for the Hundred Days. He made every effort to join the Emperor on St Helena, even trying to sneak aboard the *Northumberland*, but was eventually sent to Malta (despite British assurances to the contrary). But he was not prosecuted for treason by France and was allowed to return to his home in 1819.

Talleyrand-Périgord, Charles Maurice de, Prince de Bénévent (1754–1838). Like Fouché, to whom he is often tied, Talleyrand was a great survivor who had a taste for the flamboyant and a life of irony. Trained in the Church, he had little use for religion even as he became the Bishop of Autun in 1789. That same year he represented his diocese at the Estates-General, where he promoted the idea of the confiscation of the Church he was sent to represent. He also helped write the Declaration of the Rights of Man and of the Citizen, the seminal document of the French Revolution.

Fearing for his life as the Terror approached, Talleyrand lived overseas, including Britain and the United States, for several years. During the Directory he returned to France, where he sharpened his political skills and eventually managed an appointment as Foreign Minister. He was an early supporter of Napoleon and is probably the one who proposed the expedition to Egypt, but then neglected to inform the Sultan in Turkey of French intentions to support him.

When Napoleon took power in 1799, Talleyrand was in the thick of things and remained there for most of the remaining time of Napoleon's rule. He served as an adviser and a 'go-to' man who was in many ways indispensable to Napoleon's ambitions. But he was also convinced that only he, Talleyrand, really knew what was in France's best interests, and he engaged in possibly treasonable acts after 1807.

Talleyrand served as Louis XVIII's Foreign Minister during the First Restoration, but remained in touch with Napoleon as well. On the surface he supported Napoleon's return, but swung right back to Louis XVIII after Waterloo. He had the confidence of the King, but not of the King's advisers, and after a short time as Prime Minister was removed from any real influence. He was active in the July Revolution of 1830 and later served as ambassador to Britain.

Wellington, Arthur, Duke of (1769–1852). Wellington was born son of the Earl of Mornington, and joined the British army while also serving in the Dublin Parliament. He bought a colonelcy and was sent to India in 1797, where he served in the shadow of his brother Richard. He served with some distinction in India until 1805, when he returned to Europe as a major general. A year later he was elected to Parliament and then served as Secretary for Ireland. After some minor actions, Wellington went to Portugal in 1808, now a lieutenant general. His actions in the Peninsular Campaign made his reputation and led to great British success against the French. By 1814 he was invading southern France and had advanced to Toulouse when Napoleon abdicated for the first time.

Wellington was put in charge of the Allied forces in the north in response to Napoleon's return, but he allowed Napoleon to get between his army and its Prussian allies. While he was ultimately the victor at Waterloo, most analysts suggest that it was Napoleon's mistakes and Blücher's initiative that deserve credit for the victory. Still, Wellington was a hero to the British and played a role in the politics that followed. He argued against harming Napoleon, and eventually served as Prime Minister.

Chapter One

The End Game at Waterloo

Napoleon Returns to Cheers and Jeers

There is a common misconception that when Napoleon returned from his imperial exile on the island of Elba (he was, after all, the emperor of that tiny island), all of France rallied to his cause. This was decidedly not the case, a fact that not only complicated things before the Battle of Waterloo but also made things rather more dicey than is often imagined after that disastrous battle. This lack of universal support had been obvious from the very beginning of Napoleon's return for what would become known as the Hundred Days.

Napoleon understood the risk of moving straight north from Golfe-Juan, where he landed on 1 March 1815 on the southern coast of France, towards Paris. Straight north would take him on a route near army units that might remain loyal to King Louis XVIII and would, in any event, take him through regions that were more religious and royalist than other parts of France. Hence he decided to go on a more westerly route, through the mountains to Grenoble and then on to Lyons and Paris. But even this route, now called the Route Napoléon, saw crowds that were more curious than supportive, with more than one person questioning whether Napoleon's return was a good thing or not.

Even so, the closer Napoleon got to Paris, the better his reception was. The peasants were especially pleased to see him. As he approached the town of Digne, his valet, Marchand, tells us, 'On the 4th [March 1815], between Castellane and Digne, the peasants who heard about the Emperor's march were running down the mountain in droves; from the way they were talking, it was evident they feared the return of tithes and feudal rights.'[1] King Louis was clearly not a favorite of theirs. At Lyons, Marshal Jacques Étienne Joseph Alexandre Macdonald had been determined to halt Napoleon's advance, but declined to do so when 'surrounded by his mutinous troops, he found himself face to face with the vanguard of the Emperor, and heard behind him the great cry of a city in revolt: "Vive l'empereur!"'[2]

When Napoleon entered Paris, he might have been forgiven for being swept up by the moment, given the great crowds and cheering that met him and followed him wherever he went. Bonapartists were everywhere and royalists were nowhere to be seen. Banners cried out to the King as though from Napoleon himself, 'My good brother: there is no need to send any more troops; I already have enough!'[3] General Baron Paul-Charles-François-Adrien-Henri Thiébault described the situation in Paris as well as the ambiguity felt by supporters of the King and, one supposes, of the Emperor, as he wrote:

This scene was a final proof of the perplexity of my position. I was now the only person holding out for the King either around or in Paris; but in spite of my own feelings, in the midst of the general collapse I was determined to behave as I should have done in my own cause ... I was doomed to carry out against a giant, against one whom I had so much admired, the orders given me by pygmies whom I disdained.[4]

All Paris may have been excited by the return of the Emperor, but Napoleon was clearly optimistic when he told Marchand and others that the Allies at the Congress of Vienna would see things as he saw them and that peace was likely. Napoleon had been met by throngs of Parisians, but had not, in fact, been met in a unanimous fashion.

While Louis XVIII had, indeed, left the country once it seemed certain that Napoleon's return would be successful, Louis had also taken steps both to stop Napoleon and to ensure that royalist strongholds would continue to resist the creation of a new empire. Louis gave overall supervision of the resistance to his younger brother, the Count of Artois. He assigned additional duties to his nephews, the Duke of Berry and the Duke of Angoulême. The latter duke was placed in charge of raising armies in southern France, where royalist feelings tended to run fairly strong. Fortunately for Napoleon, most of the troops in this region were loyal to him, with only the 10th regiment of the line showing loyalty to the Bourbon cause.[5]

The Duke of Angoulême, clearly outnumbered and overmatched by the troops loyal to Napoleon, decided that discretion was the better part of valor and negotiated a truce with the Bonapartist commander, General Jacques-Laurent Gilly. The royalists were allowed to return to their homes and the duke agreed to seek exile in Spain. From just across the border, the duke awaited further developments and planned for future action.[6] Meanwhile, Marshal Brune was just able to maintain control of the major port city of Marseilles for Napoleonic France.

The most conservative region of France was the *département* in western France known as the Vendée. This region had opposed the French Revolution, both for its anti-royalist leanings and for its anti-clerical nature. Not surprisingly, the Vendée was pleased to see Louis XVIII take the throne, and not at all amused to see Napoleon return to power. Initially, regular troops were withdrawn from the area in preparation for the campaign in Belgium. Royalist forces there were well organized, however, and a general insurrection soon followed, fed by public distaste for conscription and more war. Marshal Davout, whom Napoleon had appointed Minister of War, had to put some 25,000 troops in that region to quell the royalist disturbances.[7] Minister of Police Joseph Fouché was also authorized to negotiate with the royalists in order to achieve domestic peace. General Jean-Maximilien Lamarque's regular army troops eventually defeated the royalists, and he and Fouché offered a favorable amnesty to them in return for their ceasing their armed insurrection. Domestic peace was restored, but the episode had shown how tenuous was Napoleon's hold on parts of France and how invaluable – or dangerous – was Fouché.

On the surface, at least, it seemed that Napoleon was back in charge. King Louis

XVIII left French soil for Ghent, Belgium. Marshal Masséna controlled Toulon for Napoleon; everywhere, it seemed, the royalists had been at least neutralized.

Louis was now out of France, but before he left he did what he could to turn the nation against Napoleon. On 6 March he issued a decree, published the next day in the *Moniteur*, that outlawed Napoleon and all who supported him. This decree (see Appendix I) declared Napoleon an outlaw and established punishments for those who supported him. Interestingly, it was dated 6 March, 'The twentieth year of our reign'. Louis apparently figured he had been the legitimate king after Louis XVI's son died in prison in 1795. [8]

Parisian Politics and Appointments

Napoleon's most recent Minister of War, Henri Clarke, was less than competent in the defense of Paris in 1814 and had declared for the Bourbons after Napoleon's downfall. Though Clarke had failed to obtain the portfolio of Minister of War under Louis XVIII during the First Restoration, he nevertheless had left France as part of Louis's entourage. Thereafter, his treachery was completed by his advice to the forces preparing to move against Napoleon. Louis then rewarded him with the portfolio he had sought, that of Minister of War. [9]

Napoleon appointed Marshal Davout as Minister of War, an act that points out a real difficulty facing Napoleon. He needed his best leaders with him at Waterloo, but could hardly afford to leave Paris in the hands of incompetents. This was a special concern, as those such as Minister of Police Fouché in Paris and Ambassador Charles Maurice de Talleyrand were never far from any Parisian political intrigue, particularly since Talleyrand was representing King Louis XVIII at the Congress of Vienna.

Incompetent leadership in Paris had cost Napoleon in 1814, and he did not want to see history repeated. Davout was one of his most loyal and competent marshals, so it made sense to leave him in Paris. And yet, it was probably one of Napoleon's biggest mistakes. As John G. Gallaher points out:

> Napoleon had withheld troops from the Vendée on the sound judgment that the decisive action upon which the empire would stand or fall would be with the Army of the North on the plains of Belgium, not on the Loire. This same sound judgment should have caused him to give Davout a command in the army where he would have been able to have direct influence on the course of events in the principal theater of operations. Napoleon should have realized that he would have need once again of the services of the man who had held the Austrians at bay at Eckmühl, destroyed a Prussian army twice the size of his own at Auerstädt, and withstood the crushing assault of the Russians at Austerlitz. [10]

Napoleon did what he could to secure the politics of Paris before having to face a military attack. He asked the liberal leader and his frequent critic, Benjamin Constant, to oversee the writing of a new constitution. This move disarmed his liberal critics, but led to the creation of a government less easily controlled by imperial will. The *Additional Act*, published on 22 April (see Appendix II), was widely considered by

Napoleon's strongest supporters to be a disaster for Napoleon. Its two legislative chambers were designed to be open to the public and not easy to control. Of course, one could argue that this meant that the act simply made things more democratic. Perhaps, but it also left the door open to manipulation by those who would not promote democracy but instead work to bring back a monarch far less likely to defend the liberal reforms promoted by Napoleon. In the end, it would not be a reforming emperor or a democratic republic that would benefit from this situation.

Title I of the *Additional Act* confirmed the existence of a legislative process that included the Emperor and a legislative body of two chambers. The Chamber of Peers (*Chambre des Pairs*) was a hereditary body of indefinite size. Members were appointed by the Emperor and carried on through eldest male non-adoptive descendants. The presiding officer was the Grand Chancellor of the Empire or someone else designated by the Emperor. All members of the imperial family were also members.

The Chamber of Representatives (*Chambre des Représentants*) was elected every five years by the people. It had 629 members, who could name their own presiding officer each five-year session, subject to approval by the Emperor.

In the short term, the Additional Act and its two legislative chambers reassured politicians on the left. After Waterloo, the chambers were a significant factor in Napoleon's inability to maintain control. As Count Mathieu Louis Molé, a member of Napoleon's Council of State, recounted:

> It [the adoption of the Additional Act] was a remarkable decision, which thoroughly justified what I had so often told Napoleon – that in opposing interests to doctrines he had soothed the conscience of all without converting or satisfying a single soul. From the moment men ceased to fear him and hope for a share in his immense patronage, political opinions reappeared and the century, as it were, resumed its course. Men no longer desired a ready-made constitution, discussed between a sovereign and his minister. They wanted one taken from a source in the consent of the peoples and in conformity with their wishes and understanding. The really curious point is that in 1815 Bonaparte made the same mistake that the King had made in 1814. In politics there is nothing worse than adopting principles without drawing the logical inferences from them. Sooner or later they are thrown up in one's face, and in times as enlightened as ours, governments perish when nations cease to believe in their good faith.[11]

Napoleon had taken Paris without firing a shot, and he well understood that continued peace was completely necessary. The French people demanded it and, in any event his army was greatly outnumbered by the combined Allied forces. Knowing that, Napoleon wrote to the Allies, including his former friend, Tsar Alexander of Russia, and his father-in-law, Emperor Francis of Austria, seeking peace and promising to uphold the Treaty of Paris. But neither man accepted delivery, as neither the Tsar nor the Emperor had any interest in dealing directly with Napoleon. Indeed, Metternich made a show of opening the letters to himself and the Austrian Emperor Francis at the

Congress of Vienna. Upon opening them, he declared that they would not be answered. This drama was more intended to provide a show of loyalty on the part of Napoleon's father-in-law, Francis, than to have any real impact on Allied policy.[12]

Napoleon probably did genuinely want peace. He told Hughes Maret, Duke of Bassano (who was one of Napoleon's closest advisers):

> One does not recommence a political career such as mine twice; it is in my best interest to live quietly and use the remainder of my days repairing the evils brought on France by 20 years of war ending in invasion. The misfortunes of our mother land have robbed me of my retirement; the certainty that I would be disturbed in my possession of the island of Elba made me hasten matters. I came to France without any agreement with the powers, but strengthened by the divisions existing between them. What position will Vienna take? We will soon hear of it. When the powers learn of the unanimous fashion in which I was welcomed back to France, that the Bourbons could offer no resistance, and that no one or nearly no one took up arms to ensure their retreat to the limits of the kingdom, they will think it over before responding, and if they act in haste, they may regret it. Let us not forget that the sovereigns in congress are not my only enemies; the European oligarchies fear me, and they have enough representatives in Vienna. Castlereagh and Wellington will stir them up against me and they will come to a decision to make war, so we must prepare for this.[13]

Napoleon was probably right in his fear of being disturbed on Elba. He was certainly right in his assessment that his enemies, both in and out of Vienna, would not tolerate his return. And, not surprisingly, one major reason for Allied resistance to Napoleon's return was the King's Foreign Minister and Napoleon's old nemesis, Maurice Talleyrand, who was able to focus the Allies on defeating Napoleon. It soon became obvious that war was inevitable. Talleyrand had kept up a flurry of correspondence with King Louis XVIII, telling him of the news of Napoleon's advance towards Paris and of events in Vienna. In his letter of 19 March, he broke the good news to Louis:

> I take this opportunity of informing Your Majesty that in the military conference held on the day before yesterday, at which the Emperor of Russia was present, it was decreed that Bonaparte, with whom the Allied Powers will never treat, must be stopped by prompt and enormous efforts. They have therefore decided on renewing the Treaty of Chaumont, of which I have had the honor of sending a copy to Your Majesty. But it is to be directed only against Bonaparte, and not against France, who, on the contrary, will be one of the consenting parties.[14]

Indeed, the Allied powers had decided that Napoleon must go. A few days later, on 25 March, they agreed on a treaty that bound the Allied powers to do whatever it took to defeat and remove Napoleon from power (see Appendix III).

While this declaration seemed to represent a firm consensus against Napoleon, the fact of the matter was that it came only after a great deal of difficulty. Once news of Napoleon's departure from Elba reached Vienna, there was much uncertainty as to what would happen next. No one knew for sure just where Napoleon was headed and what role, if any, King Murat of Naples would play. When word came of Napoleon's landing in France, that made things easier, but by no means easy, for the Allies. Tsar Alexander, for example, wanted to serve as commander of all the Allied forces, a role that found no support anywhere beyond his own court. Indeed, the distrust of the Russian army was such that severe restrictions were placed on its movement towards France.[15]

Even worse was Talleyrand's insistence that Napoleon be treated like a criminal, with all citizens encouraged to shoot him on sight. Wellington was alarmed at the idea that Napoleon might be murdered simply as a matter of private sport. Metternich and others were reluctant to be too nasty towards the man who was, after all, the son-in-law of the Emperor Francis of Austria. Louis XVIII had not exactly endeared himself to everyone at the Congress of Vienna, and some even considered Napoleon an acceptable replacement. Talleyrand's initial draft essentially called Napoleon a wild beast who should be hunted down – hardly a fitting end for an emperor who was the son-in-law of an emperor.[16]

Another appointment that Napoleon made upon his return was that of Joseph Fouché as Minister of Police. Fouché had been a mixed blessing to Napoleon throughout his career, but his skill as head of an extensive spy ring had often made him indispensable to the Emperor. It was Fouché's skill at keeping things together that Napoleon needed in his new administration. Moreover, most of Napoleon's advisers, including his stepdaughter, Hortense, urged Fouché's appointment. The appointment was popular among the people of Paris, and was further backed by such close advisers to Napoleon as Maret, Count Antoine Marie Chamant Lavalette and Count Pierre-François Réal, and Savary, the Duke of Rovigo. Thus, against his better inclinations, Napoleon gave Fouché a position that would come back to haunt him very quickly.

During Napoleon's exile on Elba, Fouché had kept some contact, thus retaining at least some measure of (misplaced) trust. Indeed, the King had ordered his arrest, but Fouché managed to escape. This episode only furthered Fouché's popularity with Napoleon's supporters.

Fouché appeared to support Napoleon upon his return (though he had argued to the Allies that they should put Napoleon in prison rather than on an island). Fouché's support of Napoleon, if there had ever really been any since the start of the Hundred Days, waned when he felt that Napoleon was trying to claim too much of the old imperial power and to lead France into a disastrous military campaign. Convinced that Napoleon eventually would be defeated, and determined to bring a moderate regime to power, Fouché was soon playing a double game, keeping in contact with Lord Wellington and Count Clemens Metternich of Austria. Fouché's position gave him access to all sorts of information: Davout, for example, provided him with the complete plans of the coming campaign. Fouché made good use of this information. In his memoirs, he is clearly proud of his double-dealing:

> In this decisive condition of affairs, my position became very delicate, as well as very difficult. I wished to have nothing further to do with Napoleon; yet, if

he should be victorious, I should be compelled to submit to his yoke, as well as the whole of France, whose calamities he would prolong. On the other hand, I had engagements with Louis XVIII; not that I was inclined to his restoration, but prudence required that I should procure for myself before hand something in shape of a guarantee. My agents, moreover, to M. de Metternich and Lord Wellington had promised mountains and marvels. The generalissimo, at least, expected that I should provide him with the plan of the campaign.

... I knew positively [the plans of the campaign] ... The success of Napoleon rested, therefore, on the success of a surprise; I took my measures accordingly. On the very day of Napoleon's departure, I provided Madame D— with notes, written in cipher, disclosing the plan of the campaign, and sent her off.[17]

Fouché was nothing if not clever. While serving Napoleon in the Hundred Days he maintained contact with all other factions: Wellington, Metternich, the Count of Artois and the Duke of Orléans. He truly played all sides against the middle. Of course, he would share some of this information with Napoleon, thus giving an aura of legitimacy to his double-dealings.

Lead-Up to War

Napoleon was in a quandary. War was likely, but he had to balance his need to unify his nation with his need to respond to the military threat. He was at his peak of influence; as Baron Thiébault says:

Never did Napoleon exercise a greater moral influence than at that moment. If the return from Waterloo was to complete the melancholy work of the return from Moscow, the impression made by this return from Elba was worthy of that produced by the return from Egypt [in 1798] ... [unhappily] by waiting at Paris to write a letter to the kings of Europe, which none of them would receive, to make a Constitution which deprived him of 200,000 men, to make a display at the *Champ de Mars* and play at memories when present realities were crying aloud, he gave the coalized [sic] forces time to attack him with 600,000 troops.[18]

Despite Thiébault's criticism, Napoleon probably had little choice but to stay in Paris long enough to oversee the development of a proper government and to deal with other matters. He did himself little good with the coronation event, gaudily staged to formally take back the crown, but he generally made good use of his time. He attended the opera and received numerous visitors.

One of them was the actress Mademoiselle George. She had been his favorite mistress and she idolized him. Now that he was back in power, he provided her with some financial support and they had at least one meeting. George is not as well known as Napoleon's Polish mistress, Marie Walewska, but she was one of his favorites, much to Josephine's dismay. Later, when word came that Napoleon was to be exiled in St Helena, Mademoiselle George offered to join him, but Napoleon declined the offer. An emperor does not go into exile with his mistress.[19]

Napoleon kept busy, both socially and politically. Still, his delay in Paris gave people time to become restive. The increasing inevitability of war was not sitting well with many people. Even Marshal Masséna harbored doubts, and he was hardly alone. When General Louis-Alexandre Berthier, Napoleon's renowned chief of staff, fell to his death from his window, people saw that as a bad luck omen (and it certainly deprived Napoleon of the one indispensable man on his staff). There was – and still is – some discussion of whether Berthier's fall was accidental or the result of a shove, but whatever the cause, one of the most important men in Napoleon's leadership cadre was no longer available.

Napoleon suffered another setback when his brother-in-law, King Murat of Naples, attacked the Austrians. His attack was unsuccessful and he was chased back to France. Napoleon had known nothing about his plans, but the Austrians assumed that Napoleon was behind Murat's moves. Any chance that they might have trusted Napoleon was now dashed. Napoleon was furious and refused to see Murat or accept his help at Waterloo. Given that Murat was probably the finest cavalry commander of his day, this was probably another significant mistake.

With things more or less in place in his government and in the army, Napoleon decided that his only chance was to strike quickly, before the Allies could marshal all of their forces against France and before the citizens of France could become disillusioned with the situation. One major victory and both the Allies and the French would fall into place. The British and the Prussian armies were in Belgium, but separate from each other. Thus, it was against them that Napoleon would move.

On the evening of 11 June, after a day of preparations, Napoleon received his Polish mistress, Countess Marie Walewska. It seems he gave her some good financial advice and they no doubt had tender words for each other. They would meet again in a week, but under far less favorable circumstances.

On 12 June Napoleon marched north with a force of 125,000 men. On the 13th he issued orders that outlined the coming operations. The next day, General Louis Bourmont, commander of a division of IV Corps, and several other officers defected to the enemy and gave them their plans. It was not a great start for Napoleon.

Even so, Napoleon defeated the Prussians, commanded by Field Marshal Blücher, at Ligny on the 16th, and then joined Marshal Michel Ney at Quatre Bras. There he discovered that Ney had not pursued the British, under the Duke of Wellington, who had retreated unmolested north towards Brussels. The British took positions near the small town of Waterloo, a few miles south of Brussels. Napoleon soon arrived and prepared to give battle on 18 June.

The Battle of Waterloo

Historians debate the reasons for Napoleon's defeat at the Battle of Waterloo. Of course, several copies of the plan of battle had been delivered to the Allies, so there could be no surprises. Some contend that the battle was lost two days earlier, when Marshal Michel Ney failed to pursue Wellington at Quatre Bras. Others say that it was the useless marching back and forth of d'Erlon's corps at the Battle of Ligny that sank the Empire. One suggestion is that, had General Grouchy properly kept his 'sword at the back' of the retreating Prussians after Ligny, Napoleon would not have despaired in the waning hours of Waterloo, saying 'Where's Grouchy?'

If the blame is to be found on the day of the battle itself, then there are at least an equal number of possibilities. Napoleon's plan was sound enough, but he delayed starting the battle because of very wet ground from heavy rains the day before. This delay, which no doubt seemed like a good idea at the time, allowed the Prussians to arrive just in time to change the outcome of the battle. Early in the day, Napoleon sent an increasing number of soldiers against the fortified farm on his left flank known as Hougoumont. This movement would have been useful if Napoleon was planning a flanking movement, but in the end it simply tied down too many men with too little to show for it.

Marshal Ney's foolhardy cavalry attack with no infantry support; Ney's failure to spike the British guns when he controlled them; Napoleon's lethargy and the disastrous delay in getting the battle started in the morning – all conspired to bring about the now famous ending. One of my favorite reasons for the disaster at Waterloo was the failure to use even a little artillery against Hougoumont. It would have required dismantling a few smaller guns and then bringing them through a thick wood, but the effect would have been devastating and, perhaps, decisive. Hougoumont kept far more French soldiers occupied than British, and capturing it would free up troops and give the French more options.

Napoleon seemed to be more reactive than proactive. This condition would continue to contribute to his ultimate fate, as he was reluctant to take decisive and timely action, preferring to react to the actions of others. In any event, Napoleon's last charge against the British faltered, the Prussians arrived to draw off critical numbers of French troops and devastate the morale of the rest, and what at one point seemed to be a pending French victory became a disastrous defeat.

Another intriguing debate among historians is whether or not it even mattered. Had Napoleon won Waterloo, one side of the argument goes, the Allies would simply have been delayed in their ultimate victory. I am a bit inclined towards the alternative approach, that a victorious Napoleon might well have gained the willingness of his old friend Tsar Alexander of Russia and his father-in-law Emperor Francis of Austria to 'put him on probation', with the idea being that Napoleon in control of France (but nothing else) would be better than the alternative of continued bloodshed. It is with such debates that historians enjoy their times together.

For whatever reason, and whether or not it really mattered, by the end of the day on 18 June 1815, Napoleon and the French were soundly defeated. Napoleon certainly understood that defeat, along with its larger meaning, when he declared that all was lost. Napoleon may have lost some of his ability to command, but he suffered no illusions regarding the meaning of military defeat. When he gained power as First Consul he knew that he needed military victory to maintain his popularity – and his position – and that a defeat might well drive him from office. Clearly, a defeat of the magnitude of Waterloo could have only one consequence. The only real question was how it would all play out and to what destiny Napoleon would travel.

And yet, for all that, Napoleon was of two minds, even as he raced to Paris.

Chapter 2

A Chaotic Return

Leaving the Battlefield

Waterloo was not just a defeat; it was a disaster. The French army was repulsed and sent retreating in the greatest possible disorder. Soldiers ran to save their lives, with little thought of regrouping or organizing a resistance. Only a few elements of the Guard under General Pierre Jacques Cambronne maintained their discipline and managed to cover the Emperor's withdrawal. Napoleon tried to lead them in a stand against the onrushing Prussians, perhaps even seeking to die on the battlefield, but Marshal Soult restrained him and Napoleon retreated with the rest of his army. The Young Guard stalled the Prussian advance at Plancenoit just long enough to allow Napoleon and much of his army to move south towards France and relative safety.

It should be pointed out that most of the Allied pursuit was carried out by elements of the Prussian army. Wellington's forces were exhausted, while some of the Prussian units arrived too late to play much of a direct role in the Battle of Waterloo. This was not good news for Napoleon, as it was the Prussian commander, Blücher, who was most determined to crush him once and for all. He was out for revenge and a fair amount of plunder, determined to punish the French and, if possible, kill Napoleon. But even the Prussians were only able to do so much. Their forces were limited, their supply lines questionable, and there was always the possibility, in their minds at least, that they might come upon French forces rallying to their emperor's cause. Both sides remembered 1814; both sides were determined to get to Paris first.

By late evening of the 18th, Napoleon was at the Belgian farm of Caillou. He left there soon thereafter (having sent word to Grouchy to withdraw through Namur to France), escorted by his brother Jérôme, Marshal Soult, and generals Bertrand, Drouot, Flahaut, La Bédoyère and Gourgaud. By one o'clock in the morning of the 19th, the small party had reached the Belgian town of Genappe, which was teeming with French soldiers but for which no serious defense had been organized. Had this been done, Napoleon might have been able to organize the rest of his army. He seemed interested in doing just that, but there was no time and no real chance, given the turmoil. As General Gourgaud related:

> The Emperor halted for a few moments, in the hope of restoring order, but the tumult increased with the darkness of night, and all his efforts proved vain. Perhaps, in the final result, the best course that could have been adopted would have been to make no resistance, and to retreat with the greatest possible speed. Troops of every arm were confounded together: infantry, cavalry, and artillery,

all pressed and crowded upon each other. Many carriages and caissons were overturned on the bridge, as well as in the streets. Several were even fastened together, which was a fresh proof of the malevolence that prevailed.[1]

Napoleon was barely able to get through the town before it fell under attack. Men, horses, carriages: all were jammed together and movement was slow. Napoleon and his entourage took at least an hour to move past the city. Soon in danger of being captured, he had to abandon his carriage, including the diamonds that his sister Pauline had sewn into the cushions. His valet, Ali, describes the turmoil of the moment:

> The Postilion, Horn, who drove it [Napoleon's carriage], not seeing room to extricate it from the carts and other vehicles which obstructed the road, seeing the Prussian cavalry on the point of cutting him off, and besides that seeing cannon balls and bullets falling around him, unhitched his horses, while the first footman, Archambault, took the portfolio and dressing case out of the carriage. This remained where it was, and almost immediately fell into the hands of the Prussians, who pillaged it, as well as Marchand's, which contained the Emperor's clothes.[2]

Napoleon went on by horse, escorted by an assortment of cavalrymen, through Quatre Bras, with its thousands of dead still unburied. He had sent orders for a reserve unit to meet him there, but found only the melancholy scene of dead soldiers stripped bare by pillagers. The Prussian pursuit, led by General Augustus Wilhelm Gneisenau, left little time for reflection. Depressed, even tearful, Napoleon moved on. He crossed the Sambre river at Charleroi at about five o'clock in the morning, finding there the same chaos and confusion that he earlier had seen at Genappe. Earlier orders to clear the bridge had been ignored. Food had been ransacked from wagons and the treasury wagon pillaged.[3]

Napoleon rested there with others who had joined him, including General Gourgaud, Marshal Bertrand, Marshal Drouot, Aide-de-Camp General Jean-François-Aimé Dejean, General de Bussy, General de La Bédoyère and others.[4] At Charleroi he again thought to try to rally the troops, but by now thoughts of the political situation in Paris were starting to take hold and, in any event, such an action was as yet premature. The Prussians were hard on his heels, and the soldiers at Charleroi seemed more interested in plundering and saving themselves than in preparing a defense. Their concern for their own safety was well taken. The surgeon Jean Dominique Larrey was wounded twice and almost shot. When the Prussians passed Genappe, they encountered a disorganized band of French soldiers, whom they sabred with little resistance. Prussian General Gneisenau wrote of that event, 'It was a regular hunt, a hunt by moonlight.'[5] In reality, there were only some 4,000 Prussians in hot pursuit, and the 30–40,000 retreating French soldiers should have been able to easily organize resistance. But it was not to be, and the rout continued.

So, at six o'clock on the morning of the 19th, Napoleon rode on towards Philippeville, near the French border, where upon arriving around nine in the morning he received several dignitaries and then took some much-needed sleep. Ali relates that Napoleon was 'very sad, and above all, very much absorbed in thought'.[6] Arising, Napoleon found that General Hughes Maret, Duke of Bassano, and the secretary Fleury de Chaboulon had arrived together, and other staff members were making their way there as well. One can well imagine the emotion of each reunion, such as the one related by de Chaboulon:

> By chance M. de Bassano and I took the road to Philippeville. We learned, with a joy of which we did not think ourselves any longer susceptible, that the Emperor was in the town. We ran to him. When he saw me, he condescended to present to me his hand. I bathed it with my tears. The Emperor himself could not suppress his emotion: a large tear, escaping from his eyes, betrayed the efforts of his soul.[7]

Philippeville, 80km south of Brussels, was well fortified and served as something of a rallying point for groups of soldiers making their way south into France. Soon there would be well over 10,000 men in the area, enough to produce a respectable fighting force. Napoleon took a room at the Hôtel du Lion d'Or. While there, he wrote two letters to his brother Joseph (who was acting as Napoleon's regent in Paris during the Waterloo campaign), telling of the disaster. Perhaps buoyed by being reunited with loyal members of his staff, perhaps simply thinking of survival, Napoleon's comments to Joseph in the personal letter (the other one being for the Council of Ministers and containing a summary of the battle) seemed rather upbeat, given the situation:

Philippeville, 19 June 1815

> All is not lost. I suppose that, when I reassemble my forces, I shall have 150,000 men. The *fédérés*[8] and the national guards who are fit to fight will provide 100,000 men, and the battalions of the depots another 50,000. I will thus have 300,000 soldiers to immediately oppose the enemy. I will drag the guns with carriage-horses; I will raise 100,000 conscripts; arm them with muskets of the royalists and of the unfit national guards; I will organize a mass levy in the Dauphiné, Lyons, Burgundy, Lorraine, Champagne; I will overwhelm the enemy. But they [the French] must help me, and not deafen me with advice; I am going to Laon: I will without doubt find somebody there. I have yet heard nothing of Grouchy. If he has not been captured, as I fear, I will have in three days 50,000 men. With them I will occupy the enemy, and give Paris and France time to do their duty. The Austrians march slowly: the Prussians fear the peasantry, and dare not advance too far. Everything can still be repaired again. Write and tell me how the Chamber has been affected by this horrible brawl. I trust the deputies will realize that it is their duty at this great circumstance to stand by me to save France. Prepare them to give me dignified assistance; above all, courage and firmness.[9]

It was obvious to Napoleon that the situation was desperate. Clearly the enemy would no longer be constrained by the borders of France, and defenses there would be insufficient to hold them for very long. Everything depended on establishing defensive positions further into France and, indeed, at Paris itself. Paris was the final defensive position, and Paris was also the political center from which Napoleon needed complete support. Without the political support of Paris, any military defense that he might devise would be of little use.

Politics would respond at least in part to the military situation, and so Napoleon needed to begin to prepare for a defense of Paris. From Philippeville he began to issue orders and letters to do that. He could do this now, for the first time since Waterloo, for he finally had something that resembled a working staff around him. This staff included marshals Bertrand and Soult; generals Drouot, Dejean, Flahaut, Bussy, Bassano and Reille; and secretary Fleury de Chaboulon and other administrative and personal staff. Napoleon ordered various units, such as General Jean Rapp's army of the Rhine (V corps in Alsace), General Claude-Jacques Lecourbe's corps and General Lamarque's Army of La Vendée, to move by forced marches to Paris. Marshal Grouchy was again directed to come to Laon. Other orders called for the flooding of low areas, the holding of frontier fortresses and other measures necessary to at least delay the advance of the enemy.[10] Politics was also discussed, and Napoleon, quite rightly, soon saw Fouché as a 'target for his vengeance'.[11] At two o'clock in the afternoon of the 19th, Napoleon and his growing entourage moved towards Laon, with Napoleon riding in General Dupuy's coach. Marshal Soult was left to organize the headquarters, which would then follow Napoleon. Napoleon arrived in Laon, France, on the 20th.

The retreat from Waterloo was no better for many of Napoleon's staff or, of course, his soldiers. The faithful Marchand was separated from the Emperor, as were people such as General Maret, Duke of Bassano, and Baron Fain. The latter two were on foot, a condition soon to be joined by Marchand as his coach was overtaken at Quatre Bras. He was barely able to save 300,000 francs in banknotes and had to abandon to the Allies all the other valuables, including a diamond necklace given to Napoleon by his sister, Princess Pauline.[12]

Chaos was not the only problem. The Prussians were in hot pursuit and Field Marshal Blücher had made it clear that no quarter was to be given. As de Chaboulon related:

> The Prussians, raging in pursuit of us, treated with unexampled barbarity those unfortunate beings whom they were able to overtake. Except a few steady old soldiers, most of the rest had thrown away their arms, and were without defence; but they were not the less massacred without pity.[13]

Meanwhile, the rout continued. No one knew what had happened to Napoleon and rumors of all kinds flew like cannon balls. Marchand finally caught up with Napoleon at Laon, where Napoleon had paused to rest and plan his next moves.

Where's Grouchy?

One concern to all who were with Napoleon was the fate of Marshal Grouchy, who commanded General Maurice-Étienne Gérard's and General Dominique Vandamme's two corps of about 33,000 men and 80 guns. Grouchy had been sent in pursuit of the Prussians after the Battle of Ligny, two days before Waterloo, with orders to find and attack them. While the obvious goal was to prevent the Prussians from moving in support of Wellington at Waterloo, Grouchy was slow to engage and even slower to ascertain that things were not going well with Napoleon. Urged by his subordinates, including General Gérard, to 'march to the sound of the guns', Grouchy chose instead to engage the Prussians at Wavre. Unfortunately, his action was mostly against a Prussian rearguard of no more than 17,000 men commanded by General Johann Adolf, Freiherr von Thielmann. The Prussians successfully held off Grouchy, allowing the main body of the Prussian army, commanded by Field Marshal Blücher, to become what many consider the decisive factor in the Allied victory at Waterloo.

Grouchy had achieved some success at Wavre on 18 June (he had, after all, a 33,000 to 17,000 man advantage), and when fighting ended around eleven o'clock in the evening, he was fairly pleased. Both sides prepared for battle the next day, but Grouchy seems to have felt that Napoleon had been victorious and that he, Grouchy, would push aside the Prussians on the 19th and march to join Napoleon in Brussels. This assumption was rather brash, given that he had done little or nothing to ascertain the actual outcome of the Battle of Waterloo.[14]

Grouchy's report to Napoleon of 20 June (sent from Dinant) is, perhaps not surprisingly, quite positive on his campaign against the Prussians, and he confirms that he had been prepared to march to Brussels when he finally heard the news of Waterloo:

> General Vandamme sent one of his divisions through Bielge while he took the Wavre heights without any trouble and all along my line it was a complete success. I was past Rozierne, ready to march on to Brussels when I received the painful news of the defeat at Waterloo. The officer who brought me the news told me that Your Majesty was heading towards the Sambre without telling me where you wished me to go. My whole line was engaged so I ceased the pursuit and prepared to move back. The enemy in retreat did not pursue me ... I learned that the enemy had already passed the Sambre and was on my flank; not strong enough to create a diversion useful for Your Majesty's army without compromising mine, I marched on Namur; the fourth corps marched via the Namur road on to Charleroi and the third corps went by the most direct road from Temploux. At that time the tail end of both columns were attacked, the right one had made a retrograde movement sooner than we expected and for an instant compromised the retreat of the left one. Some good dispositions made up for it ... We all entered Namur without any losses ... I put General Vandamme in charge of defending Namur, and with his intrepidity remained there until seven o'clock in the evening, so that nothing stayed behind, while I was occupying Dinant.
>
> The enemy lost thousands of men in the attack at Namur. We fought with a rare determination and the troops did their duty in a manner worthy of praise.[15]

Vandamme's actions at Namur were successful, and he eventually withdrew in good order. The movement continued, and by the 26th virtually all of Grouchy's men, some 30,000 of them, were able to join the rest of the now-reassembling French army at Laon. By then there may have been as many as 60,000 French soldiers in and around Laon. At least to some, it seemed quite possible that this army could successfully hold off, at least in piecemeal, the advancing Prussian and British armies.[16] The now-significant French army reached Paris a few days later, where they would become a pawn in the quickly evolving political developments. Whatever else one may say of Grouchy, he did, at least, get his army out of harm's way and to Paris.

Laon

At Laon, Napoleon seems to have regained a fair amount of optimism regarding his future. He sent his aide-de-camp General Charles-Auguste-Joseph Flahaut to Avesnes; there the general found some portions of the army that Prince Jérôme had managed to rally. It was still unclear if Napoleon planned to stay with the army or head to Paris. The army was the source of his strength and many of his advisers pleaded with him to stay with it, to rally his soldiers and forestall the Prussian and British advance. Do that, and the politics of Paris would take care of itself. It was a strong argument that Napoleon seemed to find persuasive.

Paris was a hotbed of intrigue and factions, and even a masterful politician like Napoleon might not prevail, especially as he was coming from a terrible loss and without his army. Caesar had known better than to return to Rome from Gaul without his army. Napoleon, Caesar's heir as a great commander, should have known better as well. General Flahaut and Fleury de Chaboulon had argued that Napoleon could not be seen as abandoning his army, that the Chambers would never forgive him for that, and that only by reorganizing his forces could he protect himself from both the politics of Paris and the armies of the enemy. Flahaut felt that Napoleon was probably finished, but by rallying the army into a formidable force he might be able to get the Allies to agree to accept his son, the King of Rome, as his heir. General de La Bédoyère, on the other hand, was convinced that Napoleon needed to make for Paris to head off any possible coup attempt and to rally the entire nation rather than just the army.[17]

Napoleon was not convinced that going to Paris was the best thing to do. He had told Bertrand that, 'If I return to Paris and dip my hand in blood, I will have to plunge it in all the way to the elbow.'[18]

De Chaboulon's account of the decision to go to Paris shows an indecisive Napoleon, perhaps too easily swayed by arguments. In his letter to Joseph he had asked not to be deafened by advice, but throughout his withdrawal from Waterloo he was treated to plenty of it, often conflicting. He seemed finally convinced that the army was not yet in any shape to oppose the enemy and that he needed to be in Paris. De Chaboulon summed up the argument to go to Paris and Napoleon's reaction to it:

... to repress your enemies, and animate and direct the zeal of the patriots. The

Parisians, when they see Your Majesty, will fight without hesitation. If Your Majesty remain at a distance from them, a thousand false reports concerning you will be spread ... The national guard and federates, disheartened by the fear of being abandoned or betrayed, as they were in 1814, will fight heartlessly, or not at all.

These considerations induced the Emperor to change his resolution. 'Well!' said he: 'Since you deem it necessary, I will go to Paris; but I am persuaded that you make me act foolishly. My proper place is here. Hence I could direct what is to be done at Paris, and my brothers would see to the rest.'[19]

Of course, it is impossible to say which decision was the better one. But one cannot help considering, given the way things worked out in Paris, that Napoleon might very well have been better off staying with the army. His presence would have doubtless rallied his soldiers far better than it rallied the Chambers. Even a minor victory against, say, a Prussian advance guard, might have silenced his political enemies in Paris and given pause to his enemies in the field as well. And, if his brothers and loyalists in Paris could have arranged for Fouché to be out of the picture, that could have made all the difference in the world.

Marchand, on the other hand, related that Napoleon wanted to go to Paris, even if staying with the army was the best thing for him to do in terms of his personal safety:

> The Emperor, solely concerned with saving the country and not his person, felt that a rapid and truthful account of events would awaken the patriotic sentiments of the representatives, and that with him there the Chambers would not despair of the salvation of the motherland. Backed by them, the nation would rise as a man and the Emperor would restore good fortune to our flag.[20]

The distinguished French historian Henri Houssaye also believed that Napoleon was determined to go to Paris, and questioned whether Napoleon even received the conflicting advice described above:

> He [Napoleon] remembered his deplorable lesson in 1814. That vote of deposition which had paralyzed him at the head of his army. He knew that if he did not return immediately to his capital to overawe Fouché, with the conspirators of all parties, and the deputies, who were hostile or blinded, his crown was doomed, as well as the country's last chance of resistance. From a military, as well as from a political point of view, his place for at least a few days was plainly in Paris.[21]

General Gourgaud was convinced that Napoleon would only go to Paris for a short time:

> Napoleon then proceeded, with all possible speed, to Paris, accompanied by the Duke de Bassano, the Marshal du Palais, Bertrand, and his Aides de Camp Drouot, La Bédoyère, Bernard and Gourgaud. At Paris he intended to remain forty-eight hours, in order to anticipate any political commotion, to which the

news of the disaster might tend to give rise; to take the most prompt measures for completing the arrangements for the defence of the capital; to prepare the public mind for the grand crisis, in which France was about to be placed; to direct on Laon all the troops that could be withdrawn from the depots and fortified places: in a word, to adopt every measure for the execution of the second plan, to which we were now reduced. Napoleon's intention was immediately to rejoin his army at Laon.[22]

Chapter 3

Paris and the Politics of Disaster

The Bad News Arrives

It was on condition of his coming out of the contest as a victor that the patriots had consented to give him their support; he was vanquished, and they considered the compact at an end.

Joseph Fouché[1]

When Napoleon had returned for the Hundred Days, he had hoped to regain his throne and rule France peacefully. It may be, however, that the best he could ever have hoped for was Allied acceptance of his son as France's new emperor. While the Allies did not accept Napoleon as legitimate, and it would therefore be difficult for them to accept his son as his heir, political and military pragmatism might nevertheless have caused them to accept such an arrangement. None other than Austria's Prince Metternich had left open that possibility in a letter to Fouché:

The Powers will not have Napoleon Bonaparte. They will make war against him to the last, but do not wish to fight with France. They desire to know what France wishes, and what you wish. They do not pretend to intermeddle in national questions, or with the desires of the nation concerning the government; but they will in no case tolerate Bonaparte on the throne of France.[2]

This letter appears to suggest that, for Metternich, speaking for the Allies, the wishes of France and of Fouché were of equal value.

After Waterloo, however, Metternich reflects the growing support for a Bourbon restoration when he advises Talleyrand to encourage the King to return quickly to France, lest the Bonapartists be successful in resisting him on the basis that he, the King, had left France.[3]

Had Napoleon been victorious at Waterloo, the Allies would quite possibly have negotiated a peace with Napoleon II as emperor with either one of Napoleon's brothers or Empress Marie Louise as regent. It is impossible to say. This was certainly Fouché's hope, and doubtless the hope of others.

Napoleon's rout at Waterloo completely changed the equation. The Allies were now in no mood to bargain away King Louis XVIII's crown. Perhaps if the government in Paris had been resolute in their determination that Napoleon II be declared emperor, perhaps if the French army had taken defensive positions around Paris, thus ensuring another bloody conflict, under those circumstances the Allies might have still considered that possibility. But as things were working out, the return of King Louis XVIII probably was inevitable.

On the day of Waterloo, Paris was receiving news of the victory at Ligny. Soon, rumors flew of victory beyond imagination: of the destruction of the Prussian army, the retreat of the British, the capture or death of Wellington and/or Blücher (the latter was, in fact, very nearly captured). Victory at Waterloo, peace in the Vendée and elsewhere, national pride and unity restored? Even Napoleon's fiercest critics in the Chambers spoke glowing words towards him, and the President of the Chamber of Deputies, Jean Denis Lanjuinais, sent Napoleon a letter of congratulations that contained assurances that even defeat would not have diminished his universal support. With victory would come peace, and who could argue with that?

But within two days, news of the disaster had reached Paris. Joseph held a meeting of the Council of Ministers and read them Napoleon's letter that outlined the disaster. The ministers felt, perhaps with great justification, that Napoleon should remain, for now, with his soldiers and organize a defense of France. They sent him a message to this effect, but Napoleon's mind had already been made up and he was on his way to Paris.

Bad news travels quickly, and soon all of Paris was buzzing with news of the disaster. Panic soon followed: what should be done? There was talk of Napoleon's abdication, of defending Paris to the last man, of making Napoleon's son emperor, of any number of options.

Fouché Adapts to Events

The hopes of Napoleon's supporters had been destroyed on the fields of Waterloo, but the plans of Fouché were in not much better condition. Fouché had been preparing for Napoleon's ultimate defeat and had even slowed or stopped legal actions against royalists that Napoleon had begun. But not even Fouché expected things to happen so quickly. As Pasquier pointed out about Fouché:

> Now, in order to bring about this result [France inviting Louis XVIII back], he needed time; it was necessary that he should accumulate difficulties which would make his co-operation valuable, and thus acquire credit for having removed them. The rapid march of events had already frustrated his combinations; he had reckoned on a war lasting three months at the very least, and on alternate successes and reverses. In lieu of which, the disaster of Waterloo had, in the space of a week, brought him face to face with a state of things he had not anticipated for two or three months.[4]

Fouché had to move quickly to preserve his own position and at the very least to soften the return of the Bourbons to power. One thing was certain: the people of France had not wanted the Bourbons in 1814, and they did not want them now. If the Bourbons were imposed by the Allies, then the government would be doomed to eternal unpopularity and, thus, ineffectiveness. Of course, this arrangement would likely doom Fouché as well, as Louis XVIII would have no particular reason not to have him shot for his role in Napoleon's return.

On the other hand, there was a possibility that Napoleon would return to Paris and find a way to rally the nation against the invading Allies. A nation in danger can be a nation unified. Napoleon could dissolve the Chambers and rule in the manner of ancient Rome's dictators, taking absolute power just long enough to see the nation through its crisis. Joseph had told the Council of Ministers that Napoleon had exactly this in mind. In this scenario, it was hard to imagine a role for Fouché other than at the lower end of a rope.

Even the Chambers might be a threat to Fouché. If a popular leader, La Fayette, for example, were to seize control of the government with the backing of the Chambers, he might declare Napoleon's son the new emperor or rally the nation against the restoration of the Bourbons. Here, too, Fouché would be in trouble. As for the Allies, it was impossible to say how they would react.

Fouché's first concern was the possibility that Napoleon might dissolve the Chambers and seize complete control of the government. If that happened, Fouché was finished. To forestall that as best he could, Fouché did what he did best: he played the various sides against each other. La Fayette and the other liberals were warned of the dangers of a dictatorship and urged to unite against any such move. He encouraged the Bonapartists to believe that all was lost, that the Chambers were united against Napoleon, and that only his prompt abdication could save the day for the King of Rome, his son, becoming the new emperor in a regency. In this effort he shared Metternich's comments that seemed to leave the door open for a regency. His basic message was simple: to save the Empire, the Emperor must go. As Fouché described it:

> To the unquiet, mistrustful, and obnoxious members of the chamber, I said: 'It is necessary to act, to say little, and resort to force; he is become perfectly insane; he is decided upon dissolving the Chambers and seizing the dictatorship.' ... I said to the partisans of Napoleon, 'Are you not aware that the ferment against the emperor has reached the highest pitch among the majority of the deputies? His fall is desired, his abdication is demanded. If you are bent on serving him, you have but one certain path to follow ...'[5]

Clearly, Fouché did not have Napoleon's best interests in mind. In the words of historian and one-time French Consul at St Helena, Gilbert Martineau, Fouché 'from the seclusion of his office and his own drawing rooms, was busy attacking the Emperor's plans with the effective weapons of treason, fear and duplicity.'[6] General Anne Jean Marie René Savary, who had succeeded Fouché as Minister of Police and served in that role from 1810 to 1814, wrote with some justification, 'It was not possible for the English to be more effectually served than they were by Fouché on the occasion.'[7] Count Montholon probably said it best when he commented, 'Had Napoleon listened to the advice of his brother Joseph, Fouché would have been conveyed from the council to Vincennes as a traitor, and the Empire, which this man destroyed, might perhaps have been saved.'[8]

Chapter 4

Napoleon's Return to Parisian Politics

Politics from the Bath

Napoleon arrived in Paris at about 5.30 a.m. on 21 June. He had sent his valet, Constant, ahead to alert the staff at the Elysée Palace of his impending arrival. Caulaincourt had rushed to meet him there, and his description of their meeting shows the desperate situation into which Napoleon had been thrust:

> The Emperor arrived early in the morning, overcome by grief, and exhausted by fatigue. He endeavored to give vent to the emotions of the heart, but his oppressed respiration permitted him only to articulate broken sentences: 'The army,' he said, 'has performed prodigies of valor! ... inconceivable efforts ... What troops! ... Ney behaved like a madman ... He caused my cavalry to be cut to pieces! ... All has been sacrificed ... I am ill and exhausted ... I must lie down for an hour or two ... My head burns ... I must take a bath!'[1]

Napoleon was exhausted and no doubt covered with the dust of the long trip to Paris. Even so, one can easily imagine the effect he would have had on the Chambers had he simply called them into immediate session and, as La Bédoyère begged him to do, shown up in uniform to rally them to the defense of the fatherland. Fouché would not have had time to properly organize the opposition, and the drama of the moment might well have carried the day. But Napoleon was different after Waterloo, far more content to react to the actions of others than to take the decisive initiative. Whatever the case, Napoleon chose to delay; this decision probably doomed his imperial position and determined his destiny. For 'Napoleon had just lost a great battle; so that the safety of the nation thenceforth depended on the wisdom and zeal of the Chamber of Representatives.'[2] That wisdom and zeal would be found missing in action, at least from the standpoint of Napoleon and his supporters.

Too restless to rest properly, Napoleon instead retired to his bath. He told Caulaincourt that he planned to call the Chambers into an 'imperial sitting' and explain the situation to them. He was certain that they would provide him with the means of saving the country. After that, he expected to return to the army. Caulaincourt had to break it to him that news of Waterloo had created a great deal of hostility in the Chambers and that it was unlikely that they would react as Napoleon had wished. Caulaincourt told Napoleon that the Chambers did not deserve his confidence and that he should have stayed with the army, to which Napoleon retorted that as of now he had no army:

I no longer have an Army. I have nothing but fugitives. I shall find men, but how are they to be armed? I have no muskets left. However, with unanimity everything may be repaired. I hope the deputies will second me; that they will feel the responsibility that will rest upon them. I think you have formed a wrong judgment of their spirit; it is French. I have against me only La Fayette, Lanjuinais, Flaugergue, and a few others. These would fain have nothing to do with me, I know. I am a restraint upon them … my presence here will control them.[3]

By now, Count Lavalette had arrived. Napoleon met him with an exclamation, 'Oh, my God!' Asked to report on the situation in the Chambers, Lavalette told Napoleon that the majority of the Chambers seemed determined to demand his abdication.[4]

Napoleon then called for a meeting of the Council of Ministers. Baron de Méneval soon arrived and found Napoleon in his bath, 'overwhelmed with fatigue and care, and yet mastering the grief with which he was devoured'.[5] His brothers Joseph and Lucien arrived soon afterwards and they gave Napoleon an idea of what the situation in Paris had become. Lucien, who had urged Napoleon to seize dictatorial powers, warned him to expect the worst from the Chambers. Napoleon had feared just that, saying 'You must count La Fayette among those: he will not fail to stir up people against me. They imagine that the Allies are only after me personally, and do not see that in parting with me they will lose France.'[6]

Napoleon was certainly right about La Fayette. In a meeting with Fouché and others on the 20th, La Fayette had already declared that, although Fouché was still giving lip-service to loyalty to Napoleon, 'There is nothing else for the Chamber but to declare itself in permanent session and to demand the abdication of the Emperor; in the case of refusal, to decree his deposition.'[7] La Fayette had become convinced that Napoleon, whom he had never supported, was going to declare himself a dictator and that only he, La Fayette, could preserve a republic in France. It would be he who would form a government (as the Allies had said they could do), once the sole object of Allied desires – that would be Napoleon – was removed from the scene. Of course, none of this was true, but La Fayette had played pivotal roles in both American and French history before and he was determined to do so again.

How had this happened? Savary relates:

Fouché directed his attention to Lafayette. He had received his offers of embarking in the work of disorganization at the period of the *Champ-de-Mai*. He kept the neophyte in reserve, and merely watched the moment to let him loose. False friends were detached to sound him. He was made to believe that everything was prepared; the chamber was on the verge of being dissolved; the imperial *cortège* was about to commence its march; not a moment was to be lost. He believed everything.[8]

While Napoleon was still in his bath, Minister of War Marshal Davout arrived. He immediately urged Napoleon to prorogue (shut down) the Chambers and operate as a temporary dictator. The Council of Ministers was waiting, so Davout went there ahead of Napoleon, who was to arrive shortly thereafter. After some delay, Davout returned to encourage Napoleon to make haste, only to be told that the meeting could start without him, his brother Joseph chairing.[9] One wonders if this was an indication that Napoleon had not really grasped the reality of his precarious situation. While the ministers and other staff waited for Napoleon, their mood was grim and they discussed various possibilities, including Napoleon's abdication.

Napoleon finally joined the meeting and a general discussion of the situation followed. Napoleon told the group that he was inclined to seize temporary dictatorial powers and then asked for their advice. Carnot was determined that France should be defended at all costs. Napoleon should rally the nation, call every person under arms to defend Paris and eventually drive the Allies out of France. If necessary, the army could withdraw behind the Loire river and continue to fight the Allies.

Caulaincourt was more pragmatic, recognizing that the unity of France and the ultimate safety of the nation was more a political question of the relationship between Napoleon and the legislative bodies.

Fouché (of course), Maret and Jean-Jacques-Régis de Cambacérès backed Caulaincourt, calling for Napoleon and his supporters to treat the Chambers with good faith and trust that it would see the necessity of cooperating with Napoleon. Count Michel Regnault, a friend and secretary to Napoleon, had no use for the Chambers, which he felt was convinced that Napoleon must abdicate and that if he did not do so voluntarily it would force the issue. Fouché had convinced him that the Chambers would not tolerate Napoleon on the throne, but that there was an excellent chance for Napoleon's son to preserve the Empire. This was, of course, highly questionable, but such were the uncertainties of the moment and the political maneuvers of Fouché that even Napoleon's most ardent supporters could be convinced to oppose him.

At this point, Napoleon's brother Lucien became rather heated and proposed that Napoleon take matters into his own hands:

> If the Chamber will not second the Emperor, he will dispense with its assistance. The safety of our country ought to be the first law of the state, and since the Chamber does not appear disposed to join the Emperor in saving France, he must save it alone. He must declare himself dictator, place France in a state of siege and call to its defense all the patriots and all good Frenchmen.[10]

In this he was seconded by Carnot and Davout, who was especially strong in his condemnation of the Chambers and wanted a single head of government rather than government by committee or legislative body. Napoleon thundered:

> The nation did not elect the deputies to overthrow me, but to support me. Woe to them if the presence of the enemy on the French soil does not arouse their energy and patriotism! ... I have no need to resort to stratagem. I have right on my side. The patriotism of the people, their antipathy to the Bourbons, who are kept in reserve for them, their attachment to my person – all these circumstances still afford immense resources if we know how to profit by them.[11]

How to profit by the feelings of the people was, of course, a major question, the answer to which never really appeared.

Caulaincourt saw that Fouché was the prime mover against Napoleon's continuing in power and did what he could to counter Fouché's moves. Fouché feared that he was losing ground, and sent notes to his allies in the Chambers warning that Napoleon was about to seize dictatorial power. Napoleon, however, was convinced that if he simply presented the situation in person, the members of the Chambers would fall into line. He outlined for them his plans for saving France, and soon there was agreement that Napoleon should go to the Chambers and seek its support. All seemed in agreement, and they even debated the type of uniform that Napoleon would wear. Various orders and documents were being drawn up, including giving the command of the army defending Paris to Davout, when disaster struck.[12]

Chamber Politics

Fouché had seen to it that the Council of Representatives went into session in the late morning of 21 June, while Napoleon was meeting with the Council of Ministers. This in itself was a clue that something was up, as they normally met in the afternoon. A person loyal to Napoleon, or at least the Empire, might well have waited to see what decisions Napoleon and the Council made and then react to those decisions. But Fouché had other plans. General Thiébault paid a visit to the Chambers and came away convinced of the eventual outcome:

> I went, therefore, to the lobby of the House [the Chamber of Deputies]. Everything was in a state of tumult and buzz, men going in and out, disappearing and reappearing, talking to people of all kinds, who, like the deputies themselves, looked as if they had been bitten by tarantulas. At that moment all disunion, any change of authority, might be fatal, and yet when I left the Chamber I could no longer doubt that this was the melancholy spectacle which the majority meant to give us.[13]

By prior arrangement, La Fayette claimed center stage, arguing that the Chamber should not allow itself to be intimidated by Napoleon and should instead declare itself in permanent session, thus removing Napoleon's ability to dissolve it and take dictatorial powers. A former commander of the National Guard, he urged that it be called to protect the Chamber from any interference. As the *Moniteur* related:

Chamber of Representatives
    Under the Chairmanship of M. le Comte Lanjuinais
    The session opened at 12.15.
    The minutes of the previous session were read and adopted.
    The President announced that M. de La Fayette and M. Lacoste had proposals to put before the Chamber.
    M. de La Fayette: 'Gentlemen, when for the first time for many years I raise a voice that the old friends of liberty will still recognize, I feel myself called

upon to speak to you of the danger to our country which you alone, at this moment, have the power to avert.

'Sinister rumors have been bruited abroad; they have unfortunately proved to be true. This is the time for all of us to rally around our ancient standard, the tricolor, the flag and symbol of '89, of Liberty, Equality and Public Order; it is that alone which we shall have to defend against pretensions from without and upheavals from within. Gentlemen, allow a veteran of this sacred cause to submit to you certain preliminary proposals, whose necessity you will, I hope, appreciate:

'Article 1. The Chamber of Representatives declares that the independence of the country is threatened.

'Article 2. The Chamber declares itself in permanent session. Any attempt to dissolve it is high treason; whoever may be guilty of such an attempt is a traitor to the country and may summarily be judged as such.

'Article 3. The army of the line and the National Guard who have fought and who are still fighting to defend the liberty, the independence and the territory of France have deserved well of the country.

'Article 4. The Minister of the Interior is requested to summon the General Staff and the commanders and senior officers of the National Guard in order to consult about giving them arms and encouraging to the full this citizen guard whose patriotism and zeal, proved over the past twenty-six years, provides a sure guarantee of the liberty, the property, the peace of the capital and the inviolability of the representatives of the nation.

'Article 5. The Ministers of War, of External Affairs, of the Police and of the Interior are requested to present themselves to the Assembly immediately.'

Tumultuous applause.[14]

The resolution was reminiscent of the famous Tennis Court Oath of 1789, an oath that eventually led to the downfall of a king. This one would lead to the downfall of an emperor. La Fayette the republican thought he had removed an emperor to preserve a republic. Instead, he had guaranteed the return of a Bourbon king whom only a small minority in France wanted. He had listened to Fouché and Fouché had played him like a fiddle. Years later, on St Helena, Napoleon would say that La Fayette 'was another simpleton, and by no means formed for the eminent character he wished to represent. His political simplicity was such that he could not avoid being the constant dupe of men and things.'[15]

One might have expected that Napoleon's supporters would have seen through this action and objected and possibly blocked any further action by the Chambers. But they were mostly silent and the Chambers voted to follow La Fayette's lead, just as Fouché had planned. The members of the Chambers had feared that Napoleon would seize power, so they countered this possible move by seizing power themselves; it was nothing less than a legislative *coup d'état* against imperial authority, to say nothing of the Constitution. As Lavalette, one of Napoleon's earliest and most loyal supporters, observed:

No hope could rest on the Chamber of Representatives. They all said they wished for liberty, but between two enemies who appeared ready to destroy it, they preferred the foreigners, the friends of the Bourbons, to Napoleon, who might still have prolonged the struggle, because they were silly enough to despise the former and fear the latter. Besides, each person took counsel only from his resentment or egotism. Some hoped to escape in the confusion because they were unknown; others thought they might draw advantage from circumstances; and the majority, foolishly trusting to the promises of the foreign Powers, were still persuaded that the Bourbons would not return to Paris, or, at least, that the King, convinced of his weakness and incapacity for government, would be so strongly bridled and fettered that he would neither be able to revenge himself nor to violate the Constitution.[16]

In the words of Napoleon's stepdaughter, Queen Hortense, the Chamber of Representatives 'discussed the principles of political freedom as though armed Europe were advancing to enforce this ideal.'[17]

Napoleon well understood the meaning of the resolution of the Chambers. By all accounts he was livid at the action of the Chambers:

The Emperor turned pale with anger. He rose, and striking his hand forcibly on the table, exclaimed, in a tone of indignation, 'I ought to have dismissed these men before my departure. I foresaw this. These factious firebrands will ruin France. I can measure the full extent of the evil. They are in open rebellion against legitimate authority. I must reflect on what must be done.'[18]

De Chaboulon adds that Napoleon commented as he retired from the sitting of the Council of Ministers, 'I see Regnault did not deceive me: if it must be so, I will abdicate.'[19] This was probably not the thing to have said, and Napoleon quickly tried to withdraw the statement. But word of his comment reached the Chambers and could only have served to increase their boldness in standing up to the increasingly weakened Emperor.

The actions of the Chambers were clearly against the constitution and probably against the interests of the French people. For whatever else could be said about Napoleon and his position at the time, he was the sole unifying force that remained in the nation, and the only hope to avoid a return of the Bourbons, a return wanted by only a small minority of people. Napoleon did, indeed, need to reflect on what his next steps should be. But time was running out. Hortense, who witnessed much of what was happening, was very concerned about Napoleon's refusal – or inability – to make a decision:

As for me my one thought was: how can the Emperor be saved? I watched him talking on and on with his brothers without ever making a decision. The longer he waited, the more he ceased to be master of his fate, but it seemed that no one, not even he, cared about what happened to him.[20]

Still unable to quite believe the foolishness of the Chambers, he confided to his brother, Joseph:

They are insane, and La Fayette and his friends are naïve politicians: they want me to abdicate in favor of my son, but that is a farce when the enemy is at the Paris gates, and the Bourbons right behind them. United we could save ourselves; divided, we are helpless.[21]

Although he was advised again to dissolve the Chambers and take advantage of the huge crowds of *fédérés* who were chanting 'Vive l'Empereur!' throughout Paris, Napoleon was not quite ready to give up on the Chambers. He sent Regnault to the Chamber of Deputies and Carnot to the Chamber of Peers, each to explain that Napoleon had returned and was preparing measures to hold off the advancing enemy. Neither man had any success. Napoleon was angry at the effort of the Chambers to gain control of his ministers, but the members of the Chambers were equally upset at the notion that Napoleon might seize power from them and rule as a dictator. Rumors again flew about the town: Napoleon was leading troops on the Chambers, Napoleon was abdicating, the Allies were at the gates, La Fayette was to be given command of the Imperial Guard.

Napoleon made another effort to obtain the cooperation of the Chambers. He sent his ministers to meet with the Chamber of Representatives, accompanied by his brother Lucien as a special minister. This group arrived at six o'clock in the evening. At Lucien's request, the public galleries were cleared and the members listened intently to his report, which included a message from Napoleon:

Message to the Chamber of Representatives
  Elysée Palace
  21 June 1815
  Mr President
  After the battles of Ligny and of Mont-Saint-Jean [what the Allies called the Battle of Waterloo], and after having prepared for the rallying of the army at Avesnes and at Philippeville and for the defense of the frontier fortresses and of the cities of Laon and Soissons, I went to Paris to consult with my ministers on measures of national defense, and to come to an agreement with the Chambers on all matters touching the salvation of the country.
  I have formed a committee, made up of the Minister of Foreign Affairs, of Count Carnot and the Duke of Otranto, to renew and follow up the negotiations with the Allied foreign powers in order to ascertain their real intentions, and put an end to the war, if it is compatible with the independence and honor of the nation. But the greatest union is necessary and I count on the cooperation and the patriotism of the Chambers and on their attachment to my person.
  I sent to the Chambers, as commissioners, Prince Lucien and the Ministers of Foreign Affairs, of War, of the Interior and of the general Police to transport this message and to give any news or information that the Chambers may require.

Napoleon[22]

Lucien related an outline of what happened at Waterloo and called upon the Representatives to join with Napoleon to save the nation from a return of the Bourbons. He asked that each Chamber appoint five members to a committee to work with Napoleon and his ministers towards the public good. When Lucien was finished, chaos took hold and there was little serious consideration given to his plea for national unity. La Fayette and others accused Napoleon of forgetting the support that the deputies had given him in the past, and several pointed out that the Allies had declared war only against Napoleon and that were he to abdicate, all would be well. To this, Lucien responded:

> Shall we still have the weakness to believe the words of our enemies? When victory was for the first time faithless to us, did they not swear in the presence of God and man, that they would respect our independence and our laws? Let us not fall a second time into the snare that they have set for our confidence, for our credulity. Their aim in their endeavour to separate the nation from the Emperor is to disunite us in order to vanquish us, and replunge us more easily into that degradation and slavery from which his return delivered us. I conjure you, citizens, by the sacred name of our country, rally all of you round the chief, whom the nation has so solemnly replaced at its head. Consider that our safety depends on our union, and that you cannot separate yourselves from the Emperor and abandon him to his enemies without ruining the state, without being faithless to your oaths, without tarnishing forever the national honour.[23]

This speech was met by more shouting and turmoil, which was calmed by the voice of La Fayette:

> You accuse us, said he, addressing Prince Lucien, of failing in our duties towards our honour, and towards Napoleon. Have you forgotten all that we have done for him? Have you forgotten that we followed him in the sands of Africa, in the deserts of Russia, and that the bones of our sons and brothers everywhere attest our fidelity? For him we have done enough: it is our duty now, to save our country.[24]

More shouting then took place, with both supporters and opponents of Napoleon trying to overwhelm the other. But in due course, each Chamber appointed a committee to study the situation, which is to say, each Chamber tossed the ball back into Napoleon's court.

When Lucien returned to see Napoleon, he had no good news to convey. He made it clear to Napoleon that the choice was either to seize complete control of the government by dissolving the Chambers or to abdicate in favor of his son. Napoleon was again indignant and inclined to stand up to the Chambers. But many who had supported this stand earlier in the day now recognized that the time for that sort of action had come and gone. Earlier in the day, Davout had strongly supported the idea of Napoleon dissolving the Chambers and ruling as a dictator, but he now counseled against any use of force to gain control of the government. Indeed, Davout had informed the Chamber of Representatives that any rumors that he, Davout, was planning to lead a military action against them were completely false and that the Emperor had ordered no such move. Caulaincourt and Maret also counseled against the use of force, arguing that public opinion would never support such a move.

Napoleon had been reflecting on his situation, and that of France, while all of this was taking place. He had talked at some length with Benjamin Constant, the liberal writer who had opposed him during the Empire but had rallied to his cause for the Hundred Days and had even helped write the new constitution. It was this liberal document that had helped rally progressives to Napoleon when he returned from Elba, but it was also this document that was used by the Chambers to defy Napoleon.

To Constant, Napoleon offered this analysis:

> The issue no longer concerns me, it concerns France. They want me to abdicate. Have they considered the inevitable consequences of such an abdication? I, and my name, are the center around which the army is grouped; if you take me away, it will dissolve. If I abdicate today, there will be no army in two days' time … The army does not understand all your subtleties. Do you suppose that metaphysical axioms, declarations of rights and parliamentary eloquence can stop them from breaking ranks? … One cannot overthrow the Government with impunity when the enemy is only a few miles away. Does anyone suppose that the foreign invaders can be put off with phrases? … If she [France] gives me up, she surrenders herself, admits her weakness, acknowledges defeat and encourages the conqueror's audacity … it is not liberty that is deposing me, but Waterloo.[25]

Savary's advice was especially convincing. He writes of their conversation, which included Benjamin Constant, where he said:

> It is possible that the proposal may be suggested to you of dissolving their sittings; but this is no longer practicable, because they have foreseen the blow, and begun by taking possession of power. At the present day, you would hardly find anyone willing to march against them. If ever they supposed you meditated such a project, they would find many wretches willing to lay violent hands upon you. Your Majesty would, besides, have no sooner succeeded in dissolving them and securing possession of the field than you would be at a loss what to do. You would not have one battalion more at command, and all the consequences of those events, which it would no longer be in your power to prevent, would be imputed to you. Since those bewildered and enthusiastic minds deem themselves so sure of doing better by following their own views, they should be taken at their word and left to shift for themselves. Besides which, I added, all minds are in such a state of excitement this evening that something new will infallibly happen tomorrow. I should not be surprised if, by way of a preliminary measure, they should send to propose your abdicating your authority.[26]

George Russell, an American student who was in Paris during this time, perhaps sums up Napoleon's position as well as anyone:

> Yes, Napoleon was in Paris – a general without soldiers and a sovereign without subjects. The *prestige* of his name was gone, and had the Chamber of Deputies invested him with the dictatorship, as was suggested, it would have been 'a barren scepter in his grip', and the utmost stretch of power could not have collected materials to meet the impending invasion. At no period did he show such irresolution as at this time.[27]

Napoleon made one last effort to reach accommodation with the Chambers. Late in the evening he sent Lucien to ask that they rally to the Emperor's cause so that he might lead the nation against the advancing enemy. Now was not the time to try to form a new government; the enemy was on the borders of France and the nation needed to rally to its defense. It would have been a perfectly reasonable request in most circumstances, but given the attitude of the members of the Chambers, molded by Fouché and La Fayette and inflamed by groundless rumors, it had no chance at all of succeeding. By now their position was pretty much set in stone: abdicate 'voluntarily' or we will force you out of power. This was the message that Lucien brought back to his brother.

Sometime after 11 p.m., as the eventful day of the 21st was drawing to a close, the Chambers sent its two committees to meet with Napoleon's ministers. Napoleon dined with Hortense, awaiting news. Not surprisingly, Napoleon was quiet, no doubt depressed from all that had transpired. Already there was talk of where Napoleon might go if he abdicated; America and Britain were the only two alternatives that seemed plausible.

Joseph presided at the meeting that included Lucien, ten ministers, and nine representatives from the Chamber of Peers as well as nine from the Chamber of Representatives. After much discussion of the general state of affairs, the group brought up the question of Napoleon's abdication. La Fayette argued for it, with Lucien in strong disagreement. The idea was rejected by a narrow margin, but a majority of the legislative representatives present voted for it, a bad omen for Napoleon.

The group did vote to have the Chambers appoint a committee to negotiate directly with the Allies, and to demand of them France's right to choose her own form of government and to remain an independent nation. At first defeated, the motion was eventually passed, with the proviso that Napoleon approve the delegation. This resolution, of course, wasn't nearly good enough for La Fayette and those who were insistent that Napoleon be required to abdicate then and there, but it was the best that the group could do. Exhausted, they ended their meeting around 3 a.m. on 22 June.

Chapter 5

Day of Decision

Hopeless Choices

Each of the Chambers reassembled around 9 a.m. on 22 June. The first order of business in the Chamber of Representatives was to hear General Grenier's report on the results of the conference at the Elysée Palace earlier that morning. Some of the members had expected that Napoleon would have arrested his most bitter foes before the meeting and, as he did not do this, they assumed he was unable to resist whatever action they chose to take. They were right, of course; the time for Napoleon to seize dictatorial power had come and gone. General Grenier also told the members that if Napoleon felt it necessary to make the ultimate sacrifice he was prepared to do so. Rather than calm the waters, this statement simply gave ammunition to those who wanted Napoleon to abdicate immediately. Many were under the impression that the meeting the night before was called to force an immediate abdication, and these people were furious to discover that this had not been the case. Some, led by La Fayette and others such as Duchesne de l'Isère, argued for the Emperor to be deposed. Others wanted to give Napoleon a chance to step down gracefully. It was clear that, one way or the other, Napoleon's time as Emperor was limited. Regnault had already gone to Napoleon to warn him of the state of affairs.

The members were not to be denied: Napoleon was through. But, as they somewhat tactfully put it, 'to save the honor of the head of state', they voted to give Napoleon one hour to abdicate. This was not as kind as it might seem. The streets were full of Napoleon's supporters, many of them armed. The army was, correctly, assumed to be loyal to the man who had led them to glory for fifteen years. To depose Napoleon would be to risk an immediate, and bloody, counteraction against the government, and woe be to those who voted for deposition. No, Napoleon would have to be given the chance, however much under pressure, to step down 'for the good of the country'.

General Jean-Baptiste Solignac, leading a delegation that included four other members, had the unhappy task of relaying that message to Napoleon, but it was not, by then, particularly unexpected. Lucien and Joseph had each urged decisive action early, but now recognized the futility of such measures and urged Napoleon to abdicate. In this advice they were joined by Regnault, Caulaincourt and Savary.

Crowds outside the palace were chanting 'Vive l'Empereur!', and Carnot still thought that Napoleon should take immediate action against the Chambers, but it was of no use. Davout, whose support for such action could have made a difference, stood by silently. He had given up on Napoleon, having been disappointed by Napoleon's lack of decisive measures the previous day and, indeed, by his decision to leave his army and come to Paris in the first place. Davout despised Fouché, but now felt he had little choice but to allow things to take their course, even if that meant that France's fate would be in the hands of someone who, in Davout's mind, was only out to preserve his own hide.[1]

Napoleon was now faced with hopeless choices. It was still possible that he could march to the Chambers with his Guard and other loyal units, supported by the *fédérés* and his ministers, and dissolve them as he had done in 1799 when he first gained power. There was no question that this action would have probably worked when he first arrived in Paris and discovered the attitude of many members of the Chambers (while he was at it, he could have arrested Fouché). Now, however, it was probably too late.

As a second option, Napoleon could also have acquiesced in the desire of the Chambers and had them negotiate directly with the Allies. But there was no reason at all to believe that they would have remained loyal to him and certainly they would have come under great pressure from the Allies to turn on their sovereign.

The third option, of course, was to abdicate in favor of his son. This was risky, as it entailed giving power to the Chambers while removing it from himself. While many in the Chambers seemed to support the idea of a regency, it was impossible to predict how they would react to pressure from the Allies in favor of the Bourbons. On the one hand, they might well rally to the cause of the Empire, if not the Emperor, and resist any effort by foreign powers to dictate their form of government or the personage of their leader.

On the other hand, there were certainly those who felt that if the Allies wanted the Bourbons, then so be it. And who could say what position Fouché would ultimately take? Further, of course, Talleyrand was never far away and quite capable of manipulating the situation to his, and the Bourbons', advantage.

Napoleon certainly considered the first option of disbanding the Chambers, but he feared its outcome. The last thing he wanted to be remembered for was that he caused a bloody civil war. And to seize power by military force would remove, at least superficially, his claim to having power by the support of the people. Such a course of action would also make it easier for the Allies to claim that their problems were with Napoleon and not France, and that now it seemed that France also had problems with the power-hungry Emperor.

In the end, Napoleon, whose spirit must surely have been broken by now, decided to go with the third course of action, abdication in favor of his son, because 'Napoleon owed it to his glory, and to the nation, which had twice confided its destinies to him, to exhibit in the fullest manner the purity of his intentions, and to prove to posterity, that if France should perish it was not at least for the interests of a single man that she was sacrificed'.[2]

Later, on St Helena, Napoleon discussed his decision at some length with Las Cases. It was clear that he was torn between taking power and abdicating, but that he feared civil war and the destruction it would have brought to France – and to his place in history:

I hesitated long, I weighed every argument on both sides; and I at length concluded that I could not make head against the coalition without, and the royalists within; that I should be unable to oppose the numerous sects which would have been created by the violence committed on the Legislative Body, to control that portion of the multitude which must be driven by force, or to resist that moral condemnation which imputes to him who is unfortunate every evil that ensues. Abdication was therefore absolutely the only step I could adopt. All was lost in spite of me. I foresaw and foretold this; but still I had no other alternative.[3]

He was right, of course. In the words of Caulaincourt, the abdication 'remedied no evil; it has not saved France from becoming the prey of conflicting parties, nor from being ruined by a feeble government. In short, the Emperor's abdication left the field open to all sorts of political speculations.'[4]

Abdication

The decision had been made, but when Napoleon received the ultimatum – abdicate in one hour or we will depose you – he was furious and thought briefly of calling the whole deal off. His steam soon blew off, much to the relief of most of those around him. Fouché was there, impassive as ever but no doubt deeply concerned that Napoleon might still foil all of his, Fouché's, plans. He was surely relieved when Napoleon turned to him and told him to write to the Chambers to be calm, as they would soon get what they wanted. Fouché did exactly that. It was now after noon and time to do what must be done. Napoleon dictated the following declaration to his brother Lucien:

Declaration to the French People

Frenchmen, in commencing the war to maintain national independence, I counted on the union of all efforts, of all wills and on the assistance of all the national authorities. I felt justified in hoping for success, and defied all the declarations of the powers against me.

The circumstances appear to have changed.

I offer myself as a sacrifice to the hatred of the enemies of France. May they be sincere in their declarations and only desire my person!

My political life is finished, and I proclaim my son, under the title of Napoleon II, Emperor of the French.

The present ministers will form provisionally the council of government. The interest I carry for my son causes me to ask the Chambers to organize, without delay, a regency by law.

All of you unite for the public good, for remaining an independent nation.

At the Élysée Palace, 22 June 1815.
Napoleon[5]

Fleury de Chaboulon made two copies; when Napoleon signed them he noticed tear stains from the emotional Fleury. A copy was sent to the Chamber of Representatives in the care of Fouché, Caulaincourt and Decrès, while Carnot, Mollien and Gaudin took a copy to the Chamber of Peers. Shortly after they left, the Count de la Borde, who was the adjutant general of the National Guard, arrived, warning Napoleon of his impending deposition. No matter, the deed was already done.

When Fouché arrived at the Chamber of Representatives, he gave the abdication to Lanjuinais, who was the president of that body. After admonishing the members to remain respectfully silent, Lanjuinais read the document to them. Fouché then took the floor and, in a statement that must surely have made some in the audience gag, proclaimed, 'The representatives of the nation must not forget, in the course of the coming negotiations, to guard the interests of the man who has presided over the destiny of our country for so many long years.'[6] Regnault then took the floor and gave an emotional speech on the greatness of Napoleon. Many wept and the rest were silent, but the speech had no influence on what would follow.

The Chamber of Representatives then voted to declare itself the National Assembly (its title under the Republic), and that an executive commission be formed to run the government, three members selected by the Assembly and two by the Chamber of Peers. Moreover, the throne was declared to be vacant; Napoleon's son was not mentioned, but the right of the nation to choose its own leader was maintained.

Fouché, of course, was behind most of what was happening, and his comments give a good sense of how he saw things and how he manipulated things in his favor:

> Here then was a change of scene; the power having passed away from the hands of Napoleon, who was to remain master of the field? I soon detected the secret designs of the cabinet; I discovered that the Bonapartist party, now under the guidance of Lucien, intended, as a consequence of the abdication, to countenance the immediate proclamation of Napoleon II, and the establishment of a council of regency. This would have been to have suffered the hostile camp to triumph. In fact, that regency which had been for so long a time the drift of all my calculations, and the object of all my desires, being now about to be organized under another influence than mine, excluded me from a share in the government. It was necessary, therefore, to recur to new combinations, and to man counter-batteries, in order, with equal address, to defeat the system of the regency and the restoration of the Bourbons. I therefore conceived the creation of a provisional government established in conformity with my own suggestions, and which, in consequence, I should be able to direct according to my own views. I presented myself to the chamber with a view of inducing it to act with decision in consecrating the principles and the laws of the Revolution.[7]

The resolution adopted by the Chamber was as follows:

> The Chamber of Representatives, considering that the common weal is the supreme law, declares:
>   1. The Chamber of Representatives, in the name of the French nation, accepts

the abdication of Napoleon.

2. The Chamber of Representatives resolves itself into a National Assembly. Delegates shall leave forthwith for the headquarters of the Allies to insist on France's right to independence, and in a special fashion on the inviolability of Napoleon's person.

3. An executive commission of five members shall be appointed, of which three shall be chosen by the Chamber of Representatives and two by the Chamber of Peers.

4. This commission shall appoint a generalissimo forthwith. The ministers will remain in office.

5. A special commission shall be entrusted with the preparation of a new constitution, which shall guarantee our national institutions, and form the basis of the past and conditions on which the throne will be occupied by the prince whom the nation shall have chosen.[8]

The omission of Napoleon's son infuriated his supporters and they, led by Lucien, objected loudly, but to no avail. Lucien pointed out (1) that Napoleon had abdicated in favor of his son, (2) the constitutional provisions for succession, (3) Article 67 of the *Acte Additionnel aux Constitutions de l'Empire* forbade any proposal to bring back the Bourbons or any other branch of that family,[9] and (4) the oaths that the members had taken to preserve the Empire: in short, that the resolution was unconstitutional and, thus, illegal. These arguments were countered by the fact that Napoleon II was not in the country, nor was his mother and presumed regent, Marie Louise; that, indeed, Napoleon II was actually a captive in Austria and that there was no guarantee that the Allies would allow his return to France.

Others pointed out that had Napoleon been killed, his son would have succeeded to the throne, and that things should be no different with a political defeat in the form of an abdication. In the end, the resolution was passed, with supporters pointing out that it did not compromise the right of Napoleon II to gain the throne should circumstances permit. This compromise was passed on the strength of that argument, but in reality the passage of this resolution doomed any chance for the continuance of the Empire.

The debate over declaring Napoleon's son Napoleon II infuriated some of Napoleon's strongest supporters. Some of their speeches may have done harm to their cause. General de La Bédoyère, for example, gave an angry speech that probably did more harm than good:

The abdication of Napoleon is not to be divided. If it is not the intention to recognize his son, his duty is to draw his sword once more, surrounded by those Frenchmen who have already shed their blood for him. Certain vile generals have already betrayed him, but woe to traitors! We who have sworn to defend him even in his misfortune, dare declare that every Frenchman deserting his flag shall be branded with infamy, his house shall be razed to the ground, and his family proscribed. No longer will there then be any traitors, nor any of those intrigues, the cause of recent catastrophes, whose authors are perhaps sitting in our midst.[10]

The Assembly sent a delegation to Napoleon to thank him for his noble sacrifice. Napoleon was understandably cool towards them, and responded with the following comments, more in the nature of a lecture:

I thank you for the sentiments you express towards me. I wish that my abdication may procure the happiness of France, *but I have no expectation of it.* It leaves the state without a head, without political existence. The time wasted in overturning the monarchy [Empire] might have been employed in putting France into a condition to crush the enemy. I recommend to the Chamber, speedily to reinforce the armies; whoever is desirous of peace ought to prepare for war. Do not leave this great nation at the mercy of foreigners; be on your guard against being deceived by your hopes. *There lies the danger.* In whatever situation I may find myself, I shall always be at ease, if France be happy. I recommend my son to France. I hope it will not forget that I abdicated only for him. I have made this great sacrifice also for the good of the nation; it is only with my dynasty that it can expect to be free, happy and independent.[11]

Napoleon made much the same comment to a delegation sent by the Chamber of Peers.

Marshal Ney

Throughout the day, the Chamber of Peers had largely followed the lead of the Chamber of Representatives. When they received Napoleon's abdication, they voted to accept it and, like the other Chamber, sent a delegation to thank Napoleon for his noble sacrifice. In an effort to rally the nation and give it hope, Interior Minister Carnot, speaking for Minister of War Davout, gave a report to the Chamber of Peers on the military situation in France. This report pointed out that Marshal Grouchy had maintained his corps (which had not been defeated in battle) in good order and that many other soldiers had rallied so that he, in fact, had a rather formidable fighting force that he was bringing to defend Paris from the anticipated Allied attack.

This was important for several reasons. If the Chambers – and the people of France – could be convinced that resistance to the Allies was still quite possible, then the new government might well order the army to defend France, or at least Paris. This would strengthen France's position in the negotiations with the Allies and probably make it less likely that foreign powers would once again impose the Bourbons on a reluctant France. Thus, resistance to the Allies for only a few days might greatly increase the possibility that Napoleon II would take the throne and the liberal Empire be preserved. This would not be to Fouché's liking, but there might be relatively little that he could do about it. But, as it happened, he had an ally in the Chambers who carried more weight on this topic than anyone else possibly could.

Marshal Michel Ney, the cavalry commander at Waterloo whose attacks both inspired and doomed the French army, had followed the stream of soldiers heading back to Paris and had arrived there not long after his Emperor. Rather than report to Napoleon or to the Minister of War (Davout) for orders, he instead went directly to Fouché to obtain passports. Ney may not have been the brightest star in the constellation, but he could certainly imagine that if the Bourbons ever returned he would be in big trouble. After all, he had accepted a position with them and then, when sent to stop Napoleon's march to Paris in April, instead defected to the Emperor and fought with him at Waterloo.

Fouché was happy to oblige, and gave Ney two passports. One of them was legitimate, made out to Ney in all his grandeur: Marshal of the Empire, Duke of Elchingen, Prince of the Moskova, Peer of France. The other one was a fake, 'just in case', made out to Michel Theodore Neubourg, merchant. Other 'servants' were listed to allow for Ney to take family members or others who needed a quick passage out of town.

His own preservation secure (or so he thought), Ney made his way to the Chamber of Peers (of which he was a member) to observe events at first hand. He arrived just in time to hear Carnot's report on the possibility of military resistance to the Allies. Ney, who was known for having a temper and for often speaking prior to thinking, immediately took the floor. Whether he sought to somehow place himself in a better light vis-à-vis Grouchy, or whether he simply felt that things were not as rosy as Carnot had made them out to be, he loudly blasted what the members had just heard.

The news ... which the Minister of the Interior has just read, is false – false in every respect. The enemy is victorious at every point. I have witnessed the disaster, for I commanded the army under the Emperor. After the results of those days of disaster – the 16th and the 18th – they dare to tell us that we ended by beating the enemy on the 18th, and that there are 60,000 men on the frontier. The statement is false. At the very most Marshal Grouchy has perhaps rallied 20,000 or 25,000 men. When they tell us that the Prussian army has been destroyed, it is not true. The greater part of that army has not been in action. In six or seven days the enemy will perhaps be in the midst of the capital. There is no other means for securing the public safety but to make proposals to the enemy at once.[12]

The Peers were stunned at this outburst and several told him privately that it had been inappropriate and would damage the morale of the troops as well as the citizens. Many were saddened to see 'the bravest of the brave' act in such a manner, and a few wondered if he were in his right mind. But no matter, the damage was done.

Scramble for Power

The two Chambers now turned to the election of their representatives to the five-member Executive Commission of the Provisional Government. Fouché, of course, was determined that he should not only be elected as one of the representatives of the Chamber of Representatives, but also end up as the head of the government by being elected President of the Commission. This was not as foregone a conclusion as he might have wished, however. There were plenty of people who deeply resented his actions, and others who simply did not want the head of the secret police running the government.

Moreover, there were plenty of other candidates who seemed likely to attract a great deal of support. Fouché did not simply wait around to see what happened. He worked actively to assure his election. As usual, he did what he could to muddy the waters. His biggest concern was probably La Fayette, whose help he had desperately needed in the beginning but whose popularity was now a threat to his own election. Fouché clearly needed to be careful in dealing with him, but he managed to remind the Bonapartists that La Fayette had led the movement to demand Napoleon's abdication (forgetting to mention, of course, who put him up to it), while reminding the royalists of La Fayette's republican past. Besides, Fouché pointed out, a man of La Fayette's stature should head the National Guard and perhaps undertake other important roles as well.

Lanjuinais, the President of the Assembly, was also popular, but Fouché managed to convince many members that they should leave Lanjuinais in his already very important post. Other possible competitors, Marshal Macdonald, for example, were dispensed with in a like manner.

As to Fouché himself? Why, to the Bonapartists he had always been acting in their best interests, to the supporters of the Duc d'Orléans he was working hard on their behalf, and to the supporters of Louis XVIII, how could they forget his connections to the Court, now in Ghent and soon to be in Paris? Somehow, he never mentioned his true feelings and goals, summed up in his comments to Pasquier, 'Nothing is better … than that the Bourbons should return; it is even necessary that they should, but under good conditions, clearly defined, firmly guaranteed, and which shall prove a safeguard of the rights, the interests, and the positions of all.'[13]

In other words, Fouché had no interest in having anyone but Louis XVIII on the throne, but only if the King could be forced to accept a constitution that placed restrictions on his power. And, of course, it was important that the King understand just exactly who had been responsible for his reclaiming the throne: Fouché! This outcome was anything but certain, however, as there was substantial opposition to the Bourbons in both houses of the Chambers. Fouché had managed to see that there were few Bonapartists in the Chamber of Representatives, but there were even fewer committed royalists to be found there. The largest block was comprised of liberals, who were probably more disposed towards putting Napoleon II on the throne than in bringing back Louis XVIII. As to the Chamber of Peers, it comprised largely people who had been loyal to Napoleon, and was likely to be even less interested in the Bourbons. But it was also in something of a state of depression and had, thus far, followed the lead of the lower house.

As can well be imagined, the election of the Assembly's members to the Executive Commission was a serious matter, and the debate and campaigning took a great deal of time on the 22nd. Fouché, apparently convinced that he had done all he could, went home to await the results. There, he was joined by dozens of people, not all of whom were supportive of his efforts, but all of whom certainly understood that he was, and would be, at the very center of power.

By early evening, Fouché was informed of the results of the election in the Chamber of Representatives. He had, in fact, been elected as one of the three members, but his 293 votes made him second to the popular liberal (and devout supporter of Napoleon) Carnot. General Paul Grenier had been elected to the third position. Carnot would not be at all interested in bringing back the Bourbons. The Chamber of Peers, who took until a little before 3 a.m. on the 23rd, elected (in the second round) Minister of Foreign Affairs Armand-Augustin-Louis de Caulaincourt, Duc de Vicence (fifty-two votes) and Nicolas-Marie Quinette, Baron de Rochemont (forty-eight votes) to be their representatives to the Provisional Government. Lucien Bonaparte had come third with eighteen votes. Quinette's selection was the biggest surprise of the election. It may also be worth noting that the five-member commission had three regicides. Carnot, Fouché and Quinette had all voted for the death of Louis XVI in 1792.[14]

When the commission met later in the morning of the 23rd, at the Tuileries Palace, Fouché was at his best, though he took a significant risk to achieve his goal. He was, of course, determined to be the head of the Provisional Government by virtue of being President of the Executive Commission. But the popular Carnot had received more votes than Fouché and wanted to be President as well. That seemed a foregone conclusion to all but Fouché. Counting on the goodwill of all there and on the other members not suspecting him of being up to anything (and why they would not suspect this is anyone's guess), Fouché called for an election of President of the Executive Commission and announced that he would vote for Carnot. This all seemed like a gesture designed to bring early unity to the Commission. In a magnanimous gesture, Carnot declared that he would vote for Fouché. This cannot have been a serious comment, simply a friendly gesture, but it immediately backfired. Grenier, Caulaincourt and Quinette, who would probably have been willing to support Carnot, instead declared for Fouché, who was elected. In the words of the official law published that day, 'La *Commission du Gouvernement* se constitue sous la présidence de M. le duc d'Otrante'. (The Commission of the Government is constituted under the presidency of the Duke of Otranto.)[15]

Carnot had been outwitted, but he was by no means the only person Fouché had bested that week. It had been an amazing several days, and there was much more to come, but Fouché had thus far been completely victorious and had seemingly supplanted Napoleon as the most powerful person in France. He was now free to work towards his ultimate goal, the restoration – with significant conditions – of Louis XVIII.[16] Fouché had certainly shown what he was capable of doing, much to the surprise of some:

> On the one side was France, her representatives, her army, and a decided superiority of position; on the other was Fouché, whose store of subtle talent appeared to multiply itself in proportion to the emergencies. How he managed

to be named a member, and even president of the 'Commission of Government' I do not now remember, but, undoubtedly, it was by some clever trick and legerdemain, only practicable at such a moment of national stupefaction and bewilderment.[17]

Those who were surprised at Fouché's emergence should not have been, nor should they have been surprised at the results of his activities. As Napoleon's valet Louis Marchand related:

The provisional government had been named: names like Caulaincourt and Carnot reassured decent people, but that of the Duke of Otranto (Fouché) gave cause for concern. That minister was habitually surrounded by intrigue and treachery.[18]

Chapter 6

Napoleon II, Emperor of the French

Fouché Takes the Reins

Fouché had been put into a very powerful position, but he was not in complete control of all events and all eventualities. There was still a great deal of support for declaring that Napoleon II was taking the vacated throne, as per the constitution. If this happened, all sorts of things might follow, none of which were what Fouché had in mind. Fouché still had to deal with the existence of the Chambers, the strong Bonapartist feelings on the part of many in those bodies, and the crowds of people in the streets crying out 'Vive L'Empereur!', each day seemingly more loudly than the last. In addition, people like Pasquier seemed intent on pushing for an immediate declaration for Louis XVIII, a move that Pasquier felt was the only way to assure peace at home and abroad. To this suggestion, Fouché replied:

> Do you imagine that I am not as well aware of this as yourself? But we have been so taken by surprise. He has been crushed so quickly that he has not given us time to mature any plans, and it is impossible to convert the public mind in a day. Moreover, we must be careful of the feelings of the army, which we must not frighten away, but which we must see to rally to our cause, for it might yet do a great deal of harm; if people will only not hurry too much, all things will be settled for the best and to the satisfaction of all.[1]

Fouché moved quickly to organize the government. Marshal Davout, who was still Minister of War, was given the responsibility for the defense of Paris; he was now Commander-in-Chief of the Army. Marshal Masséna, who had not rallied to Napoleon's cause for the Hundred Days, was made commander of the National Guard.[2] So much for La Fayette's being indispensable for that role. Drouot was given command of the Imperial Guard. Fouché brought to an end all efforts to prepare defenses to the city of Paris, a move that should have telegraphed his ultimate intentions to one and all.

On the morning of the 23rd, the Bonapartists in the Chamber of Representatives made their final push to preserve the Empire. In keeping with the constitution, they demanded that Napoleon's son be declared Napoleon II. This in itself would not be a disaster to Fouché's plans, but if they followed this declaration with the creation of a Regency Council, he would be in trouble, as that Council would doubtless replace the Executive Commission of which he was President. In Fouché's view, at least, this would increase the likelihood of the Allies not accepting the new government and, thus, a continuation of the war. It also meant that if the Bourbons were restored to the throne, it would be by force rather than by the 'will' of the people (well, the 'will' of Fouché, anyway).

The question of taking an oath of office was raised, and the question then was: to whom should the oath be taken? There was also the question of in whose name the Provisional Government would act. Seizing upon this opportunity, the Bonapartists pointed out that Napoleon II should, by virtue of Napoleon's abdication and the constitution, be the head of state, and moved to have the Chamber declare him so. One of the implicit possibilities, one might say threats, in such a move was that since Napoleon abdicated in favor of his son, any move to prevent that from happening could well lead to Napoleon deciding to nullify the abdication and take power again. The popular support for Napoleon seen in the streets of Paris, and the likelihood that most of the army would rally to his cause, was not lost on the members. The debate raged back and forth, with the supporters of Napoleon II appearing to get the upper hand.

Then Jacques-Antoine Manuel, whom Fouché had asked to represent his interests in this debate, took the floor. Following the instructions of Fouché, Manuel, a brilliant speaker, argued that while it was certainly fine and proper to proclaim for Napoleon II, as a practical matter he was in no position to take the throne yet, and that therefore the Executive Commission should still continue to run the government, rather than a Regency Council. Perhaps because they had been defeated so often that they were desperate for a victory, perhaps because they were simply duped into thinking that this declaration without teeth would actually mean something, the Bonapartists accepted his argument and the Chamber passed the following resolution:

> The Chamber of Representatives, deliberating on the various proposals made during the meeting and referred to in its minutes, passes to the current agenda, as follows:
>
> First: that Napoleon II has become Emperor of the French as a result of the abdication of Napoleon I and according to the Constitution of the Empire.
>
> Second: that the two Chambers wish, by the decree dated yesterday concerning the appointment of a Commission of provisional government, to assure the nation of the guarantees that it desires, in the present unusual circumstances, for its liberty and peace through an administration which has the full confidence of the people.[3]

Shortly thereafter, the Chamber of Peers adopted the same resolution. Napoleon's son was, at least in name, Emperor of the French. It would soon be clear that 'in name' was about all it was, as the *Commission du Gouvernement* soon decreed that actions taken by various government bodies and officials should be issued not in the name of Napoleon II, but 'in the name of the French People',[4] and by the 28th they were doing the same thing.[5]

Spectator's Misgivings

If the members of the Chambers were pleased, Napoleon was certainly not. He had been speaking with Hortense at the Elysée Palace, where she had been encouraging him to act quickly regarding his future plans. Regnault came in to report to the Emperor, who asked him what was happening:

'The attitude of the members is a thoroughly satisfactory one,' replied the chamberlain with a satisfied air. 'Napoleon II has been proclaimed amid much enthusiasm.'
'But,' interrupted the Emperor, 'what is being done?'
'The articles of the constitution are being discussed.'
    'Ah,' exclaimed the Emperor, rising abruptly, 'we have gone back to the days of Byzantium. People stop to discuss when the enemy is at the gates.'[6]

As usual, Napoleon was a step ahead of those around him and had seen through the wool that Fouché had pulled over all other eyes. But there was little he could do but grieve for what he knew must surely follow for France, and plan for his own, uncertain, future.

Colonel Francis Maceroni offers an intriguing suggestion as to why the effort to install Napoleon II ultimately failed:

Austria was pledged to support Napoleon II, defensively and offensively; but I am inclined to believe that Napoleon did not wait for the proper and decisive guarantees from the Emperor Francis, which would have irremediably compromised the latter [Fouché], and so broken up the coalition. The Emperor of Russia was also favourably disposed to that arrangement, as he looked upon the Bourbons as too much enthralled by England to enter with him into such plans of commercial and political aggrandizement as the British government might object to.[7]

The idea of appealing to Austria and even Russia sounds attractive on the surface, but it seems quite unlikely that the ruler of either country would be willing to stand up to the Bourbons at this point. Perhaps that would have worked before Waterloo, but by now it was simply too late.

The Chambers had not voted for a regent, but, in reality, they already had a very powerful regent in Fouché. Caulaincourt saw this clearly in the early meetings of the Commission, and wrote, 'Fouché, who was president of the provisional government, of which I was likewise a member, was regent *de facto*. He was the central point of every intrigue; and by a thousand hidden springs he controlled the deliberations of the assembly.'[8]

Caulaincourt might have been reasonably expected to compete with Fouché for power and influence in the new government. After all, he had long served Napoleon and had a level of prestige and intellect that could at least come close to matching that of Fouché. But for whatever reason, Caulaincourt chose to play a relatively limited role. Pasquier, a devout royalist, argued that this was because:

The Duc de Vicence [Caulaincourt], who might have disputed him [Fouché] the position, judged the situation too well not to perceive that the only service he could render his country was to carefully pave the way for the transition, and to prepare without too much jarring the return of the only government which could once more restore some little peace to France, and effect a reconciliation between her and Europe. His personal position, his horror of intrigue, and his low estimate of M. Fouché's character, inspired him with a great reserve; so he remained a quiet spectator of his actions, exercised supervision over him, and contented himself with giving him a helping hand, whenever his doings seemed to tend to the only goal which it was of the highest consequence to attain.[9]

Perhaps not surprisingly, Caulaincourt has something of a different take on the situation:

> The government committee, of which the Duke of Otranto was president, held its sittings at the Tuileries. It would be impossible to describe the misery I suffered during the last days of the crisis. I was not now, as in 1814, supported in the painful conflict by the consciousness of being useful to the Emperor. Now, all I could do was to obtain some little mitigation of the vexations to which he was exposed. I was like a sentinel stationed to watch the approach of danger, and to use my efforts to avert it.[10]

In other words, Caulaincourt, dispirited, had pretty much given up. Napoleon II was a non-starter, Napoleon I was on the way out, and the restoration of the Bourbons, almost assuredly in the personage of Louis XVIII, was now a foregone conclusion by anyone who was paying attention. That it would happen peacefully (which had certainly not been a foregone conclusion) was almost entirely the work of Fouché:

> However, no one knows at what cost of violent clashes and bloody encounters this inevitable solution of Louis' restoration would have been accomplished, if there had not been at the center of the drama the one necessary man to guide the events into the proper channel for a peaceful solution ... During the whole three weeks of the critical transition, from June 20 to July 8, Fouché played the greatest political game of his whole life with a perspicacity, a cool composure, and a Machiavellian ingenuity which makes one of the most thrilling spectacles in French history – but not one of the most edifying.[11]

Chapter 7

The King Returns

Armistice

While Napoleon, Fouché and others were concerned with politics in Paris, the Allies were advancing in that direction. Initially, the Prussians took up hot pursuit of the withdrawing French forces. Napoleon's army had offered little in the way of resistance and the Prussians steadily made their way towards the French border. Wellington, his forces having borne the brunt of the fighting at Waterloo, held back for a time before making a serious move forward. The Austrians made some minor forays from the east, and the Russians were still some distance away.

With Napoleon defeated and on the run, there was no need for the British or Prussians to move too fast. It was hard to say what kind of resistance they would meet with when they crossed the border into France. Moreover, as Napoleon was presumably still in charge of organizing the defense of France, it made good sense to wait until the Russians and Austrians were ready to move in from the east. So for a time, up to the 22nd at least, the British and Prussians were content to consolidate their forces on the border. This would also give Fouché time to undermine Napoleon, and Louis XVIII time to move into position to reclaim his throne.

All of that changed, however, with news of Napoleon's abdication, published on 22 June 1815. This news meant several things. First, it meant that the greatest military mind of his day was no longer in control of the French army. That control passed to Marshal Davout and his staff. Davout was one of Napoleon's finest marshals, but he was no Napoleon. Besides, Davout was in charge of the army, but he was not in charge of policy. That power was Fouché's alone (his other commission members notwithstanding), and it was not at all certain that Fouché would be interested in a spirited defense of France, or even of Paris.

Napoleon's abdication affected more than just the leadership of the army. It was a crushing blow to its morale. Most soldiers probably anticipated that they would become involved in a defense of the fatherland, and most probably expected that this defense would be led by Napoleon. There was good reason to feel that Napoleon could rally the army and successfully defend France, at least to the point of forcing some serious negotiations that might lead to either his retention as emperor or the accession of his son to the throne. After all, there had been a constant stream of soldiers from Waterloo, armies in the rest of the country were rallying to Paris and, most important of all, Marshal Grouchy and his army of perhaps 25,000 men had marched into France in good order and would soon form an excellent nucleus for any defensive effort. All of this was still true after Napoleon's abdication, but no leader could match Napoleon, and, in the words of Gourgaud, 'As soon as this news became known to the army, consternation and despair spread through the ranks.'[1]

Ironically, on the 22nd, the very day that Napoleon's abdication was published, Marshal Grouchy issued a proclamation to his soldiers. It was well received by them, as it lauded their performance and promised a vigorous defense of the fatherland:

Soldiers! Victors at Fleurus, at Wavre, at Namur, you have beaten the enemy everywhere you have encountered them. Your valour has seized their military trophies from them, and they cannot boast of having ravished a single one of yours. Strengthened by reinforcements and once more under the leadership of the chief of the Empire, you will soon take the offensive as you desire. Defenders of our beloved country, you will preserve its sacred soil and all France will proclaim your right to gratitude and love.

I am happy to have been your leader wherever you have won your glory in these great events and I wish to pay to your valour the meed of praise due to it. In your name I give your pledge to our country that, faithful to your oath, you will perish rather than see it humiliated and enslaved.

Long live the Emperor!

Marshal commanding the right wing of the army, Grouchy[2]

When Grouchy learned of the abdication, he issued another proclamation, calling on the army to rally to the cause of Napoleon II, but it was not to be.

All of the effects of Napoleon's abdication served to encourage the Allied forces in the north to continue their move southward, and that is exactly what they did. On the 23rd, Wellington and Blücher met at Catillon, France. Wellington was already playing politics, a role that suited him almost as much as military leadership. He had King Louis XVIII with him, and was already promoting Louis's return to power and a significant role in the new government for Fouché. Louis had been preparing to move quickly to Antwerp had Napoleon been successful at Waterloo, but events had made that trip unnecessary, and Louis was headed south. He received words of encouragement and pledges of support from people such as Joseph Lainé, who had been President of the Chamber of Deputies, and other assorted political types who had deserted Napoleon when the winds of fortune shifted.

Blücher was less interested in politics and more interested in whipping the French and, with any luck, capturing and executing Napoleon. There were French soldiers at border forts. Wellington had little interest in them, but Blücher had wanted to destroy the border forts and claim their plunder. Both men, however, quickly agreed that it was urgent that they march without delay on Paris. Bypassing French forces that were too weak to offer much resistance, the British and Prussian armies began to move rapidly towards Paris.

The Russians were not yet a major factor in the area, and the Austrians had made only minor efforts in support of the other Allies. Still, they were on the Rhine, and military realists, including Davout, were certainly aware that, in time, the Allies could bring to bear overwhelming forces against the French near Paris or, for that matter, anywhere else. Even the most spirited and successful defense of Paris would bring only short-term relief from the Allied onslaught, and it seemed unlikely that the Allies would not choose to press their advantage.

By the 28th, the Prussians were near St-Denis, with Wellington several days, perhaps as much as a week, behind. The Prussians were actually over-extended and subject to an effective attack on their flank, but by now Davout was disheartened and interested only in achieving an armistice. When the Prussians chose to avoid the good defenses to the north of Paris and instead move through St-Germain and Versailles to the lesser-defended southern border of Paris, Davout had an excellent opportunity to defeat them. As Gallaher points out:

> Davout … realized at once that Blücher's army was in an extremely vulnerable position. Stretched out from Versailles, through St. Germain, to St. Denis it could be attacked and forced to fight at a numerical and tactical disadvantage. Wellington's army was approaching Paris from the northeast, but could not have taken part in a battle west of the city before the second. The army wanted to fight. If they could defeat the Prussians and throw them back upon the English, they would be revenging Waterloo and checking the advance on Paris all in one blow. But Davout decided not to undertake a major engagement.[3]

It is difficult to justify Davout's reluctance to take on the Prussians. True, any victory would be short-term and he clearly did not want any more French bloodshed in what, to him at least, seemed a lost cause. But a defeated Prussian army would have given rise to French morale and might well have improved the French negotiating position for both an armistice and a future government. On 2 July, General Exelmans led a cavalry attack that virtually wiped out a Prussian brigade. Still Davout did nothing, even though he certainly knew that a victory was likely and useful. By the fourth, it was too late. An armistice was declared, and the French army was forced by its terms to withdraw south from Paris, beyond the Loire river. The Allies would soon occupy Paris. The army's morale now deep into an abyss, desertions were at record levels. As Gourgaud relates:

> The possession of Paris might still have been retained with the federal troops and the national guard, which would have raised our force to upwards of one hundred and twenty thousand men: conditions advantageous for the army, and which would have guaranteed the rights of the people, might then have been obtained. But it may truly be said, that after the departure of Napoleon the army lost all its zeal; the Marshals were divided in opinion, and no one among them had sufficient preponderance for such a crisis. The Provisional Government and the Chambers had, through the whole proceedings, been betrayed by Fouché, and the party which maintained intelligence with the enemy. Carnot acted an upright part, but he allowed himself to be easily deceived.[4]

Deceived Carnot certainly was. When Louis returned to Paris, Fouché, as Minister of

Police, sent Carnot a letter indicating that his fate was to be placed in internal exile under close surveillance. An outraged Carnot sought out Fouché and their famous exchange pretty much says it all. Carnot: 'Traitor! Where do you require me to go?' Fouché: 'Simpleton! Where you please.'[5]

Royalist Supporters and the White Terror

It was not just the advance of the British and Prussian forces that put military – and political – pressure on Paris. Royalist supporters in the south had been waiting for an opportunity to 'liberate' southern France in the name of Louis XVIII. News of Waterloo prodded them into action. The Duke of Angoulême, headquartered just across the border in Spain, had been in touch with royalist sympathizers throughout southern France. Augmented by bitterness at economic difficulties in the south, conscription and other similar issues, many people in that region were anxious to see the return of royal authority. The news of Waterloo, helped by the presence of a British fleet in the harbor and attacks on soldiers by royalist thugs, led General Jean-Antoine Verdier, Napoleon's local commander in Marseilles, to abandon the city to the royalists almost two weeks before Louis XVIII returned to Paris on July 8.[6]

Marseilles 'liberated', the royalists now turned their attention to another major port city, and one with strong Napoleonic connections, Toulon. It was here so many years earlier that Napoleon had driven out the British and their royalist sympathizers and re-established government control on behalf of Revolutionary France. Toulon promised to be a difficult proposition for the royalists. A strong garrison of soldiers loyal to Napoleon was commanded by Marshal Guillaume-Marie-Anne Brune. Though Brune had not always been in favor with Napoleon, he had rallied to the Bonapartist cause for the Hundred Days and was determined to hold the city, even against a superior royalist/British force. News of Waterloo did not cause Brune to swerve in his determination, and Napoleon's abdication was likewise ineffective at changing his mind. Royalists, supported by British forces led by none other than Sir Hudson Lowe (who would later become governor of the island of St Helena while Napoleon was there in exile), opened negotiations with Brune. When Brune heard that the Army of the Loire had been dissolved, he saw the writing on the wall, and agreed to royalist demands that he remove his troops from the city.

As was the case in Marseilles and elsewhere, what was known as the White Terror followed the departure of Napoleonic troops. Violence was frequent, kangaroo courts common, and anyone with a tie to Napoleon or the Revolution was suspect. Untold numbers of people fled, while others were murdered or executed.

As for Brune, his fate was little better. Given a safe conduct pass to Paris, he could have easily steered clear of dangerous areas and arrived in Paris unmolested. But for some reason Brune decided to go through the city of Avignon, then in the control of what can only be described as royalist mobs who were a law unto themselves. When Brune was recognized, the mob demanded blood. The mayor and the prefect tried to protect him, but he was pulled from his hotel room, killed in the streets and his body tossed into the river.[7]

Vengeance

The murder of Brune and of many other Bonapartist supporters (or, in some cases, presumed supporters) was no small matter, and drew the attention of Louis XVIII, as well as of leaders of the Allies. Louis issued two proclamations on the subject. The first, on 25 June, made it clear that heads would roll, with its talk of menacing dangers and reprisals against those who supported Napoleon (see Appendix IV).

But Louis was soon joined by Talleyrand, who soundly advised him to be more tolerant of those whom he would lead, and on 28 June King Louis issued a second proclamation, now countersigned by Talleyrand, which was more conciliatory in nature, talking of restoring peace and tranquility (see Appendix IV).

Still, this proclamation made it clear that those directly responsible for Napoleon's return and its aftermath could anticipate 'revenge'. And this from a man whom Chateaubriand had a year earlier described as 'a prince known by his learning, inaccessible to prejudices – a stranger to vengeance'.[8]

Royalists were not the only ones who were up in arms about how things were going in France. Napoleon's supporters were dismayed by his abdication, incensed at the conduct of royalists in some parts of France, and outraged by the increasingly likely return of a Bourbon king, especially Louis XVIII. While the white (Bourbon) flags of the royalists flew in the south, the Vendée and elsewhere, in places such as Brittany Napoleon's supporters set altars with busts of Napoleon in their homes. In Alsace, Lorraine, Champagne and the Midi, Bonapartists rioted, killed royalists and otherwise expressed their anger. Soldiers swore oaths to the Emperor. But none of it mattered. The Empire was finished.

Nor, it must be said, was all the violence on the part of the various French factions. The ousting of Napoleon and the return of the King did nothing to keep Allied soldiers from continuing to move into France. The Austrians and Prussians were especially vindictive towards the populace:

> … roaring, drinking, pillaging, ransacking, and raping, with utter disregard as to who was on which side. Entire cities were sacked and what soldiers could not take with them, they destroyed, including farmers' crops in the fields. 'We have conquered France,' Canning told Madame de Staël in brutal terms, 'France is our prey, and we want to so weaken her that she will not be able to move for another ten years.'[9]

On the 23rd, the French provisional government sent an emissary telling Blücher of Napoleon's abdication. Since the Allies had declared war on Napoleon, as opposed to France, surely Blücher would cease and desist from his plunder. That was wishful thinking, and the onslaught continued. Blücher was not to be denied his pound of flesh.[10]

Later, in Paris, it would take Louis XVIII's personal intervention to keep Blücher from blowing up the Pont de Jéna [Jéna Bridge], dedicated to Napoleon's 1806 victory over the Prussians.

Clearly, Wellington and Blücher had very different approaches to relations with

France after the war. As the German historian Peter Hofschröer puts it:

> The Duke considered himself to be the liberator of France from Bonaparte and an ally of Louis XVIII. The Prussians, who had suffered years of occupation by the French, saw the matter differently. Wellington was at war with Napoleon, while the Prussians considered themselves to be at war with France, particularly as the provisional government that replaced Napoleon did not prove cooperative. As well as revenge, they wanted to plunder France's resources as compensation for their own losses and see to it that French military power was so weakened that it would no longer be such a threat to Prussian security. Such variances in political objectives led to different military strategies. While Wellington was happy to send Napoleon into exile on St Helena, the Prussians wanted him strung up on the nearest tree.[11]

Wellington himself recognized as much. In a letter to Sir Charles Stuart, dated 28 June 1815, he wrote:

> The Parisians think the Jacobins will give him over to me, believing that I will save his life. Blücher writes to kill him; but I have told him that I shall remonstrate, and shall insist on his being disposed of by common accord. I have likewise said that, as a private friend, I advised him to have nothing to do with so foul a transaction – that he and I had acted too distinguished parts in these transactions to become executioners – and that I was determined that if the Sovereigns wished to put him to death, they should appoint an executioner, who should not be me.[12]

Bourbon Politics

Louis XVIII's proclamations notwithstanding, it was not always clear that he would automatically return to the throne after Napoleon abdicated. After all, it was arguably his mistakes that had led to Napoleon's return in the first place. His refusal, over the objections of his allies, to pay Napoleon his pension certainly leaps to mind, along with his treatment of veterans of the *Grande Armée*. His popularity among the French was not exactly universal and the Allied leaders had at least some questions regarding how wise it would be to reinstate him on his throne. For a time, it seemed that there was at least some possibility of putting Napoleon II on the throne, with his mother as regent. This was never really likely, however, and soon thoughts began to center on a restoration of the Bourbons, most probably in the person of Louis XVIII.

The news of Waterloo reached London on 21 June and the news of Napoleon's abdication arrived four days later, late on 25 June. Naturally enough, both pieces of news brought great joy to most British citizens, and certainly to their leaders. But the immediate response to the news was simply to continue the military campaign. True, there was a Provisional Government headed by Fouché, but there was also a formidable French army in the field and until it had been neutralized, peace was not truly at hand. Foreign Secretary Lord Castlereagh drew up instructions that the military campaign was to remain active until the French had capitulated. Naturally enough, Castlereagh was primarily concerned with British security, which he pointed out would be greatest if Napoleon was dead or captured and Louis XVIII was back on the throne. The least secure option would be Napoleon in America and 'some other government' than Louis XVIII on the throne. In that case, Castlereagh suggested, France might have to be partitioned to assure British security.[13] The fact that French prisoners of war were sent to England was a sure sign that the war would continue. British public opinion seemed to want the war to continue and to want Napoleon and his supporters to be dealt with severely. Government policy was, from the very beginning, designed to make Napoleon a prisoner.

The British took other steps upon hearing the news of Waterloo, steps that would prove decisive in the end game of Napoleon's Hundred Days. Admiral Lord Keith, commander of the Channel Fleet, heard of Waterloo on 24 June. Not one to await instructions when action was required, Keith immediately sent every ship that was ready to sail to blockade the French coast. Not on his watch would Napoleon leave France, at least not unless his superiors wanted it so. These actions were quickly confirmed by Keith's superiors. Keith and the Admiralty understood that catching Napoleon would be difficult if 'he embarks like Hamlet "naked and alone"' but they were determined to make every effort to prevent his escape.[14]

The continuing war aside, Wellington the politician soon became a dominant force in the politics of succession, or what eventually became Bourbon politics. Wellington had always had a good eye for politics and was closely aligned with Castlereagh. But he – and the Foreign Secretary – each realized that the other Allies had to play a role and that France herself, in one personage or another, would need to be included in the process.

Britain had always believed in maintaining a continental balance of power. That goal was one reason for their continual opposition to Napoleon, and that goal was fundamental to Wellington's actions after Waterloo. In his goals, he had two major allies: Prince Metternich and Prince Talleyrand. Metternich and Talleyrand had been in close correspondence. Indeed, Metternich had sent Talleyrand a long and firm proclamation to the French people from Karl Philipp, Prince of Schwarzenberg making it clear that Austria would never accept Napoleon on the throne of France (see Appendix V). The proclamation, which arrived about the time of Napoleon's abdication, also makes it clear that Austria, at least, expected retribution against those French citizens who had taken up Napoleon's cause. Note the irony of a representative of the old feudal order talking about the 'disasters of the middle ages'. Historical accuracy was not a primary goal, it seems. But the primary goal is quite clear: convince France to dump Napoleon.

King Louis XVIII had been spending his time in exile in the beautiful medieval city of Ghent, Belgium. There, with his loyal advisers, he awaited developments and kept up correspondence with his supporters. He was slow to communicate with Fouché in Paris, however, causing Fouché to say in exasperation to Pasquier:

Now, when and how are we at last going to be able to communicate with those people at Ghent? They are such a bungling lot. How is it that they have no agent here? Should they not already have entered into communication with me? They must be aware of my sentiments, which they must have learnt from more sources than one.[15]

Fouché wasn't the only person anxious from the very beginning to see Louis take a more active role. Wellington was certainly interested in the King's beginning to act like a sovereign instead of an exile, and Talleyrand was determined to put him back on the throne – and himself back into major influence. Talleyrand had represented King Louis XVIII at the Congress of Vienna, which was where he was when Napoleon returned. He kept up a flurry of letters to the King, informing him of every little detail of events, both large and small, in Vienna. His efforts were not ignored, and Louis and members of his court kept Talleyrand informed of their movements. A letter from Louis to Talleyrand, written in Ostend on 26 March, shows the precarious nature of Louis's position, his delusion regarding his popularity, and his closeness to Talleyrand (see Appendix VI).

Restoration

Talleyrand and Fouché each imagined, with great justification, that the King's return would be in their best interests. They had little future in an empire run by Napoleon I or, for that matter, Napoleon II. Whether or not the King's return was in the best interests of France was far more questionable. Talleyrand understood that Louis could be somewhat unrealistic as to his popularity with the French people. Talleyrand was in Vienna when Napoleon returned to France, but would soon move to rejoin his King.

Wellington, too, wanted the King restored, but quickly and without restrictions. Fouché, of course, wanted to ensure that this action would gain him a position in the new government, so he was determined to make it seem to Louis that all was made possible by Fouché. It is also true that Fouché was concerned with the nature and appearance of Louis's return. He did not want it to seem that the King was back on the throne only because the Allied powers put him there – a view he shared with Wellington. That would not make for a stable or popular government. Moreover, Fouché believed that in order to avoid the mistakes of 1814 that led to Napoleon's return, it would be important for Louis to be seen as a constitutional monarch, rather than one who ruled by divine right or, worse, because of the support of outside powers. Fouché and many others recognized that Napoleon's return was helped greatly by public unhappiness with Louis, at least as much as it was by the fondness of the French for their former emperor.

The Prussians, incidentally, didn't appear to care whether Louis was restored to the throne or not. On 3 July (the day the Armistice would ultimately be signed), the Provisional Government sent General Jacques Tromelin to meet with General Gneisenau, Blücher's Chief of Staff. General Tromelin's report pretty much sums up the Prussian attitude:

I arrived about five o'clock at the Prussian headquarters at Senlis.

Graf Gneisenau, Army Chief of Staff, received me haughtily and told me that, as the army was on the move, he could not allow me to return to Paris; I was only allowed to write to the Provisional Government, leaving the dispatch open. I found the Prussians more concerned with reaping the benefit of their victory than in making the Bourbon cause triumph. They did not even take the trouble to conceal the lack of interest that it inspired in them. 'We are here by right of conquest and it is as victors that we wish to enter Paris,' he said to me … 'It doesn't interest us whether you take back the Bourbons or restore the Republic, for we have not forgotten that three months after having restored Louis XVIII he threatened us about Saxony. We are waging war against Napoleon because no agreement with him is sacred and no firm peace may be expected from him … After having destroyed him, we no longer care. You may choose any government you like, except that of Bonaparte and his family.'[16]

While in Ghent, Louis had attempted to create an image of a moderate monarch who had been wronged. Chateaubriand had joined him there and published the newspaper *Journal Universel*, a royal answer to the now imperial *Moniteur Universel* in Paris. Chateaubriand published material, including a 12 May *Report to the King* by his ministers, designed to portray Louis as committed to liberal and constitutional measures to assure individual liberties upon his return. This was necessary to counter the feelings of ultra-royalists, led by the Count of Artois, who wanted to return to the days of absolutism. Moreover, he quickly accepted the treaty adopted by the Allies on 25 March (see Appendix III). This treaty did not really guarantee that the Allies would support Louis's return, but Louis tried to use that as a way to make it appear not only that the Allies supported his return but also that, since they were allies, the invading troops should withdraw as soon as it was clear that Napoleon was out and Louis was in.[17]

All of this was necessary, as Louis's restoration was by no means a given, though he certainly had the advantage of having been on the throne for a year. There was important support for Napoleon II in some quarters, and for the Duke of Orléans, a powerful pretender to the throne who had a reputation as a moderate and at least the possible support of some of the Allies. He might well have emerged as the 'compromise candidate' for the throne. Head of a different branch of the Bourbon dynasty, he had served his exile in London, where he had felt free to criticize what he considered the reactionary actions of Louis XVIII. His support was strong enough that even Fouché felt compelled to go through the motions of considering him as France's new king. But Fouché was never really serious about that, hoping only to use the Duke of Orléans, as he did Napoleon II, as leverage for a more moderate, constitutional King Louis XVIII.

Additionally, many in and out of the government were determined that France should not have any ruler forced on her. Preliminary proposals for an armistice had made the point that the Allies were only fighting Napoleon and that the government was not likely to stand for any Allied coercion on the matter.

Chapter 8

The Allies Take Command

The Politics of Armistice

During this time – while the Allies had been advancing, the King had been preparing for his return and the royalists had been beginning to seek their revenge – Fouché had been doing a delicate dance in Paris. He was convinced that only he had the ability to bring about the kind of transition that he felt was best for France. Napoleon's quick defeat at Waterloo had hampered Fouché's plans, but his selection as head of the provisional government gave him the power to achieve his goals.

Fouché had to act carefully, but he had to act quickly. After all, the British and Prussian armies were heading towards Paris, and the French army was anxious to fight them. The first order of business was to try to get the Allies to negotiate a ceasefire or armistice. On 23 June he sent the Baron de Vitrolles to see King Louis to assure him that he, Fouché, was working for Louis's restoration. Louis was making his way south towards Paris, and was soon joined by Talleyrand at Mons. This meeting did not go well. Talleyrand, rather than immediately presenting himself to the King, preferred instead to sleep and see Louis the next day. But when at dawn he realized that the King was leaving without him, he quickly went to Louis and they had a brief meeting. Talleyrand, it seems, wanted Louis to go to Lyons, while Louis, more logically, wanted to head straight to Paris. Paris it would be.

At the same time, the Commission of Government sent a delegation to Wellington that consisted of La Fayette, D'Ageson, General Sébastiani, Comte de Pentécoulant, Comte de la Forêt and Benjamin Constant. Their instructions included, among other things, French insistence on 'the safety and inviolability of the Emperor Napoleon out of its territory'.[1] They were prepared to negotiate the location and nature of Napoleon's future, so long as it was something that Napoleon would find reasonable.

The delegation pressed for an armistice, but on the evening of the 29th received instead this letter from Wellington:

Headquarters of Prince Blücher
June the 29th, 1815, 11½ at night
Gentlemen:
I have the honour to acquaint you, that having consulted Marshal Prince Blücher on your proposal for an armistice, his highness has agreed with me, that, under present circumstances, no armistice can take place, while Napoleon Bonaparte is in Paris, and at liberty; and that the operations are in such a state, that he cannot stop them.

I have the honour, etc,

Wellington[2]

At about the same time, Fouché sent a rather unusual messenger to Wellington. Frances Maceroni was a British citizen who had served as an aide-de-camp to King Murat of Naples, one of Napoleon's marshals and his brother-in-law. Maceroni was convinced that his mission was to prevent further bloodshed, so he undertook it with vigor. He carried a message to Wellington, which, among other things, assured him that Fouché was for the King and urged the British army to get to Paris before the Prussians arrived and tried to sack the city.[3]

Maceroni's trip to visit Wellington was quite an adventure, and even included a run-in with Blücher, who was none too pleased that the French insisted on dealing with Wellington rather than with the Prussian commander. At one point, Blücher's aide, Gneisenau, exploded:

What, nobody but the Duke of Wellington? Always the Duke of Wellington? Have they forgot that there is a Prince Blücher? That there is a Prussian army? They shall feel that there is a Prussian army! They have felt it! They shall again smart under it![4]

Eventually, Maceroni met up with Wellington and dined with him. His relating of the story of that meeting pretty much sums up the situation as it existed. He had reminded Wellington that the Allies were only fighting Napoleon and that he, Wellington, should therefore wait for the French Provisional Government to make its case to the other sovereigns before attempting to force Louis on them (Louis was, of course, traveling with Wellington's army). Wellington replied:

The duke, in the presence of Lord March, Colonels Hervey, Freemantle, Abercromby and several other officers, replied: 'I can give no other answer, than that which you know I have just given to the deputies. Tell them (the commission of government) that they had better immediately proclaim the King (Louis XVIII). I cannot treat till then, nor upon any other condition. Their king is here at hand: let them send their submission to him.'[5]

Fouché's efforts to ingratiate himself with people close to Louis paid off. He had been quite concerned with his role in a future government run by Louis XVIII and had lobbied at great length to be, among other things, Minister of Police. On 5 July, two days after the Armistice was signed, he went to Neuilly, where he met with Wellington, Molé, Pozzo di Borgo, Talleyrand and others. Talleyrand greeted Fouché coolly, but the two discussed the nature of the King's return and the level of moderation towards those who supported Napoleon to be shown by the King. Hoping to calm the fears and anger of the French army, Fouché argued for retention of the tricolor flag, but that argument was rejected. Fouché also argued for amnesty towards people such as Marshal Ney, but in the end that argument also was rejected.

The issue of the tricolor flag was actually an important matter to the French army, and it probably would have served the King well to have granted the request. But the negotiations were an uneven match for, as Marshal Macdonald observed, 'The days of the temporary government were numbered.'[6]

Count Molé, who also counseled moderation, sums up the dance of Fouché, Wellington and Talleyrand:

> I was tickled at the simple-mindedness of the Duke of Wellington, who argued vehemently without suspecting Fouché's private motives. Talleyrand, who could understand them all right, supported the Duke of Wellington in the discussion, but only casually, for the sake of form, being a man who knew quite well what Fouché wanted and how it would all end. The whole question boiled down to the single point whether the Duc d'Otranto [Fouché], in order to become the King's Minister, would agree to break with his party and agree to the policy of severity which was being demanded of him. It was clear that he would argue as much as possible about each of his actions, that he wanted to appear forced into doing those he could not get out of, and lastly that he was hoping to do under the King what he had done under Bonaparte, i.e., save his popularity from the wreck by persuading people that he saved them from far more evils than he caused them.[7]

Wellington was aware that Fouché was running a risk and that there were some in Paris, including on the Commission, who might well cause Fouché and Caulaincourt harm for talking to him. The Duke was having none of it, writing to the Commission that if anyone did any harm to Fouché or Caulaincourt, the Duke would 'hang up the other three on his arrival in Paris.'[8]

Fouché's role was still undetermined, but the next night he met with Talleyrand, who offered him the position of Minister of Police. It seems that various advisers to the King, including his own brother, had been touting Fouché's attributes, and the King, probably with a great deal of reluctance, accepted Fouché as his Minister of Police.

On 6 July, Talleyrand presented Fouché to Louis. As Chateaubriand wrote, 'It was vice leaning on the arm of crime, the trusty regicide, on his knees, put his hands, which had pushed Louis XVI's head under the knife, into the hands of the brother of the martyred king; the apostate bishop was guarantor of the oath.'[9]

In his discussions with Wellington, the new Minister of Police was told in no uncertain terms what Napoleon's fate was to be:

> ... the king having condescended to continue me in my office of general police; but he did not disguise from me that all kind of measures were taken, in order that Napoleon might fall, as a hostage, into the power of the allies, and that it was required of me that I should do nothing to favour his escape.[10]

On the 7th, Fouché forced the disbanding of the Provisional Government, claiming that he had no choice in the matter. The arrival of Prussian troops made his point for him, though the Provisional Government did pass a resolution that they were leaving only because the Allies were so determined to put Louis back on the throne. If that was true, it was only because of the efforts of Fouché: Waterloo had not necessarily guaranteed Louis's return. As Sauvigny puts it so very well:

> This was Fouché's final lie and final treason, because no more now than in 1814, did the Allies intend to impose on France a regime contrary to the wishes of the nation. Thus the Restoration was besmirched with an initial stain that it was never able to wash away. Our fine Duke of Otranto had thus worthily crowned his work by succeeding, in one single act, in betraying the cause of the Revolution out of which he had come, the cause of the Empire which had brought him his highest honors, and the cause of the monarchy where he hoped to find a dominant place for himself.[11]

While it is true that Fouché richly deserves a great deal of criticism, it must also be said that he may have managed to find a path that would, at least, prevent further bloodshed. A Napoleon riding to the defense of Paris, or perhaps any other military effort to allow France a greater say in her own destiny would have led to significant loss of life on the part of the French and Allied armies. Whether the end result would have been any different is impossible to say.

Fouché is not alone in being condemned by both peers and historians. Count Molé offers a succulent description of Talleyrand's questionable career:

> Of all the ex-ministers, M. de Talleyrand was the only one who joined the Opposition. He has a weakness for ministerial power and will never find himself shut out without experiencing a violent longing to be in again. What a strange destiny is his! Passing from treachery to treachery, from perjury to perjury, he finds himself once more under the banner of loyalty. After betraying the Bourbons, the nobility and the Church for the Revolution and Mme. Grand, sold the Directory to Bonaparte, and Bonaparte to the Bourbons, for whom he found a crown for the second time, and instead of thanking god or the devil, in whom he believes much more than in God, for so many miracles, instead of enjoying with dignity retirement and his immense wealth, instead of occupying his leisure and old age in mentally renewing the past, he became the centre of every intrigue and offered himself successively to all parties.[12]

Las Cases says simply, 'M. Fouché must have a furious partiality for clandestine operations … he has in fact always shown the greatest obliquity in affairs of moment.'[13]

On 8 July 1815, Louis XVIII entered Paris. There were no joyous celebrations to match those given upon Napoleon's return from exile on Elba. The Hundred Days had begun with a bang but, in Paris at least, it would end with a whimper. The American student George Russell describes the scene:

> I then hastened across the garden to await his [Louis's] arrival at the Tuileries, standing near the spot where, three months before, I had seen Napoleon. The tricolor was no longer there, but the white flag again floated over the place so full of historical recollections. Louis XVIII soon reached this ancestral abode of

his family, and having mounted, with some difficulty and expenditure of breath, to the second story, he waddled into the balcony which overlooked the crowd silently waiting for the expected speech, and leaning ponderously on the railing, he kissed his hand, and said in a loud voice, 'Good day, my children.' This was the exordium, body, and peroration of his address, and it struck his audience so ludicrously that a laugh spread among them until it became general, and all seemed in the best possible humor. The King laughed too, evidently regarding his reception as highly flattering. The affair turned out well; for the multitude parted in a merry mood, considering His Majesty rather a jolly old gentleman, and making sundry comparisons between him and the late tenant, illustrative of the difference between King Stork and King Log.[14]

Chapter 9

Napoleon's Farewell to Paris

Contemplating Decisions

This period of time was marked by a great deal of indecision on Napoleon's part. It seemed for some time that he simply did not know what to do or where to go. Hortense and Madame Mère, among others, noticed this with some concern: all understood that the longer Napoleon stayed in Paris the less control he had over his own fate. Hortense argued against his going to England, but thought America would be a good place if he moved quickly. She also suggested that perhaps the Austrian Emperor Francis, his father-in-law, or Russian Tsar Alexander would remember happier times and give him comfortable asylum. Napoleon rejected Russia and Austria, but seemed interested in America and England. But no decision was forthcoming, and Napoleon continued to stay at the Elysée Palace in Paris.

Time, however, would not wait for Napoleon to move of his own accord. Napoleon's presence at the Elysée Palace was quickly becoming a difficult situation for all concerned. In the days before and after the abdication, its courtyards and the surrounding streets had been filled with people offering their support. Cries of 'Vive l'Empereur!' were heard day and night. Napoleon in Paris provided a dangerous counterweight to the power of Fouché and even to the approaching King Louis XVIII. The French army had been defeated at Waterloo, but there were plenty of soldiers rallying to the cause. Marshal Davout, were he to declare for Napoleon, would be a formidable commander and, of course, Wellington was always presumed to have said that Napoleon's presence was worth 40,000 men. In the short term, at least, all sides recognized that Napoleon's close proximity to Paris and the French army was at the very least problematic. As de Chaboulon put it:

> The Duke of Otranto, however, and the deputies who had concurred with him in pulling down Napoleon from his throne, did not look on his residence at the Elyseum without alarm. They dreaded, lest, emboldened by the daring counsels of Prince Lucien, by the attachment the army retained for him, by the acclamations of the federates, and citizens of all classes, who assembled daily under the walls of his palace, he should attempt to renew a second 18th Brumaire. They demanded of the chamber, therefore, by the mouth of M. Duchesne, that the *ex-Emperor* should be desired, in the name of their country, to remove from the capital.[1]

Napoleon had abdicated on 22 June. By the next day the Provisional Government, encouraged without much subtlety by Fouché, decided that Napoleon had to go. This was not an altogether inappropriate desire. There had been some demonstrations in front of the palace, especially by some of the *fédérés*, whose fervor might be difficult to control. At one of these demonstrations, Chancellor Pasquier saw Napoleon, and his description of the once-powerful emperor is a poignant reminder of how far Napoleon had fallen – and how fast:

> I saw him [Napoleon] one day make his appearance on the terrace. I had not seen him since my farewell conversation with him in 1814, on the eve of his departure for the French campaign, and I could not help falling a prey to the deepest emotion, on seeing him reduced to coming forward and replying by repeated bows to acclamations springing from so low a source. There are few more melancholy, more touching, and more heartrending sights than that of a man, so long the center of so great a glory and of such prodigious power, reduced to such humiliating straits. His naturally grave physiognomy had assumed a somber aspect; occasionally he endeavored to smile, but the expression of his eyes reflected the sadness which pervaded his soul.[2]

The Provisional Government wanted him out of town. Napoleon, however, was not anxious to leave, though he certainly understood that his presence was difficult for the Provisional Government and with that being the case his own situation could be potentially dangerous. Indeed, in some respects Napoleon seemed unconcerned even for his own safety. There were very few troops around him and almost nothing of a personal bodyguard. If the Provisional Government had been able to put together a force of soldiers loyal to them (perhaps a difficult task), they could have forcefully removed Napoleon or even done him bodily harm. To break this impasse, the Provisional Government sent Davout to visit Napoleon and to try to convince him to leave. Davout went to Napoleon on 24 June, finding what few soldiers were around him in disreputable condition, a situation that outraged his sense of military decorum and, no doubt, saddened him on behalf of his former leader.

Napoleon was less than amused to see his old comrade-in-arms, at least in these circumstances. He exploded in anger, pointing out that he could have easily retained power had he been willing to take advantage of the soldiers in the vicinity. That he had declined to do so for fear of starting a civil war seemed, in his eyes, to have been forgotten by the Provisional Government. Moreover, he had abdicated: what more did they want of him?

Davout pointed out to Napoleon that the point was not the feelings of the Provisional Government, or the fear of a civil war. The problem was, as he saw it, that the Allies had a hard time taking Napoleon's abdication seriously since he, Napoleon, insisted on remaining in the center of the action, ready at a moment's notice to make a move to regain power. If Napoleon really meant his abdication, and wanted to do what was best for France in this most difficult of times, he would withdraw to the comforts of his former home, Malmaison. At that, the two men parted, having seen each other for the last time.

Time to Go

It is difficult to say if Davout's visit was the turning point in Napoleon's decision to leave Paris. De Chaboulon would have us believe that it was Napoleon himself who came to that decision, writing 'Napoleon himself, however, was aware that his presence at Paris, and in an imperial palace, might give the allies room to question the sincerity of his abdication, and be detrimental to the re-establishment of peace. He determined, therefore, to remove.'[3]

Marchand says much the same thing:

> After the abdication, the Emperor remained a few more days at the Elysée. The next day and the following there were many carriages in the courtyard. The third day they decreased, but the public turmoil around the residence increased. The Emperor thought that such demonstrations could hinder negotiations, and that his abdication could be slandered by his enemies who feared the people's manifestations in favor of their elected choice, and thus withdrew almost stealthily from so much proof of love and affection by retiring to Malmaison.[4]

There may have been other factors involved in Napoleon's determination to leave. While in Paris he was far more likely to be in personal danger then he would be in the relative seclusion of Malmaison, especially given his lack of personal protection. More than one person feared that the Provisional Government – for which read Fouché – would take steps against Napoleon. Fouché would probably be better off if Napoleon were either dead or in the custody of the Allies. Savary, whose business it was to know such things, firmly believed that Napoleon was in danger as long as he stayed in Paris, and that Fouché was the source of that danger:

> I was too well aware of Fouché's evil intentions towards the Emperor not to ascribe to him some sinister projects, and I accordingly took measures to obstruct them.
>
> I had never been the dupe of his protestations, and clearly perceived that he was about to avail himself of his position to effect the Emperor's irretrievable ruin: for this course of conduct was calculated to answer any project he might meditate, wither in favor of the elder or the junior branch of the house of Bourbon, or even of the regency. The Emperor's death was indispensable for the security of his own life. He was too deeply versed in the science of revolutions to expose himself to a fresh return. I was engaged in conversation with the Emperor during the whole of the 23rd, representing my uneasiness on this subject, and I did all in my power to impart the same feeling to him, and to procure his adopting the determination of instantly taking his departure …
>
> The Emperor began to suspect the possibility of such a guilty course being actually meditated, and he immediately made every preparation for his departure.[5]

Whatever the case, Napoleon determined to leave the Elysée Palace and repair to Malmaison. On the evening of the 22nd he requested the Minister of Marine to place two ships, at anchor in the harbor near Rochefort, at his disposal for travel to the United States. The next day he had General Bertrand apply to Fouché for passports to leave France for the United States. Time was becoming a critical concern. The Allies were closing in, the Provisional Government couldn't be trusted, assassins were said to be behind every lamppost and the British were beginning to close off the French coast. As early as 3 June, Vice Admiral Sir Henry Hotham had sent Captain Maitland and the *Bellerophon* to keep an eye on developments near the Île d'Aix.[6]

In some ways, Napoleon was in a real quandary. The Provisional Government wanted him not only out of Paris but also out of the country (assuming it didn't actually want him dead or perhaps captured). But the British were beginning to take steps to prevent Napoleon from leaving France. Normally, deposed monarchs are able to settle where they like, but after Napoleon's return from Elba, it seems that he was to be subjected to different rules.

Before he left Paris for Malmaison, Napoleon prepared the following address for his soldiers, sent from Malmaison, which was never actually either delivered to them or published in the *Moniteur*, given its inflammatory nature:

Soldiers!

When I yield to the necessity that forces me to leave the courageous French army, I take with me the happy certainty that through the eminent service the motherland expects from it, it shall justify the praise even our enemies cannot deny it. Soldiers! Although absent, I shall follow your actions: I know each corps, and none can win some reported advantage without my doing justice to the courage it displays. You and I have been slandered, and men unworthy of appreciating your work saw in the signs of attachment you showed me a zeal of which I was the sole object. Let your future services teach them that it was the motherland above all you were serving in obeying me, and that if I share in any way in your affection, I owe this to my deep love for France, our common mother. Soldiers! Only a few more efforts and the coalition shall dissolve. Napoleon will recognize you through the blows you strike. Save the honor and the independence of France, remain to the very end as I have known you for the past twenty years, and you shall be invincible.[7]

This was no call to civil war, as his departure prevented that. But Napoleon did hope and expect that the army would continue to fight the invading Allied forces. Only by doing that could they possibly forestall having Louis inflicted upon them. If there were any hope of a throne for Napoleon II or even a republic, the army would have to fight to preserve strength at the negotiating table.

Napoleon also had Bertrand arrange for a collection of books to be prepared, and the letter is quite instructive as to the nature of Napoleon and his plans for the future:

To M. [Antoine-Alexandre] Barbier
    Librarian to the Emperor
    Paris, 25 June 1815

The Grand Marshal begs M. Barbier to be so good as to bring to Malmaison tomorrow:

1. The list of 10,000 books and engravings, such as those of the voyages of Denon and the Egyptian Commission, of which the Emperor had several thousand copies.

2. Some works on America.

3. A detailed bibliography of everything that has been printed about the Emperor during his various campaigns.

The Emperor's traveling library must be brought up to date. It ought to include the books carried on each campaign, and to be supplemented by a number of works on the United States.

The Grand Library must contain a complete set of the *Moniteur*, the best encyclopedia, the best dictionaries.

This library should be consigned to an American house, which will forward it to America by le Havre.

By order of the Emperor, the Grand Marshal of the Palace, Bertrand[8]

That done, Napoleon was resigned to leave Paris for his former home in Malmaison, nine miles away. His stepdaughter Hortense had been living there, and she had continually urged him to join her there. As he prepared to leave, he met with Caulaincourt, asking him to continue to look out for his interests in Paris. It was a sad departure:

'Remain where you are, Caulaincourt,' said he, on taking leave of me. 'Do whatever you can to prevent mischief. Carnot will second you. He is an honest man. For me, all is at an end. Strive to serve France, and you will still be serving me. Courage, Caulaincourt. If you and other honorable men decline to take an active part in affairs, that traitor, Fouché, will sell France to foreigners.'

'All is over. All is consummated,' said I, completely dispirited. 'I will remain, Sire; but only because I hope for the possibility of being yet useful to Your Majesty.'[9]

In the early afternoon of 25 June, Napoleon left the Elysée Palace. He left quietly, perhaps out of fear for his safety, perhaps out of melancholy. It may be that he realized that he would never return to Paris alive. Napoleon rode in Grand Marshal Bertrand's carriage, along with Bertrand and the servant Noverraz. They left by the Champs-Elysées, while Napoleon's own carriage left on Rue du Faubourg-Saint-Honoré with Generals Gourgaud and Montholon and Count de Las Cases. This was all a ruse – just in case of trouble. Once safely out of town, Napoleon switched to his own carriage for the remainder of the trip. It was a sad trip. As Count Montholon put it, Napoleon was acting almost as though he were a fugitive.[10]

Marchand stayed behind to gather up some of Napoleon's personal belongings. These included numerous images of Napoleon's son, a few other works of art, and Napoleon's favorite silver washstand. This latter piece Marchand felt compelled to hide in his overloaded carriage, lest it attract attention. Marchand visited Marie

Walewska and arranged a visit with the Emperor the next day. His duties in Paris accomplished, Marchand and his now groaning carriage made their way to Malmaison.[11]

Chapter 10

Malmaison

Recollection and Protection

Napoleon's arrival at Malmaison must have been bittersweet for all concerned. He was greeted by his loyal stepdaughter, Hortense, who had encouraged him to move there and arranged for all to be prepared for his arrival. This was something of a risk to take, as she had won the favor of the Allies and had not been subjected to harassment or penalties after Napoleon's first abdication. Indeed, this had been guaranteed by treaty, but that was the same treaty that guaranteed Napoleon an adequate pension. By showing this loyalty to Napoleon, she ran at least some risk of losing her protections. On the other hand, the Allies and the Provisional Government wanted Napoleon out of Paris, and soon out of France altogether, and Malmaison was a natural way station on that journey. Hortense, ever loyal to Napoleon, even put her children up with a friend to allow her to devote all of her attentions to Napoleon.

And then there was the question of Josephine. This beautiful home had been Napoleon and Josephine's love nest. Napoleon had never really stopped loving Josephine and had mourned deeply her death while he was on Elba. This is not to denigrate his love for his second wife, Marie Louise, or even his Polish mistress, Marie Walewska. But his relationship with Josephine was special, and Malmaison was a symbol of that relationship. To many, Josephine had been Napoleon's good luck charm. She represented the best of his reign, his success as general, his whirlwind of reforms during the Consulate, and the earlier, happier, years of the Empire. When they divorced, the Empire was perhaps at its military, social and moral peak. Napoleon perhaps mused, as he pondered his fate in the melancholy halls of Malmaison, that it was his divorce from Josephine that marked the beginning of his terrible downfall.

With the weight of these memories and thoughts heavy upon him even while in Paris, Napoleon had specifically asked Hortense not to put him up in Josephine's suite. That would have been too much to take. She complied with this wish, putting Napoleon in a separate wing from the former imperial suite. One cannot help imagining that this action did little good. Josephine's influence was everywhere, most notably in the gardens. She had been famous for her beautiful gardens, resplendent with one of the widest selection of roses to be found anywhere in the world. She was long gone, but gardeners had faithfully maintained her gardens. When Napoleon walked among those roses in these last few days of his time at Malmaison, the melancholy must have hung heavily in the air. On one such walk, the day after he arrived, he said to Hortense:

'Poor Josephine! I cannot become accustomed to this place without her. It always seems as though I were going to catch sight of her behind the next hedge, picking the flowers she loved so dearly. Poor Josephine!' Noting how this topic depressed me he added: 'It is true she would be very sad if she could see the way things are going at present. There was only one subject we ever disagreed about, her debts. How I used to scold her about them! She was certainly the most charming person I have ever known. She was a true woman with all the qualities that word conveys, quick, lively and so good-hearted. Have another portrait made of her for me. I want it as a medallion.' I promised to have this done.[1]

Hortense and others continued to worry about Napoleon's security. There were only a handful of armed men and, while their willingness to fight was not in doubt, their ability to protect Napoleon against any serious effort on his person was dubious, at best. This concern was at least somewhat reduced when, late on the 25th, General Nicolas Beker arrived and asked to see Napoleon. The Provisional Government had earlier in the day delivered the following letter to the General:

Paris, June 25, 1814, 4 p.m.

General,

Please be advised that the government commission has named you to command the guard of the Emperor Napoleon at Malmaison.

The honor of France requires that his safety and the respect owed him be assured. The interest of the nation demands that malicious people be prevented from using his name to foment trouble.

General, your acknowledged character is the government's and France's guarantee that you shall fulfill both tasks. You are invited to proceed immediately to Malmaison, take command of the guard, and take all dispositions required to accomplish these goals.

Sincerely, etc.

Minister of War Prince of Eckmühl (Davout)[2]

Beker's arrival was good news and bad news. The good news was that the Provisional Government had recognized the need to provide security and had sent a good general to take command of the Imperial Guard members protecting Napoleon. This gave Napoleon and his entourage some assurance that the Provisional Government did not plan to do Napoleon any harm.

The bad news was, of course, that this action made it clear that Napoleon was no longer master of his own destiny and was, in fact, a prisoner. No matter how polite Beker was – and he treated Napoleon with all respect and dignity – this basic fact was impossible to ignore. It was also clear that Beker's primary mission was to ensure that Napoleon left Malmaison as soon as possible and that he, Beker, was to provide him with a military escort on his way out. Of course, Beker's presence also made it clear that Fouché would be able to monitor all of Napoleon's movements, lest the former emperor decide to gamble on one last roll of the dice.

Beker had risen under Napoleon but then had the bad judgment to be critical of some of Napoleon's decisions. This did not go down well, and he was put on half-pay (a sure sign an officer was on the way out) and then forced to retire. After Waterloo, however, Napoleon needed all the men he could get, and Beker was reinstated to serve in the defense of Paris. Beker understood the difficulty and delicacy of his mission and did not really want to accept it. It was Davout, who trusted Beker and knew he would afford Napoleon the safety that Davout wanted for his former Emperor, who insisted and was therefore responsible for Beker's arrival on the scene. Whatever else may be said about his loyalty to Napoleon, Davout wanted Napoleon and his family protected from any vengeance that might ensue after the coming restoration of the Bourbon monarchy.[3]

Montholon, incidentally, suggests that Beker actually encouraged Napoleon to leave Malmaison, take command of the army, and 'resume the sword of Marengo and Austerlitz, and to march boldly against the enemy'.[4] This seems unlikely, though Napoleon would shortly volunteer to do exactly that. Caulaincourt, who was privy to Beker's appointment, says that the mission was to 'watch the movements of the prisoner'.[5]

Many years later, Beker told Marchand:

> When I accepted this mission, it was only in order to serve the Emperor and protect him; I did not then suspect what was revealed to me a few days later, that the Duke of Otranto and the Prince of Eckmühl were negotiating with royalist agents.[6]

Final Goodbyes

While Napoleon was at Malmaison, he was visited by many of his friends and associates from happier days. His brothers Joseph, Lucien and Jérôme gave him much-needed familial support, and he was also surrounded by military and political supporters, including Bertrand, Savary, Lallemand, Montholon and Gourgaud. Count Las Cases was there, as well as an assortment of ladies, mostly wives of the men in attendance.

Perhaps Napoleon's most poignant visit was that from Countess Marie Walewska. The two had met in Poland in 1806 and had quickly fallen into bed. At first an affair of convenience and politics, the relationship developed into a true love story. She remained in love with Napoleon and they wrote to each other often. In 1809, she joined him in Vienna for a few weeks and became pregnant with Alexander Florian Joseph Walewski (in Polish, the ending -ka is feminine, -ki is masculine). Marie had visited Napoleon on Elba and had even offered to stay with him there. He declined the offer, still hoping that his wife and son would be allowed to join him in exile. That, of course, did not happen.

On Wednesday, 28 June, Marie, still under 30 years of age, and their young son Alexander came to visit Napoleon, a visit that had evidently been arranged some days earlier by Marchand:

'The atmosphere was very sad,' recalled Alexander Walewski some years later. 'I can still see the Emperor … every single feature of his face … He took me in his arms and I remember a tear ran down his face … But I cannot recall what exactly he said to me on that occasion.'[7]

Whatever was said in that hour-long farewell, it was certainly emotional. Hortense relates that after the meeting, 'She [Marie] was all in tears. I shared her grief and invited her to stay and lunch alone with me so that people might not see her in such a state.'[8] One can only speculate, but it seems possible that she once again had asked to join Napoleon in his exile and had once again been rebuffed, however gently. Had she been able to join him on St Helena, perhaps that period of his life would have been happier and longer. It is impossible to say.

Visits of old friends aside, Napoleon was becoming more and more depressed during his stay at Malmaison. Part of this was the memory of happier days with Josephine, but it went beyond that. Caulaincourt's comment on the situation is touching in its description of Napoleon's emotions:

All that could rouse the indignation of a lofty spirit, all that could lacerate a mortal wound, was studiously put into practice, and this treatment had wrought the wished-for effect – that of impairing his energy. His mental suffering was extreme. 'My removal to this place,' said he, 'is an additional annoyance to me. Every object that presents itself to my eyes revives some distressing recollection. This Malmaison was the first considerable property that I became possessed of. The money with which I purchased it was my own earnings. It was long the abode of happiness; but she who was its chief ornament is no more – my misfortunes killed her. Ten years ago I little foresaw that I should one day take refuge here to avoid my persecutors. And who are these persecutors? Men whom I have loaded with favors; men whom I have raised from humble to exalted stations. I made myself what I was, but they are only what I made them. What recollections I shall carry with me from France.'[9]

The Fouché Sidestep

Napoleon was staying at Malmaison merely to await official documents – passports – that would allow him to leave France and migrate to the United States of America. In retrospect, one might wonder why he didn't move quickly to Rochefort, hop on one of the available French ships, and head out for America. It would seem unlikely that the French ship captains would deny the former Emperor the opportunity to sail for America, so far from the politics of Europe. It was the delays Napoleon suffered waiting for passports as much as his own indecision that led him to his unhappy fate on St Helena. Napoleon and his followers pleaded with the Provisional Government to provide the passports immediately, but they were not forthcoming. If only Napoleon had foreseen this possibility and made provision of passports a condition for abdication. But the election of Fouché and Wellington's direction to Fouché that the Allies wanted custody of Napoleon meant that Napoleon would wait in vain for the dignity and assurance that passports could give.

It was one thing to leave France without a passport. That could probably have been done with little difficulty. But then there was the question of what would happen when Napoleon and his entourage reached the United States. While one suspects that the American government would have accepted him as an imperial refugee, it is quite possible that they would have denied his request to settle there and ordered his ships to leave American waters. Given the nature of American attitudes towards people wishing to immigrate, and the pro-Bonapartist feelings of at least some segments of society (for example, in New Orleans), this action seems unlikely, but it was, nevertheless, a concern. Napoleon could then have attempted to enter a nation in Latin America, but it would have been a real blow to his dignity to have to wander the seas looking for a home. Convinced as he was that passports would be forthcoming, he chose to wait. It was a terrible, if understandable, decision.

Incidentally, Las Cases suggests that Napoleon had planned to leave for America all along. Indeed, this plan had been in effect since his days on Elba:

> Even at the time of Napoleon's first renunciation of the throne, a wish was entertained by not a few of his friends that the Emperor would adopt the resolution of choosing the United States for the future residence of himself and his family, when he was sovereign of the island of Elba, and the apprehensions of the European courts seemed to have no end so long as he remained in Europe; and there were even an abundance of indications that, notwithstanding the treaties concluded with him, it was in contemplation, in more quarters than one, to adopt violent measures against him; these wishes and demands were reiterated ... On the second renunciation of the throne, this plan was to have been actually carried into execution. Joseph Bonaparte set off in haste before Napoleon, and New York was fixed on as the general rendezvous for the whole of the rest of the family, as well as of those persons who might not deem it advisable to remain in France ... the brothers and sisters of Napoleon, particularly Joseph and Lucien, possessed considerable wealth, and nothing more was sought for in America than to live free from care and secure from all further persecution, and to follow the calm pursuits of agriculture and literature.[10]

On the 26th, Fouché's Provisional Government issued a decree that, on first blush, seemed to give Napoleon permission to depart to the United States. But included in its wording were ominous indications that all was not as well as Napoleon might hope:

Decree of the Commission of Government
Paris, 26 June 1815
Article I. The Minister of Marine shall issue orders that two frigates in the port of Rochefort may be armed for the purpose of transporting Napoleon Bonaparte to the United States.

Article II. He shall, if he requires it, be provided with a competent escort as far as the place of embarkation, under the orders of General Beker, who is directed to watch over his safety.

Article III. The director-general of the posts shall on his part issue the orders connected with the service of the relays of horses.

Article IV. The Minister of Marine shall give the requisite instructions for the purpose of insuring the immediate return of the frigates as soon as the landing shall have taken place.

Article V. *The frigates shall not leave the roadstead of Rochefort until the passes shall have arrived.*

Article VI. The Ministers of Marine, of War and of Finances are charged, each one in what concerns him, with the execution of the present decree.

[Signed] The Duke of Otranto, Count Grenier, Count Carnot, Baron Quinette, Caulaincourt, Duke of Vicence.[11]

Note the key words in Article V, italicized by Savary, that make it clear that Napoleon is free to go to the coast, but no farther. ('Roadstead' and the more often used term 'roads' refer to sea channels, not land highways.) This is not really a surprise, of course, as it was fairly clear from the beginning that the Allies and their new lapdog, Fouché, were not really interested in allowing Napoleon his freedom, any more than they were truly interested in declaring his son the Emperor Napoleon II. This became more and more clear as circumstances unfolded. Napoleon was no longer in control of his fate, a circumstance that was perhaps obvious to him at the time. That may explain his seeming lack of concern and hurry to leave for the coast. To what end would he be leaving? But the Prussians were coming, and that, in the end, would be reason enough to go.

Savary relates a series of conversations with both the Minister of Marine and Fouché. The latter, of course, did what he could to appear to be trying to help Napoleon while never actually doing what desperately needed to be done, namely to provide the necessary passports. Fouché's response to Savary provides yet another decisive piece of evidence as to his real intentions regarding Napoleon. Told that Napoleon was anxious to leave France and wanted passports to go to America, Fouché claimed to be hearing of that idea for the first time, a claim that did not fool Savary. Fouché's comments were disingenuous at best:

Fouché replied to me with his usual levity of language, which failed, however, in its object of deceiving me.

'You are quite right,' he said. 'The Minister of Marine has written to me, but I did not exactly comprehend what he asked, and I forgot to mention the subject to my colleagues. It is too late to settle the matter today, but you may rest assured that at the sitting of tomorrow morning it shall be terminated, and I shall send an immediate answer to the Minister of Marine.'

'I will therefore return tomorrow,' was my reply. 'But as for the passports, this point depends wholly upon yourself. The Emperor, who is in a hurry to be off, has directed me to ask them of you.'

'With respect to the passports,' rejoined Fouché, 'that is another question. Where does the Emperor intend to go?'

'Where else can he go,' I resumed, 'but to America? I thought you were aware of it.'

'I know it!' said Fouché, 'this is the first time the subject is mentioned to me. He [Napoleon] is quite right, but I will not take upon myself to let him depart without adopting every precaution for his safety: otherwise, I should be blamed if any accident were to happen to him. I will apply to Lord Wellington for passports for him, as it behooves me to protect my individual responsibility in the eyes of the nation. I should never be forgiven for acting without the requisite precaution.

I [Savary] could not avoid observing to him that what he proposed to do would take up some time: the Emperor would relieve him from every kind of responsibility, and by hurrying his own departure, would alone be blamed for any consequences that might result from the course he adopted ... Caulaincourt ... recommended that I should urge the Emperor to take his departure as speedily as possible ... 'How can the Emperor take his departure,' I said, 'unless he be provided with the means of doing so? He wishes it, and only waits for the frigates and the passports.' – 'Let him be off,' was Caulaincourt's reply, 'he can never start too soon.'

'In that case,' I resumed, 'why is not his application complied with? There is no reasonable motive for the refusal, and the consequences must necessarily recoil upon the guilty authors of it.'

M. de Caulaincourt made no reply, and we separated.[12]

Fouché was, once again, playing a double game. Who could possibly imagine that he would 'not exactly comprehend' what the Minister of Marine was asking, or that he 'forgot to mention the subject' to the Commission of Government? The fate of Napoleon was one of the items foremost on the thoughts of all members of the government and, indeed, all of France, and there is no way that Fouché would not be right on top of that situation. But in his conversation with Savary, he may have tipped Napoleon off about the need for haste. Fouché had sent General Jacques Tromelin on a mission to the Allies to seek passports for Napoleon. At least, that was the official reason. Numerous people at the time, as well as historians since, contend that the real mission was to tip off the Allies that Napoleon was preparing to leave and that if they wished to prevent his departure from France they had better act quickly. Caulaincourt's warning that Napoleon could 'never start too soon' would certainly seem to suggest that the game was afoot and that Napoleon held an increasingly weak hand.

Of course, Fouché's game was also made obvious by the fact that he now insisted that he needed to get passports from the British. He had seen fit to give French passports to Marshal Ney, and there was no reason in the world why he could not do the same for Napoleon. No reason, that is, other than his desire to have Napoleon available unless the Allies should decide they no longer wanted him.

That night, General Beker took Napoleon a copy of the resolution by the Provisional Government referenced above. The next day, after again meeting with Fouché, and again hearing words without substance, Savary returned to Malmaison to inform Napoleon of what happened and to warn him of the increasing dangers. The Allies were closing on Paris, the British were patrolling the seas, Rochefort was being watched carefully. The British and the Prussians were already debating Napoleon's fate, with Prussian Field Marshal Blücher greatly desiring to execute Napoleon on the spot, while Wellington was more interested in keeping Napoleon in captivity. Napoleon's time was running out, if it had not already done so.

On 27 June, Grand Marshal Bertrand wrote to Napoleon that the frigates were being made available, and that arrangements had been made to pay for the costs of the voyage. Fouché also gave permission to Bertrand to take the following items from the Tuileries Palace, with it being very clear that nothing more was to be allowed:

> A complete table service of twelve settings, the porcelain known as 'Headquarters', six sets of table linen for twelve in damask cloth, six sets of kitchen linen, twelve pairs of high-quality sheets, twelve pairs of ordinary sheets, six dozen towels, two travel coaches, three saddles and bridles for general officers, three saddles and bridles for grooms, 400 books to be taken from the Rambouillet library, various maps, and 100,000 francs for travel expenses. This was what the government was granting to the man who had governed France with so much glory, and given considerable fortunes to those who surrounded him; the very man who was allowing these modest belongings to be taken had received from him an income of 200,000 pounds.[13]

The Primacy of Passports

Napoleon was determined not to leave Malmaison without passports. In some respects this was a reasonable decision. What would be the point of going to Rochefort or the Île d'Aix if he could go no further? At Malmaison he was close to his army and the people of Paris. It would be difficult, at least in the eyes of some, for a new French government or the Allies to do him harm while he was staying at Malmaison. But isolated a long way from Paris, he would be even less the master of his fate than he already was. Napoleon was quite prepared, even anxious, to leave. But it would not be simply to walk into a trap.

Accordingly, on the 28th, Napoleon sent one of his aides, General Flahaut, to see Fouché and Davout. His mission was to inform the government that Napoleon would not leave without proper guarantees that would be represented by the receipt of passports to the United States. Failing that, he would stay and seek the protection of the honor of France.

Not surprisingly, Flahaut's mission was a complete failure. Fouché was incredulous and Davout actually threatened that if Napoleon would not leave immediately he,

Davout, would go and arrest him in person. Thus had the loyalty of the man completely shifted. Napoleon, when told later in the day of Fouché's and Davout's response, simply shrugged it off with the comment, 'Let him [Davout] come,' and continued his day as before. He was reading as much material as possible on America, and receiving a steady stream of guests, including his mother, his uncle Fesch and assorted generals.

While Napoleon refused to move from Malmaison without passports, the Allies were moving closer and Napoleon was in danger of being captured. The Provisional Government seemed to move in several directions at once. It assured Beker that it anticipated that Wellington would soon issue the requested passports and that the said documents would be forwarded to Napoleon at Malmaison or, better still, at Rochefort. One might reasonably question such promises, but then the Minister of Marine arrived with the following letter from Fouché:

To the Minister of Marine
   Paris, 27 June, in the forenoon
   Monsieur le Duc,
   It is of the utmost importance that the Emperor should take his departure. The enemy is fast approaching, and is perhaps already at Compiègne. The Commission wishes that you should immediately repair to Malmaison and prevail upon the emperor to depart, as we could not be answerable for any movement that might take place. With respect to the clause of Article V of yesterday's decree respecting the passes, the Commission authorizes you to consider it as one of non-effect. All the other clauses are maintained in force.

[Signed] The Duke of Otranto

P.S. It would be important that the Emperor should take his departure *incognito*.[14]

This last suggestion should certainly have alerted Napoleon to the dangers of his forthcoming trip. He must have well remembered how he was treated on the way from Paris to the coast as he left for exile in 1814. No leaders, especially those recently deposed, are universally loved, and Napoleon was no exception. The other problem with the letter, of course, is that it seemed to suggest that Napoleon did not want to leave, when he had made it quite clear that leaving was exactly what he wanted to do.

That said, the revocation of the requirement that the frigates would not be available without proper passports was welcome news. The last barrier to departure had been lifted. Indeed, Minister of Marine Denis Decrès also brought with him detailed orders authorizing two frigates to take Napoleon to the United States (see Appendix VII), which he read to Las Cases.[15] The Prussians, when they came, would find an empty Malmaison and the Americans would soon find a most interesting immigrant in their midst. It was almost too good to be true.

It wasn't true, of course. Whether it was meant in good faith or not cannot be firmly proven either way, though given Fouché's nature one could certainly draw a conclusion in the negative. Decrès's orders referenced above were important and seemed to be the final word on the matter (though, as we will note below, they may have contained a poison pill). But shortly thereafter, a dispatch from the Minister of Marine arrived, informing Napoleon of a letter from Fouché stating, 'in consequences of the dispatches we have received this morning the Emperor cannot quit our ports without a pass. He must wait for it in the roads. Accordingly, the decree of yesterday remains in full force, and the letter which we wrote to you yesterday for the purpose of cancelling Article V is null and void. You will adhere to the text of our letter of yesterday'.[16] The nature of these all-important dispatches is not mentioned, but in fact Fouché had been alerted by his delegation to the Allies that Napoleon was not to be allowed to leave France. Fouché had received a dispatch from Laon dated the 26th which read in part:

> After conversations which we have had with the aides-de-camp of Prince Blücher the decision arrived at, and which we are loath to repeat, was that one of the great difficulties would be the person of the Emperor. They think that the Powers will demand guarantees and precautions against his reappearance on the scene. They claim that their people are even demanding security from his undertakings. It is our duty to observe that we think that his escape, before the conclusion of negotiations, would be considered as an indication of bad faith on our part and could materially compromise the safety of France. We have, further, the hope that this matter can be concluded to the satisfaction of the Emperor also, since they have made so few objections to his abode and that of his brothers in England that they seem to prefer it to residence in America.[17]

Minister of Marine Decrès goes on to say that he had been given a letter from Fouché:

> To the Minister of Marine
> Paris, 27 June, at noon
> The Commission recalls to your recollection the instructions it transmitted to you an hour ago. You are to attend to the execution of the decree such as it was yesterday drawn up by the Commission; in virtue of which decree Napoleon Bonaparte is to remain in the road of the Île d'Aix until the arrival of the passports.
> It is of consequence for the welfare of the state, which he cannot view with indifference, that he should remain there until his fate and that of his family shall be regulated in a definitive manner. Every means shall be employed in order that this negotiation may turn out to his satisfaction. French honor is interested in it. In the meanwhile, however, every precaution should be adopted for the personal safety of Napoleon, and for his not quitting the residence temporarily assigned to him.

> Accept, M. le Duc, &c
> The Duke of Otranto,
> The President of the Commission of Government[18]

Decrès continues:

It results from the foregoing, that the Commission conceives it indispensable for Your Majesty's safety that you should proceed on board the frigates at the Île d'Aix; and for the progress of the negotiations, that the frigates should not sail until the arrival of the passports.

Whilst I communicate this state of things to Your Majesty, I am on the point of returning to the Tuileries. I shall represent there whatever Your Majesty has stated to me, and ask for the orders of the Commission, in case that Your Majesty, on arriving at the Île d'Aix, should desire to be immediately conveyed to England on board a frigate or any other vessel, instead of remaining in those roads.[19]

The cat was clearly now out of the bag. Fouché had alerted the Allies that Napoleon was at Malmaison and was soon to leave for Rochefort, hoping to go to America. While it would be possible that the Allies could capture Napoleon at Malmaison, that would risk a general uprising of both the people of Paris and of the army. Even Davout might be inspired to go into battle in the name of French honor and his old Emperor; certainly others would do so. But in Rochefort, on the tiny Île d'Aix, or in a French vessel sitting in a harbor, Napoleon would be a sitting duck. The Provisional Government might have, at one point, hoped that Napoleon would escape safely to America (though it is doubtful that Fouché ever truly felt this way), but this letter removes all doubt that the decision was no longer theirs – or Napoleon's – to make. Negotiations might well be in order, but they would be rather one-sided. Napoleon's fate was up to the Allies, most especially, as it happened, the British.

General Beker, meanwhile, had received yet another letter regarding Napoleon's status, this one from Davout:

From the Minister of War
  Paris, 27 June 1815
  General,
  I have the honor to transmit to you the subjoined decree [presumably that of the 26th referenced above], which the Commission of Government desire you to notify to the Emperor Napoleon, at the same time informing His Majesty that the circumstances are become imperative – and that it is necessary for him immediately to decide on setting out for the Île d'Aix.

This decree has been passed as much for the safety of his person as for the interest of the state, which ought always to be dear to him.

Should the Emperor not adopt the above-mentioned resolution, on your notification of this decree, it will then be your duty to exercise the strictest surveillance, both with a view of preventing His Majesty from leaving Malmaison, and of guarding against any attempt upon his life. You will station guards on all the approaches to Malmaison. I have written to the chief inspector-general of the gendarmerie and to the commandant of Paris to place such of the gendarmerie and troops as you may require at your disposal.

I repeat to you, General, that this decree has been adopted solely for the good of the state and the personal safety of the Emperor. Its prompt execution is indispensable, as the future fate of His Majesty and his family depends upon it.

It is unnecessary to say to you, General, that all your measures should be taken with the greatest possible secrecy.

[Signed] Prince of Eckmühl
Marshal and Minister of War[20]

Another letter from Davout, sent later the same day, instructed General Beker to remain with Napoleon as long as he was on the Île d'Aix, and promised that a passport would be sent to Napoleon at that location. Passport or no, Napoleon was being urged to leave. Lavalette told him, 'Depart nevertheless … Your presence on board the ship will still have a great power over Frenchmen; cut the cables, promise money to the crew, and if the Captain resist, have him put on shore, and hoist your sails. I have not the least doubt but Fouché has sold you to the Allies.'[21]

Napoleon still had people who were interested in his welfare. Marshal Davout and his army were still near Paris, and neither Davout nor his soldiers were interested in seeing any harm come to their former Emperor. But defending him was becoming increasingly difficult, as the British and, especially, the Prussians were drawing ever closer. Napoleon was kept aware of their movements on an almost hourly basis, lest he needed to make a sudden departure. But save for leaving, he was in no position to do very much about the gathering storm around Paris.

Davout, however, commanded a formidable force and was prepared, if necessary, to defend Paris. Barricades were being erected (making it more difficult for Napoleon to remain in contact with events in Paris) and other measures were being taken. The Prussians were becoming an immediate threat to Malmaison. Indeed, Blücher had sent a detachment in the direction of Malmaison specifically to seize Napoleon. They arrived just hours too late.[22] Davout sent Beker the following order:

Order of the Minister of War to General Beker:
General,
You will take the command of a body of the Guards at present at Ruel and proceed to burn and completely destroy the bridge of Chatou.

By means of the troops at Courbevoie, I shall also cause the bridge of Besons to be destroyed, and send one of my aides-de-camp to superintend the operations.

Tomorrow I shall send some troops to St. Germain, but in the meantime guard yourself against an attack by that road. The officer who is the bearer of this letter is commissioned to bring me back a report of the execution of the order.

The Prince of Eckmühl[23]

The noose was tightening, and burning bridges would only delay, not halt, the oncoming Prussians. The bridges were quickly destroyed, and not a moment too soon. The Prussians shortly reached the destroyed bridges and were forced to look for a better crossing, away from the road to Malmaison. But for Davout and Beker, they might well have surprised Napoleon that very day. Napoleon had dodged a bullet, but it was about time to go. A look around Malmaison would tell the story. Once filled with those seeking favor and, perhaps, hoping that Napoleon would somehow avoid the fate that was closing in on him, Malmaison was no longer home to those who were now seeking their destiny with the new government.

Chapter 11

Heading South

An Offer They Could Refuse

By the evening of the 28th, Napoleon had become resigned to the need to leave Malmaison and head south to Rochefort and the Île d'Aix. He was to leave in secret: no one must know that Napoleon was on the road. Was this due to a desire to ensure his safety, or to keep the people from rallying to his cause? Perhaps it was a little of both. Minister of State Count Berlier had given the following letter to Beker:

> The Commission of Government hereby commands all officers, civil and military, to give free passage to Lieutenant-General Count Beker, member of the Chamber of Deputies, travelling to Rochefort, accompanied by his secretary and one servant. They are expressly enjoined not to cause or suffer to be caused any delay, and to throw no obstacles in the way of his journey, but on the contrary to render him aid and assistance in case of necessity.
>
> > Given at Paris, 26 June 1815
> > Berlier (seal)[1]

Perhaps Napoleon was aware of the danger to his person and prepared to see to it that he did not fall into the hands of the Prussians or, perhaps, a royalist mob along the way. He had been warned more than once that Fouché was negotiating with representatives of Louis XVIII and that Davout was less than enthusiastic about confronting the Allies. For their part, the Allies seemed intent on moving on Paris and, no doubt, Malmaison. On the 28th, Napoleon had called his valet, Marchand, into his room and gave him a small vial of red liquid. Napoleon had attempted suicide in 1814, and Marchand had no doubt that this vial contained what Marchand called 'instant death'. Napoleon's doctor, Jean Corvisart, had visited Napoleon earlier in the day and the two of them had been alone for some time. Corvisart had brought a certain M. Maingault, who was to be Napoleon's doctor, but it is likely that he also provided the vial. The ever-faithful Marchand arranged a way for the vial to be just inside Napoleon's jacket. This, naturally enough, was quite depressing to Marchand, but the poison was never used.[2]

Thiébault suggests that the druggist Cadet Gassicourt had given Napoleon poison before Waterloo, which Napoleon had taken on 21 June and then asked Gassicourt to negate the effects, which he did. Many years later, Gassicourt told Thiébault that he feared that the poison hastened Napoleon's death on St Helena.[3]

Marchand made arrangements for the Emperor's table service and other material to be loaded into two carriages. Fouché had listed what was allowed to be taken, but Marchand and M. Colin, the controller of Napoleon's household, put in all of the silver that was available. Years later, on St Helena, Napoleon would seem to have a virtually endless supply of silver, a fact that can be traced to Colin's devotion to his Emperor.[4]

The morning of the 29th began as one might expect Napoleon's last day at Malmaison would begin. His brother Joseph paid him a visit and they had a long and no doubt emotional talk. Other visitors jockeyed for the chance to pay their respects to the Emperor, and messengers kept Napoleon and his staff as up to date as possible on the latest position of the Prussians.

Then General Michel Brayer and his division marched by Malmaison. The soldiers cried out, 'Long Live the Emperor! Down with the Bourbons! Down with the Traitors!' and expressed their interest in following their Emperor once more. General Brayer met with Napoleon,[5] but in any event, the support shown by these soldiers, along with the realization that the Prussians were over-extended and isolated from the British, inspired Napoleon to action. Marshal Grouchy's three corps were well positioned to drive the Prussians back, and Davout's army, of perhaps 117,000 men, could rally to put the Allies on the run. The Prussians had foolishly put themselves in a position to be utterly destroyed. After that, the French could turn and face Wellington, who had only a little over 50,000 men.

Suddenly, Napoleon's spirits picked up. Here was the chance he'd wanted, the chance to lead France to one last, great victory. Those damned Prussians, the cause of his defeat at Waterloo: he'd show them what was what. The Prussians had walked into a trap, and who better to spring it on them than France's greatest general? Davout, of course, was as aware of the situation as Napoleon and had concluded that the best that could be gained was a temporary victory. Where Napoleon saw the destruction of the British and, especially, the Prussian armies, Davout saw a temporary saving of Paris and a victory that would only last until the Austrians and Russians arrived. While French numbers seemed strong, they were poorly organized and not in a position to carry out an offensive operation of that magnitude.

Those who felt that even a French victory at Waterloo would have been only temporary would naturally side with Davout. Those who felt that a French victory at Waterloo might have changed history would be with Napoleon. The Emperor, of course, had made his determination. He did not want a civil war, and was not interested in leading soldiers on a fool's mission. But a defeat of the hated Prussians and even of the British could cause the Russians and, especially, the Austrians to reconsider their approach. Napoleon was certainly not going to return to power, but a major French victory might give France a greater say in its destiny. It could be Napoleon's one last, great gift to the nation.

Napoleon immediately halted preparations to leave and summoned General Beker. He proposed to Beker that he would volunteer to lead the army against the Prussians in the name of his son, Napoleon II. After driving them from the gates of Paris, he would retire to private life. Beker was amazed to hear of this plan, and could only imagine the lack of enthusiasm with which it would be received in Paris. He tried to get out of being the messenger for such a proposal, suggesting that Napoleon should send one of his personal aides-de-camp. But Napoleon, rightfully, wanted Beker to do the job. After all, Beker was the general assigned to watch over Napoleon and thus could be assumed to have the confidence of the government and, indeed, of Fouché. So Napoleon pressured Beker to accept the assignment. He told the general:

> You will explain to them that it is not my intention to resume possession of power. My only wish is to defeat and crush the enemy, and compel him by means of our victory to give a favourable turn to the negotiations. As soon as this result shall have been obtained, I shall depart, and quietly proceed on my journey.[6]

Like so many before him, Beker was learning just how difficult it was to say no to Napoleon.

Beker left for Paris, but the trip was not easy. The roads were crowded, even for a general, and the bridge at Pont de Neuilly had been barricaded. But after crossing the bridge on foot and then obtaining a carriage for the remainder of the trip, the general arrived at the meeting of the Commission of Government. Fouché and the others were amazed to see General Beker before them. After all, he was supposed to be on the way to Rochefort, escorting Napoleon out of the area.

They were even more amazed when they heard why he was there. There are numerous accounts of what happened. Montholon, who must be read with caution, is probably as accurate as any in this case, when he relates Beker's words to the Commission:

> Gentlemen, the Emperor sends me to inform you that the situation of France, the wishes of all true patriots and the cries of the soldiery, demand his presence to save our country. It is no longer as Emperor that he demands this, but as a General, whose name and reputation may still exercise a powerful influence over the fate of the empire. After having repulsed our enemies, he promises to retire to the United States to accomplish his destiny.[7]

Napoleon evidently sent a letter with Beker that outlined the basic strategy, and added:

> In abdicating power I did not renounce the most noble right of a citizen, which is to defend my country. The approach of the enemies to the capital leaves no doubt with regard to their intentions and their bad faith. Under these serious circumstances I offer my services as a general, still looking upon myself as the first soldier of my country.[8]

If Napoleon thought that the logic of the situation would sway Fouché, or that Davout or other members of the government, such as Caulaincourt, would rally to his cause, he was sadly mistaken. Fouché was in charge, his agenda was paramount, and he was having none of it. Fouché and the others received the proposal with a sense of dread, fearing that Napoleon would upset the delicate negotiations and bring greater ruin upon France. Perhaps Fouché also feared that this would compromise the return of Louis XVIII or, worse yet, compromise the position of the person most important to Fouché – himself. Napoleon was mad!

After raging against Napoleon for the proposal, and sarcastically pointing out that Napoleon's promises were less than trustworthy, Fouché and the others turned on Beker. How dare he bring such a proposal when he was supposed to be escorting Napoleon to Rochefort? Didn't he realize that Napoleon was in danger? Beker was shown various reports by generals that told of Allied advances virtually to the gates of Malmaison itself.

When Fouché asked Beker who was with the Emperor when the proposal was drawn up, he replied that Hughes Maret, the Duke of Bassano, had been there. Indeed, Maret had been set to making preparations for Napoleon to take charge of the army, so sure had Napoleon been that his offer would be accepted. Napoleon had changed into his Chasseurs of the Guard uniform and waited for confirmation of the acceptance of his offer.

That acceptance was not, of course, forthcoming. Fouché, Davout and all the rest were determined more than ever that Napoleon should leave – now – and they told Beker that in no uncertain terms. Beker, reasonably, requested some kind of written response to give to Napoleon. Fouché, now disgusted with the entire affair, dashed off a note, not to Beker, not to Napoleon, but to Maret, the Duke of Bassano:

> As the Provisional Government cannot accept the offer that General Beker has just made on behalf of His Majesty, for reasons that you yourself will appreciate, I pray you to use the influence you have always had on him to advise him to leave without delay, as the Prussians are marching on Versailles, etc.
>
> [Signed] The Duke of Otranto[9]

Alone in his study, Napoleon received Beker and heard his report. He must have been both sad and angry, to say nothing of tempted to call Fouché's bluff and ride to the head of the army. Most of his entourage hoped he would do exactly that. But in the end, he was resigned to his fate. When Beker convinced him that his offer had been well understood and decisively rejected, Napoleon knew the game was up and it was, at long last, time for him to leave Malmaison to meet his fate. 'These people do not understand the state of men's minds when they refuse my offer; they will repent of having done so … Give the necessary orders for my departure, and when all is ready, you will inform me.'[10] Napoleon then changed into civilian clothes and waited, spending a few moments with Joseph. Caulaincourt paid him a visit and describes Napoleon's state of mind:

> His attitude was indicative of dejection, and his whole appearance betrayed the efforts he had made to conceal the grief which inwardly preyed upon him. It was evident that he suffered the utmost extreme of mental misery. I shuddered as I read the anguish depicted in his looks. His glory and his dignity were insulted

– his feelings and affections were violated. He was now sinking under the lassitude consequent on the efforts he had made to conceal his real emotions. He summoned all his energy to struggle against his pitiless destiny, and to subdue the irritation continually created by the circumstances of his position.[11]

Marchand, as close to Napoleon as anyone at this time, relates the scene for the next hour:

> Once back in his quarters, accompanied by the Grand Marshal, he said: 'These people are destroying France.' He removed his guard chasseur's uniform, donned a brown coat with blue pants and riding boots, and placed a round broad-brimmed hat on his head. The Emperor was chatting while dressing, with the calm of a serene soul that had wished until the very end to defend the interests of the country. He went into the drawing room where he found Queen Hortense, whose tears moved him, and who proved full of devotion and kindness. He went out with her into the garden, but did not want her to go any further. He embraced the princess for the last time, said a final goodbye to the few friends who were there, as well as to Mmes de Vicence [Caulaincourt], Caffarelli, and Walewska, handed his horse to his equerry Baron de Montaran, and walked away from friends who were all bursting into tears as he approached the small park gate. A coach hitched to four post horses that was to be preceded by Amodru, a groom acting as outrider, had been waiting there for nearly an hour. The Emperor climbed in, followed by General Beker, the Grand Marshal, and the Duke of Rovigo [Savary], who were accompanying him.[12]

One of Napoleon's most loyal supporters, General Charles de La Bédoyère, had planned to join him in exile. He had spoken to the Chamber of Peers with great emotion, even anger, in support of Napoleon and of his son, reminding the members of the oaths they had taken to defend the Emperor. Napoleon tried to convince him to join him at least as far as Rochefort. But the general had come to believe that the King would be lenient on those who had supported Napoleon, and was reluctant to flee with or without his young family. He was wrong, of course, and was caught up in the furious move for revenge that resulted in his execution on 19 August.

Queen Hortense had sewn a diamond collar into a ribbon that Napoleon could use as a belt. Napoleon had been reluctant to accept them, but Hortense had insisted. In the end, she had proved to be as loyal as anyone to Napoleon. Another symbol of loyalty, Marchand, put 20,000 francs and a full complement of pistols in Napoleon's coach. Saint-Denis rode above. At 5.30 p.m. on 29 June, the Emperor's coach left Malmaison for the last time. Moments before, General Beker sent Davout the following letter:

General Beker to the Minister of War

My Lord, I have the honor to inform you that the Emperor is on the point of entering his carriage to accomplish his destiny. I shall take care to announce to your Excellency the day of our arrival at Rochefort, and shall not set out on my return to Paris until I have seen the Emperor on board.

[Signed] Count Beker[13]

To maintain secrecy, 'a little traveling carriage of the most ordinary and most modest sort had been prepared for him, and carriages with coats of arms and other carriages were to receive the persons who composed the suite and carry the baggage of each of the travelers'.[14] Soon to follow would be numerous coaches carrying Napoleon's personal belongings and that of his traveling companions, some forty-eight people in total. They left at slightly different times and by different routes, but all were headed for Rochefort.

The Trip to …?

Napoleon's coach headed for Rambouillet. He deliberately carried little in the way of luggage, wishing to appear to be out for a day's excursion rather than a lengthy trip. Napoleon's coach traveled alone; again, the desire to avoid standing out was paramount. Two other coaches carrying the Emperor's effects, General Gourgaud, Marchand and others followed about two hours behind.

The other part of the convoy, which included the more formal imperial carriages that would be more likely to attract attention, left by another gate and headed towards Rochefort via Angoulême, Orléans and Tours. This group of carriages included Montholon and Las Cases, among many others.

Napoleon's carriage traveled in silence. It was a hot and humid day, and they could hear the sound of guns in the distance. One can only imagine the anguish and apprehension felt by all of its occupants. It is easy to imagine that nerves were on edge and that tempers could flare. At one point, Napoleon noted that his courier, a man named Amandru, was carrying a knife with an Imperial Eagle on it. When told to put it away, Amandru became angry. He went ahead, supposedly to get horses at the next relay, and was never seen again. The horses were nevertheless obtained, though with a potentially dangerous delay of a quarter of an hour or so, and the carriage continued on. The once loyal Amandru was replaced by the still loyal Santini.

The Emperor and his entourage passed near Versailles and St-Cyr and at one point encountered some Polish cavalry. Although it seems likely that some of the postilions who provided fresh horses along the way must have recognized him, Napoleon arrived at Rambouillet without further incident.

General Beker had been given explicit instructions that Napoleon was not to dally along the way, but when his carriage reached Rambouillet at about eight or nine o'clock in the evening, Napoleon expressed a desire to spend the night. He was doubtless exhausted, both physically and mentally, and in need of rest. Beker could hardly refuse, especially as they were sufficiently far from Paris that the Emperor's safety was not, at least for the moment, in doubt. Napoleon's carriage entered the grounds of the castle and the small entourage went in. There they were greeted by M. Hébert, who had served as valet to Napoleon during the Egyptian campaign.

Napoleon had little to eat beyond a cup of tea and soon, after a brief meeting with Bertrand, went to bed. All who were with him could see that he was completely disheartened by the events that had so rapidly overtaken him, and during the meal there was nothing but silence.[15] Saint-Denis reports that Napoleon was 'restless all night'. He also observed the vial of poison that Napoleon was still carrying with him, as well as the diamonds given him by Hortense.[16]

Gourgaud arrived several hours later. Though he was also no doubt exhausted, he was sent back a few miles to obtain news of events to the north. All of Napoleon's entourage were depressed, ate little, and soon went to bed as well.

The next morning, 30 June, Napoleon arose in better spirits. Bertrand had collected a few more books and maps for the journey. Napoleon wrote to his librarian, Barbier, to send more books to Rochefort. Following the loss of Amandru, one of the secretaries, M. Rathery, pleaded the illness of his wife as just cause to abandon Napoleon. Napoleon was understanding, but canceled the pension that had been promised. This money went instead to Colonel Bellini and his wife. The good colonel had been with Napoleon on Elba and volunteered to join him yet again in his exile. Napoleon, though touched, declined, fearing that the size of his entourage had become too large.

Napoleon had to endure yet another touching goodbye, this time with his old valet, Hébert. Napoleon had a long memory of and loyalty to people such as Hébert. He left this good man a large sum of money in his will.[17]

By six o'clock Napoleon was once again on the move. Little of consequence happened along the way. They did stop and purchase some cherries for refreshment; it was a very hot day and the cherries were no doubt very welcome. A few people evidently recognized the Emperor, and at one point some gendarmes warned them of brigands and actually offered to accompany them, a kind offer that Savary declined. Little else happened until they arrived at Tours late in the evening. There they stopped to rest and to obtain further information as to events in Paris. Count Miramont, who was prefect of the region, assured them that no news or suspicious activity had been noted and that Napoleon could be assured that he would delay anyone seeking the Emperor and send Napoleon a quick warning.[18] Count Miramont invited Napoleon to spend the night there but, perhaps bowing to an increased sense of urgency, Napoleon pressed on to Poitiers. The conversation with Count Miramont had taken perhaps an hour, so the horses and the rest of the entourage were rested.

When they arrived at Poitiers, Napoleon rested at the Hôtel de la Poste outside of town. It was eleven in the morning, but he wanted to rest until midday. While there, General Beker sent a letter by fast courier to the Maritime Prefect at Rochefort, alerting him of Napoleon's impending arrival and requesting that he be prepared to greet the Emperor. Local officials checked the group's internal passports, but otherwise the stop was uneventful.

Not so their arrival at St-Maixent. There, a large crowd appeared, curious at the arrival of a coach from the north and anxious for any news. The local sentry demanded the passports and did not return them as quickly as was normal. It seems that the local officials were at least a little suspicious of the nature of the passports and their bearers. It took the intervention of General Beker to get the passports – and a safe conduct pass – returned. It was a close call, as Savary relates: 'There is no doubt that General Bertrand or I should otherwise have been compelled to answer for ourselves; we, and necessarily also the Emperor, must infallibly have been recognized.'[19]

Napoleon's carriage made a rapid departure from St-Maixent, but their adventures were not over. Shortly thereafter, it became necessary to disembark from the carriage to lighten the load for the horses as they ascended a very long and steep hill. The sun had just set and the walk was no doubt a welcome relief from being cooped up in the carriage. A local man, probably a farmer, kept staring at Napoleon and asking Saint-Denis who that fellow was. Saint-Denis said simply that the group consisted of officers headed for Niort, but the man was not convinced that there wasn't more than that to the situation. The encounter no doubt made Napoleon and his followers nervous, though the man was a supporter of Napoleon and had expressed unhappiness with the arrival of the Bourbons.[20]

Around 8 p.m. in the evening of 1 July, an exhausted Napoleon arrived in the city of Niort. Here he determined that he would spend the night and was therefore taken to the Boule d'Or inn, which was at best modest accommodation. Napoleon was given a room above the kitchen. By now hungry, Napoleon accepted a modest dinner and then retired. In the middle of the night, two gendarmerie officers came looking for Savary and Beker, but nothing significant came of their visit. Not long afterwards, the carriages containing General Gourgaud, Marchand and the baggage arrived. It had been delayed and was quite late.

Beker, in the meantime, sent a fast courier to Paris with the following report:

Letter from Beker to the Provisional Government
  Niort, 2 July 1815

  In order to hasten my report to the Provisional Government, I am informing it by special courier that the Emperor has arrived in Niort, tired and very concerned about the fate of France.

  Without having been recognized, the Emperor was greatly touched by the concern with which people were inquiring of him along the way, and the expressions of interest made him say several times: 'The government doesn't know the mood in France, it was too anxious to have me leave Paris, and had it accepted my proposal, things would have turned around: I could still exercise in the name of the nation a great influence on political matters, by backing up the government's negotiations with an army for which my name would serve as rallying point.'

  Arriving in Niort, His Majesty was informed by the Rochefort maritime prefect that, by doubling its cruisers and its vigilance since June 29, the British squadron had rendered impossible any exit by vessels. The Emperor had General Beker write the following letter to the prefect:

  'In these conditions, the Emperor wishes the Minister of the Navy to authorize the captain of the frigate he will be boarding to communicate with the commander of the British squadron should extraordinary circumstances render this move indispensable, as much for the Emperor's personal safety as to spare France the pain and shame of seeing him removed from his last refuge and delivered into the hands of his enemies.'

Under these difficult circumstances, we are anxiously awaiting news from Paris. We hope the capital will defend itself and that the enemy will give you time to see the outcome of the negotiations undertaken by your ambassadors, and to reinforce the army to cover Paris (this sentence and the last were dictated by the Emperor). If in this situation the British cruisers prevent the frigates from departing, you may call upon the Emperor to serve as a general, as his only consideration is being of use to the motherland.

[Signed] Lieutenant General Count Beker[21]

It is hard to say how serious Napoleon really was about this offer to serve as a general. It may have been a ploy to put pressure on Paris, or it may have been an act of desperation. As we will shortly see, it received the only possible reply from Paris, namely outright rejection.

The next morning, 2 July, proved more eventful than most on the trip thus far. Napoleon's brother Joseph arrived, as did General Lallemand, who confirmed that General de La Bédoyère had decided not to rejoin the Emperor. By now, Napoleon's presence in the city was not a secret, and the prefect, M. Busche, came by to insist that Napoleon take up quarters at the prefecture building. Napoleon agreed and spent the rest of the day there. Numerous military officers came by to ask Napoleon to lead them once again to victory, a suggestion that Napoleon graciously declined. He was no doubt tempted, but with each mile from Paris his ability to make a difference diminished, with a destiny before a firing squad the more likely outcome. If the Provisional Government summoned him (as he suggested in the letter above), he would answer the call. Otherwise, he would continue his move south. He was beyond the point of taking any direct initiative of that nature.

Still, these offers were gratifying to Napoleon and made the peril of his situation a bit more bearable. He was surrounded by family, friends and supporters. Countess Bertrand arrived to join her husband. Crowds acclaimed the Emperor wherever he went. For a day, it seemed that time stood still.

Chapter 12

Parisian Follies

Allied Pressure

Time had not, of course, stood still. In Paris, things were moving with great rapidity. The effort to obtain an armistice had met with resistance by the Allies, and not surprisingly, Napoleon's status was in the center of it all. The letter from the Allied Foreign Ministers makes that clear:

> Letter from the Allied Foreign Ministers to the French Plenipotentiaries
> Hagueneau, 1 July 1815
> According to the stipulation of the treaty of alliance, which says that none of the contracting parties shall treat of peace or an armistice but by common consent, the three courts that find themselves together, Austria, Russia and Prussia, declare that they cannot at present enter into any negotiation. The cabinets will assemble together as soon as possible.
> The here powers consider it as an essential condition of peace, and of real tranquility, that Napoleon Bonaparte shall be incapable of disturbing the repose of France, and of Europe, for the future, and in consequence of the events that occurred in the month of March last, *the powers must insist that Napoleon Bonaparte be placed in their custody.*
>
> > [Signed] Walmoden
> > Capo d'Istria
> > Knesbeck[1]

The Chamber of Representatives, perhaps suddenly realizing that Napoleon's departure had deprived them of their ace in the hole, attempted to dictate terms to the Allies. It was the theater of the absurd, as they were in no position to dictate terms to anyone. Perhaps they were merely posturing for history:

> Declaration of the Chamber of Representatives
> 2 July 1815
> The troops of the allied powers are about to occupy the capital.
> The Chamber of Representatives will nevertheless continue to sit amid the inhabitants of Paris, to which place the express will of the people has sent its proxies.
> But, under the present serious circumstances, the Chamber of Representatives owes it to itself, owes it to France and to Europe, to make a

declaration of its sentiments and principles.

It declares, therefore, that it makes a solemn appeal to the fidelity and patriotism of the national guard of Paris, charged with the protection of the national representatives.

It declares that it reposes itself with the highest confidence on the moral principles, honor and magnanimity of the allied powers, and on their respect for the independence of the nation, positively expressed in their manifestoes.

It declares that the government of France, whoever may be its head, ought to unite in its favor the wishes of the nation, legally expressed, and form arrangements with the other governments, in order to become a common bond and guarantee of peace between France and Europe.

It declares that a monarch cannot offer any real guarantees if he does not swear to the observance of a constitution, formed by the deliberations of the national representatives and accepted by the people. Accordingly, any government that has no other title than the acclamations and will of a party, or is imposed on it by force, any government that does not adopt the national colors and does not guarantee:

The liberties of the citizens;

Equality of rights, civil and political;

The liberty of the press;

Freedom of religious worship;

The representative system;

Free assent to levies and taxes;

The responsibility of ministers;

The irrevocability of sales of national property, from whatever source originating;

The inviolability of property;

The abolition of titles, of the old and new hereditary nobility, and of feudal claims;

The abolition of all confiscation of property, the complete oblivion of opinions and votes given up to the present day;

The institution of the Legion of Honor;

The recompenses due to the officers and soldiers;

The succor due to their widows and children;

The institution of a jury; the indefeisibleness of the office of judge;

The payment of the public debt;

Would not ensure the tranquility of France and of Europe.

If the fundamental principles announced in this declaration should be disregarded or violated, the representatives of the French people, acquitting themselves this day of a sacred duty, enter their protest beforehand, in the face of the whole world, against violence and usurpation. They entrust the maintenance of the arrangements, which they now proclaim, to all good Frenchmen, to all generous hearts, to all enlightened minds, to all men jealous of liberty, and, in fine, to future generations.[2]

Even so, it was as much in the interests of the Allies as of France to reach some kind of accommodation, and on 3 July an armistice was reached that called for the withdrawal of the French army and the peaceful entry of the Allies into Paris (see Appendix VIII).

An Unwanted Emperor

Beker's report from Niort on Napoleon's arrival in that city and his second offer to lead French troops into battle as a mere general (the first having been made the day he left Malmaison) was received with a response that was even less enthusiastic than the response to Napoleon's first offer. Fouché quickly dashed off letters to the Minister of Marine and General Beker:

Paris, 4 July 1815
  Minister of Marine
  The Commission sends you a copy of the letter it has written to General Beker. It is the wish of the Commission that you should transmit the necessary instructions to Rochefort, *in order that military aid may be furnished to General Beker, as well as any other assistance he may require towards the accomplishment of his mission.* You will find enclosed the letter addressed to General Beker. The minister of the interior and of war are apprised that the courier you dispatch will take charge of the instructions they have to issue in reference to the same subject.

[Signed] The Duke of Otranto
Carnot
Count Grenier
Quinette
Caulaincourt, Duke of Vicence

Paris, 4 July 1815
  General Beker,
  The Commission of Government has received the letter you have written to it from Niort under the date of the 2nd of July. Napoleon must embark without delay. The success of the negotiations mainly depends upon the positive assurance the Allied Powers wish to receive of his actual embarkation, and you are not aware to what extent the safety and repose of the state are compromised by this procrastination. *Had Napoleon taken his departure immediately*, we have before us a report from the maritime prefect of Rochefort stating that there was a possibility of succeeding on the 29th. The Commission therefore places the person of Napoleon under your responsibility. *You must employ every measure of coercion you may deem necessary*, without failing in the respect due to him. Accelerate his arrival at Rochefort and make him instantly embark. As to his

offer of services, our duties towards France and our engagements towards foreign powers do not allow us to accept of them, and you must no longer mention the matter to us. Lastly, *the Commission conceives it to be inexpedient that Napoleon should communicate with the English squadron. It cannot grant the permission which is asked on that subject.*

Accept, &c,

[Signed] The Duke of Otranto[3]

These letters make it clear that the Provisional Government wanted Napoleon out of their hair as quickly as possible. Whether they wanted him in the hands of the British, on his way to America, or simply dead may be debated, though the Allies were making it clear that they wanted to gain control of Napoleon and were not interested in his escaping to the United States. Perhaps Fouché wanted it both ways. One can understand their concern. While at Niort, Napoleon had again been urged to lead an army to Paris to defeat the traitors and the invaders. Napoleon might have had as many as 20,000 to 25,000 men under his command, with the expectation that others would join him, certainly when he reached Davout's soldiers near Paris. Moreover, perhaps there would have been what Montholon describes as '100,000 fanatical peasants' marching in his support.[4] Perhaps, but if Napoleon had been unwilling to take command of troops near Paris over the objections of the Provisional Government, he was certainly not willing to do so now except at the request of the government, which he had now sought for the second time. However, despite the Provisional Government's urgent direction to General Beker to put Napoleon on a ship, the necessary passports did not accompany these directives. The moment came and went, much as other, more important, moments during this tragic period had come and gone with no action taken.

In any event, Napoleon spent the night of the 2nd in Niort. That evening saw a gala dinner in his honor, with regimental bands, songs and a generally festive time. General Gourgaud was sent ahead to Rochefort to ascertain the possibilities for leaving for America. The party lasted until 11 p.m., after which Napoleon told Marchand to have the carriages ready to leave at four in the morning.[5] The evening had been fun, nostalgic even, but time was being wasted.

At 4 a.m. on 3 July, Napoleon said goodbye to the prefect and left Niort, escorted by a platoon of the 2nd Hussars. He left the city as though a reigning monarch, given all honors and salutes, cheered by throngs of supporters. A few miles later, he bid the Hussars farewell, giving each man a gold napoleon.

Rochefort

By afternoon, Napoleon arrived in Rochefort and immediately took up quarters in the Maritime Prefecture's headquarters, where Baron Casimer de Bonnefoux received him as Emperor. Bonnefoux had not been loyal to the Empire, having quickly declared for the Bourbons in 1814 and again in 1815, and he was well aware that

Louis XVIII would soon be back on the throne. Still, this was Napoleon, and both the military and the populace in the area were quite loyal to him. Prudence dictated that he receive Napoleon with all courtesy and hope that he would soon be gone. He showed Napoleon to his quarters, still decorated in the Empire style. Napoleon had stayed there in 1808 on his return from Spain. It no doubt brought back many memories of happier days; even Spain seemed a success then. But Bonnefoux was playing a double game, telling Napoleon that all was ready to set sail but that the winds were unfavorable and the British ships made any immediate departure impossible. That was not true, but at this time Napoleon had no way of knowing any better.

That night and early the next day, all the carriages arrived, and the day after, Joseph again joined his brother. The final dance was about to begin.

Napoleon felt fairly secure in Rochefort, at least for the moment. The Emperor was quite popular in that city, as during his reign he had done much to promote its wellbeing. Marshes had been drained, roads and buildings built: the local economy had prospered during Napoleon's rule and the people remembered it well. Word of Napoleon's arrival soon spread. There was no need for or possibility of secrecy now, and the people thronged to pay him homage. Large crowds gathered below his window and he would routinely feel obligated to show himself and wave at the friendly people. Cries of 'Vive l'Empereur!' were heard regularly.

At the Elysée Napoleon had shrunk from such demonstrations, knowing that they served to remind Fouché and the royalists of the danger of having him so close at hand. Here in Rochefort, though, he was far from the politics of Paris and surrounded by admirers. Napoleon virtually held court in his new quarters, with only Bertrand, Savary and Gourgaud given ready access to his person. It was just like the old days.

It was perhaps a little too much like the old days. It was a fantasy that served only to delay the inevitable. Napoleon was, in fact, running out of time. There was no time to delay. More than once in his past – most memorably in Russia – delays and indecision had cost Napoleon dear. Napoleon needed to act and act quickly. To hell with the Provisional Government, passports, or anything else! Get out of the country! Savary[6] contends that Napoleon wanted to leave right away, yet Marchand tells us, 'The Emperor was calm and appeared indifferent to what was going on.'[7]

The situation was not something about which one should have been calm. Not only were the British ships lurking and the King returning, but also the very fact that the Provisional Government had sent him to Rochefort should have sent warning signals to Napoleon. France had plenty of other ports, several of which were probably easier to leave from undetected. Why Rochefort, run by a local official who had shown loyalty to the Bourbons and near which there were British ships on the lookout? Napoleon should have suspected the worst and made a run for it. Forget the passports: arrive in America, with her pro-French and anti-British feelings, and ask for *her* mercy. That would seem to have been far more likely to be forthcoming.

To be fair, it is likely that it would take at least some time for everything to be loaded onto the two ships at their disposal. But Napoleon would take far more time than necessary. In Niort he had received a letter from Bonnefoux alerting him that there were British ships guarding the coastline. At this point their numbers were limited, but more were most certainly on the way, as by now the British must have an idea of Napoleon's presence in Rochefort.

Why Napoleon stayed so long will be forever a mystery. Napoleon must have understood the situation and the need for speedy action. The idea that they needed time for luggage to arrive was mentioned, no doubt to the exasperation of one and all. Montholon, along with all the others who eventually ended up in St Helena or worse, was amazed at how long they stayed in Rochefort:

> The reasons of our sojourn at Rochefort till the evening of the 8th of July, when we embarked to go on board the *Saale*, are a mystery which I have never been able to fathom, for I can never bring myself to believe that we remained five days at Rochefort to wait for some boxes, directed by mistake to La Rochelle.[8]

Of course, one reason Napoleon delayed was that he was still anticipating the arrival of passports. He may well have felt no great need to hurry until they arrived. Another reason was that he felt secure in Rochefort. There were large numbers of soldiers stationed in the area, virtually all of whom were loyal to their Emperor. In this security, he could easily wait for the passports. As Savary, who was a general, describes the situation:

> A regiment of marine artillery was quartered at Rochefort; a regiment of sailors was encamped at the Île d'Aix, in Rochefort road; fifteen hundred national guards were at La Rochelle; Niort was occupied by a corps of cavalry; and there were about three thousand men of the gendarmerie, horse and foot soldiers, in the vicinity of that town. The greater part of their officers and subalterns had served under my orders, and had received their appointments from me. General Clausel was at Bordeaux with some regiments of infantry under his command. All of these troops transmitted to the Emperor the expression of their regret and devoted attachment. Personal services were tendered to him: offers were made to follow his fate.[9]

Napoleon was certainly grateful for these expressions, but graciously declined them. He had no interest in starting a civil war – now he would run the risk of having to fight French armies loyal to either the Provisional Government or the King – and in any event it was clearly too late for him to attempt to influence events in Paris. And as to offers to join him in his fate, Napoleon realized that his entourage was already quite large and he was not interested in making it any larger.

Options

Napoleon had a number of options to consider, all of which would have a greater likelihood of success if taken sooner rather than later. He met with all those who might be of help in reaching a decision: Savary and Bertrand, whom he trusted completely, Beker, whose support he might well need, and Bonnefoux, Vice-Admiral

Count Pierre Martin and other local officers, who knew the situation and the capabilities of available ships better than anyone.

The most obvious course of action was to board a ship and leave immediately. The *Saale* and the *Méduse* were standing in waiting. They had been equipped for a long journey and were prepared to make a run for it just as soon as Napoleon gave the word. At this stage, the British blockade, such as it was, consisted of the brig *Myrmidon* and the 74-gun frigate *Bellerophon*, commanded by Captain Frederick Maitland. The *Bellerophon* had a distinguished history but was, in fact, an older frigate that was not especially fast. The French ships, most especially the *Saale*, were much newer and faster. While outgunned, they would have an excellent chance of making good a successful escape – *if* no further British ships arrived on the scene. There were several passages to the open sea that could be taken, and the current contingent of British ships could not hope to control them all.

On the other hand, there was certainly danger in making a run for it. If there was a confrontation between the *Bellerophon* and either of the French ships, blood would certainly be spilt and one or both ships could possibly be sunk. This possibility would not necessarily prevent the Emperor from making good his escape, but it would mean that at least some of Napoleon's entourage would not make it out of France alive. Could Napoleon expect that sacrifice of his supporters, and, especially, their families? Almost to a man, Napoleon's staff urged him to go, but Napoleon wanted no more bloodshed on his behalf. Or, at least, that is what appears to be a major factor in his indecision. Marchand says as much:

> Much time had been wasted in Rochefort, and the delay can only be blamed on the uncertainty of the orders issued by the Provisional Government, the passports that were expected, the unfavorable winds, and the blockage of the exit by British vessels.
>
> Had he been alone, the Emperor would not have hesitated on the choice to be made; as early as Niort he had said: 'As soon as Marchand arrives, I will go to Rochefort and board the first ship I find there sailing for America, where people can come and join me.' Steered away from this solution, he came to have with him women and children, hence his hesitation.[10]

A seemingly obvious solution to that problem would be to leave all families and non-military supporters at Rochefort, with the hope that they could eventually make their way to the United States. This would require families to separate, with the men marching into the face of possible disaster, but that was hardly unusual for military men and their families.

While Napoleon was in Rochefort, the Danish sloop *Magdaline* made an appearance. She was commanded by Captain Besson, who was, as it happens, French. The good captain was anxious to take Napoleon to freedom, his son-in-law and another man were naval officers who would readily serve on the crew, and it seemed a very real possibility. The ship was fast, and the British would naturally enough be concentrating on keeping an eye on the French ships. Indeed, three ships could leave at the same time via three different routes. If the sloop were intercepted and boarded by the British (there was no possibility of offering combat), Napoleon could hide in a cask stowed with many similar such containers. He could breathe through tubes; water could be available in flasks kept with him. Only a prolonged delay by the British would lead to his likely discovery, and this delay seemed unlikely. Las Cases was put in charge and an actual contract drawn up. But Napoleon's pride and sense of dignity evidently prevailed, and he declined the opportunity. He wished to sail as a retiring monarch, not a fugitive. This is perhaps understandable – Napoleon was an emperor, after all – but his decision removed one of his possible choices from serious consideration and pushed him ever closer to his ultimate destiny.

The captain's son-in-law and his comrade also volunteered to take Napoleon to the United States in two smaller ships that were really designed for fishing. Las Cases tells the story and explains why it was doomed to failure:

> During the interval, everything on our part which the imagination can suggest was exhausted, for the purpose of discovering means of escaping from this port and gaining the open sea. Even the desperate idea was suggested of crossing the ocean in two light and frail fishing barks. Young pupils of the marine, animated by the most fiery courage and an enthusiasm which sets all obstacles at defiance, had come to offer their services on such a hazardous design, and to man the boats. The Emperor adopted the plan, but in the moment of departure we found ourselves compelled to abandon it. For among other difficulties, the seamen informed us that it would be absolutely necessary to land on the coasts of Spain and Portugal to take in fresh water.[11]

Another option was to take the corvette *La Bayadère*, which was anchored at the mouth of the River Gironde. General Lallemand was sent to investigate that possibility and reported that Captain Baudin of that ship would be delighted to accommodate the Emperor. General Lallemand's description of this entire period, including Napoleon's time with the British before leaving for St Helena, is quite instructive and can be found in Appendix X. Like others in Napoleon's entourage, Lallemand was distraught over Napoleon's lack of action to protect his future.

Other vessels were also available, including the American ship, the *Pike*. A flotilla could be formed and they could all leave at once, obviating any possibility of an effective British blockade. Napoleon seemed interested in this possibility, but nothing ever came of it. Instead, he preferred to wait.

Chapter 13

Inching Towards Departure

A Waiting Game

While in Rochefort, Napoleon and his entourage made plans to leave, but were slow to take decisive action. Savary cashed in drafts for 100,000 francs, and Napoleon fretted over the fact that the Provisional Government had not approved sending him the furniture and books he had requested. He organized his household, assigning various tasks to those loyal supporters who were still with him. It was almost as if he had planned to stay there forever. That, of course, was completely out of the question.

On 5 July, Napoleon's brother Joseph arrived in Rochefort. Joseph had already made arrangements for his departure, having maintained a small entourage of three people (a Spanish doctor, a valet and an American interpreter) and having put his valuables into safety. He was planning to go to America and urged Napoleon to do likewise, rather than to allow himself to be turned over to the British. Joseph recognized the danger of further delay in Napoleon's departure and urged him to leave at the soonest possible moment, preferably now. Napoleon, said Joseph, should take only Bertrand along with him, as the others could easily join him later. The two brothers and their small group could leave together. The ships were being loaded and this could have been done. Indeed, Joseph would eventually leave on the 25th from Royan and arrived in America with no difficulty. Of course, he had passports with false names, but one suspects that Napoleon could have had something of the sort forged if need be.

Joseph also suggested that the two could exchange identities and Napoleon could leave while Joseph remained behind and pretended to be Napoleon. This could throw the British off and might have worked. Things were quickly coming to a head, but Napoleon could not bring himself to move. Many days were completely wasted, with Napoleon considering first one option, then another, all the while playing at his pretend Imperial Court as though nothing were amiss.

Things had been moving quickly in Paris. The armistice had not been well received by all of the people of Paris, many of whom no doubt still longed for their Emperor to lead the French army against the invaders. On 5 July the Commission of Government published a declaration to the French people, calling for unity and explaining that they had done all they could to defend the interests of the people and of the nation. Whether or not anyone was buying it is a matter of conjecture. But the fact that the Committee even produced it speaks of the disintegration of French control over the country's own destiny. Having rejected Napoleon as Emperor and as general, they were now about to see the results of Fouché's double dealing. (See

Appendix IX.)

On 6 July the Commission of Government, clearly worried about Napoleon's status, sent him the following resolution:

Decree of the Commission of Government

Extract from the dispatch of the Ministers of the Department of the Secretary of State

Paris, 6th of July 1815

Considering the urgent nature of existing circumstances, and that it is of the utmost importance that Napoleon Bonaparte should immediately quit the French territory, with reference to his personal safety no less than to the interest of the state, the Commission of Government decrees as follows:

Article I. The Minister of Marine will renew the orders he has already given for the embarkation and immediate departure of Napoleon with two frigates destined to that mission.

Article II. If, in consequence of contrary winds, the presence of the enemy, or any other cause, the immediate departure should be prevented, and there should be a probability of succeeding in effecting Napoleon's removal by a small vessel, the Minister of Marine will give orders for immediately placing one at his disposal, on condition that said vessel should sail within twenty-four hours at latest.

Article III. If, however, owing to the inconveniences which might be felt on board a small vessel in unfavorable weather, Napoleon should prefer being conveyed immediately either on board an English cruiser, or to England, the maritime prefect of the fifth district will afford him the means of doing so, on his written application; and in that case a flag of truce will be forthwith placed at his disposal.

Article IV. In any case, the commander of the vessel destined to convey Napoleon is forbidden, on pain of treason, to land him on any point of the French territory.

Article V. Should the commander of the vessel be compelled to return to the coast of France, he will adopt every precautionary means requisite for preventing Napoleon from landing. In case of need, he will apply to the civil and military authorities for assistance.

Article VI. General Beker, who has been made responsible for the custody and personal safety of Napoleon, is not to quit him until he has sailed beyond the Pertuis; and if Napoleon has demanded to be taken on board of the English cruiser, or to be conveyed to England, he is not to quit him until he shall have lodged him on board the said cruiser, or landed him in England.

Article VII. As long as General Beker shall be on board the vessel destined to receive Napoleon, the commander of the said vessel shall be under his orders, and attend to all the requisitions the said general may make to him with reference to the object of his mission, and the spirit of this decree.

Article VIII. The Minister of Marine is charged with the execution of the present decree, and with its transmission to General Beker, who is to conform, in what concerns him, to the clauses which it contains.

The Duke of Otranto, president
Count Grenier
Caulaincourt, Duke of Vicence
Carnot
(For the secretary attached to the Minister Secretary of State),
Quinette[1]

This can be seen in more than one way. On the one hand, clearly Louis XVIII will be along just any day now, and when that happens there will be no further possibility of Napoleon receiving assistance from the French government, and any military individual or unit that assists him will be guilty of treason. For now, at least, the Commission of Government was the legitimate French government.

On the other hand, this could be Fouché's way of forcing Napoleon to take actions that would be likely to put him into the hands of the British. Documents quoted above seem to indicate that this was the desired outcome of all that had occurred. Further, the Commission of Government sent orders to take Napoleon away from France, but *still* neglected to send the needed passports to allow him to leave legally.

Tentative Moves

On 4 July Beker had written the following letter to the Provisional Government:

Rochefort, July 4, 1815

I have the honor to inform the Commission of Government that the Emperor arrived here yesterday morning at eight o'clock, having received from all the inhabitants of the districts through which we passed the strongest testimony of their respect, of their regret, and enthusiastic attachment to his person.

Immediately after our arrival at Rochefort, the superior officers of the navy declared it to be impossible to sail from the roads (sea passages) of Aix, as long as the English kept such a large number of cruisers on the station in sight of our ships.

In consequence of this opinion of a council of war, preparations are being made to get ready a corvette lying in the Gironde and to arm a brig, in order to take advantage of either of these opportunities, should the cruisers remain off the Pertuis, and leave the mouth of the Gironde open, so as to favor the escape of the corvette.

As the success of this maneuver is all but certain, he is anxious to obtain passports, which the English, interested in the departure of Napoleon, can no longer refuse. Prince Joseph having come incognito to Niort to take leave of his brother, set out again for Saintes, from whence he proposes to retire in a country-seat in the interior of France, to await the determination of the fate of his family. The prince has been compromised by one of the *garde du corps* who raised a mob against him and some persons in the suite of the Emperor on their way to Saintes, in order to go to Rochefort. The movement was suppressed by the National Guard, who caused both the persons and carriages to be set at liberty.

The Emperor is in perfect safety at Rochefort; he does not show himself, although the inhabitants exhibit a great desire to see him, in order to express their gratitude for all the benefits which he has conferred on this country.

We are in expectation that M. Otto will obtain the passports, and whilst waiting for his arrival, the best means are adopted to take advantage of any changes favorable to the Emperor.

[Signed] Count Beker, Lieutenant General[2]

Note the inconsistencies in the letter. On the one hand, plans to sneak out of France are moving ahead. On the other, Napoleon expects the requested French passports to arrive any day, just as soon as the British relent and allow the French government to issue them. All the while, General Beker received multiple dispatches from Paris to get Napoleon on the move. The Provisional Government was nearing its end, and Napoleon definitely should not be in France when Louis XVIII took charge again. Meanwhile, the British net was strengthened by the arrival on 7 July of HMS *Slaney*. Now Napoleon's options were yet again narrowed.

The problem mentioned with Joseph was another indication of Napoleon's narrowing options. It seems that Joseph had actually been mistaken for the Emperor and that a royalist had attempted to capture him. Already some elements of society were being emboldened to take actions against their former emperor.

On 8 July Napoleon asked Beker for his advice and received this reply:

'Sire,' answered General Beker, 'I am not in a position to give an opinion or advice to Your Majesty, and for this reason I abstain. In a case so important, in which there are chances to run, I might, perhaps, have reason at some future time to reproach myself with the consequences of my advice in the resolution adopted, should that resolution, instead of conducting you to America, cause you to fall into the power of the English. The only advice which I dare venture to give Your Majesty is that of adopting a prompt determination and of carrying into effect, as speedily as possible, the plan which you may adopt.

'The fate of France is unhappily determined; Your Majesty may wait until agents are sent in your pursuit; from that moment the scene changes, Sire; the powers which I now hold from the Provisional Government cease, and Your Majesty will be exposed to new dangers, of which it is difficult to foresee the result.'

In pronouncing these words, the General was so affected that his words produced a strong sympathetic emotion on the Emperor in his turn.

'But General,' said he; 'should these events occur, you are incapable of giving me up?'

'Your Majesty,' answered General Beker, 'knows that I am ready to lay down my life for you; in such a case, however, my life would not save you. The same people who crowd under your windows every evening and oblige you to show yourself would, perhaps, prefer cries of another kind if the scene were changed. Then, Sire, I repeat it: Your Majesty, already threatened, would be completely compromised – the commanders of the frigates, receiving orders from the ministers of Louis XVIII would disregard mine, and that would render your safety impossible. Reflect upon the urgency of the circumstances, Sire, I beseech you.'

'Well!' said the Emperor, 'since it is so, give the necessary orders for proceeding to the Île d'Aix.'[3]

No doubt in great relief, Beker immediately wrote to the Provisional Government that Napoleon was heading to the Île d'Aix to be in a better position to take advantage of any opportunity to depart at a moment's notice.

Beker's refusal to give any specific advice on what Napoleon should do probably signaled that he did not feel free to advise as to Napoleon's best interests, perhaps because of his loyalty to the government. Napoleon did ask whether or not the general would turn him over to Louis XVIII, but apart from that bottom line he may not have considered the implications of the general's refusal to give advice. That refusal, especially when accompanied by a warning about falling into the hands of the British, should have raised numerous alarm signals to Napoleon. Apparently they did not, except as to the danger of delaying until Louis XVIII might capture him on French soil.

Departure from Rochefort

On the afternoon of 8 July Napoleon said farewell to his supporters in Rochefort. He thanked Bonnefoux for his hospitality and offered him the imperial carriage, which could not be taken to the ship. Perhaps fearful of mob action should he be seen in such a carriage, Bonnefoux declined the honor. Napoleon then offered him a gold snuffbox with an 'N' made of diamonds. This token Bonnefoux accepted, but only after being assured that it was empty. What difference that would have made is anyone's guess.

That absurd farewell dispensed with, Napoleon took a carriage to Fouras, where he boarded a longboat from the *Saale* that was to take him to the Île d'Aix. It was low tide, so Napoleon left the mainland on the back of a sailor named Beau. A small monument with a commemorative plaque was erected on the spot by Baron Gourgaud, and was still there in 2005. Napoleon was joined by Beker, Bertrand and Gourgaud. Other boats eventually picked up the remaining members of his group.

The 8th was an important date for more than this move. On that day the Provisional Government breathed its last breath as the Prussians entered the courtyard of the Tuileries Palace. Napoleon was out of options: it was time to act. Instead of heading to the island, however, Napoleon had the boat take him to the *Saale* itself, where he arrived at 8 p.m. If the winds were favorable, perhaps they could leave now. Napoleon boarded the ship with all honors. He inspected the ship, asked questions, and then dined. Captain Pierre-Henri Philibert was gracious, declining only to fire the normal cannon salutes, which would, of course, have told the nearby British ships what was happening. The ship was ready to depart whenever Napoleon was ready, but the captain's enthusiasm was perhaps less than might be hoped. As Ali noted in his memoirs:

> The Emperor was very uncomfortable on board the frigate. The officers did not appear favorable to his cause; the captain was far from being satisfied at seeing on his ship the great misfortune which had come to take refuge there. Knowing the events which had just happened, and foreseeing all the results which might flow from them, he thought it well to walk warily. Consequently I think that when the emperor decided to live on the Île d'Aix, Captain Philibert must have exclaimed, 'Ah! Now I can draw a long breath!' Moreover, the ship was extremely badly kept; it showed its commander's negligence.[4]

The next morning, the 9th, Napoleon awoke to discover that the hoped for shift in the winds had not occurred, and that there was no possibility of sailing for America. He could see two British ships blocking the channel. With little else to do, after breakfast Napoleon and some of his staff took longboats to the Île d'Aix, where he spent part of the day inspecting the fortifications and receiving the accolades of the local populace. He reviewed the drill of a rather surprised detachment of Marines who had turned out for their Sunday parade. He then inspected the fort, which he had personally ordered constructed, and noted that the British ships were, unsurprisingly, out of cannon range. For Napoleon, it would be the last time that he would truly be treated as Emperor.

Having completed all that he could do on the island, Napoleon returned to his ship. It had been an enjoyable day, perhaps, but nothing further had been accomplished towards obtaining his departure. Indeed, things were turning sour. Admiral Bonnefoux was waiting for Napoleon on the *Saale* and presented Napoleon with a letter from Minister of Marine Denis Decrès, his last before being replaced by the new, royal, government:

To the Maritime Prefect
Paris, July 6th, 1815
Sir:

It is of the utmost importance that the Emperor should leave the soil of France as quickly as possible. The interest of the state and the safety of his person imperatively require it.

Should circumstances not permit his departure in one of the frigates, it will, perhaps, be possible for a pilot boat to deceive the English cruisers, and in case this method be deemed suitable, it is not necessary to hesitate in putting one at his disposal, in order that he may set out in twenty-four hours.

Should this plan be unacceptable, and should he prefer going on board one of the ships of the English squadron, or directly to England, he is requested to address to us a formal and positive demand in writing, and in that case you will immediately put a flag of truce at his disposal, in order that he may adopt either of these alternatives.

It is indispensable that he should not disembark on French territory, and you cannot be too precise in your instructions on this point to the commander of the vessel on board of which he may now be, or on which he may embark.

I forward you a decree on this subject, which has just been passed by the government, and send a copy of the same to General Beker. The terms are such that I have nothing to add, beyond what I have already said to you, to remove all difficulties in the way of his departure, as far as is in your power. I cannot too strongly repeat, his departure is a matter of the greatest urgency. He must not, however, be allowed to depart in a pilot boat for the United States, or in a flag of truce for the English squadron or for England itself, until he shall have made a formal and positive request in writing to that effect. This restriction, with which he will be made acquainted by General Beker, will make him feel that one of the great reasons for the urgency of his departure is founded upon the interest taken respecting his personal safety.

Should a flag of truce be sent, you will draw up the sailing orders according to the usual form.

I subjoin an extract from the decree of the government, which you will append to the instructions of the commander of the flag of truce, in order to regulate his conduct. You will, in like manner, give this extract to the commander of the boat for the United States, should the Emperor select that alternative.

You will be careful to appoint as commander of the vessel a good officer who understands how to combine the greatest firmness of purpose with the observance of the respect necessary in such a delicate affair.

Accept Sir, the assurance, etc.

The Duke Decrès

PS: It is well understood that if the departure of the two frigates be possible, no changes have been made in the orders given for conveying him to the United States in that manner.[5]

This letter certainly makes it clear that Napoleon needed to leave, and appears to authorize him to leave just about any way he can, including surrendering to the British. The request that he make a formal and positive request for such actions would seem to be simply an effort to give the government cover, as they must have realized that there was no way for communications to go back and forth between the *Saale* and Paris in a timely fashion. It was becoming clear to all that the British option was probably the only option really left to Napoleon, but just how that would play out was anyone's guess.

Of greater significance is what is not mentioned. Note that once again we have a letter from Paris that makes no mention of the requested passports. In this case, however, the omission is of greater significance. As of 30 June, the British had formally denied the request for passports and Fouché must certainly have known this by the time this letter was sent.

Preliminary Overtures to the British

Napoleon spent the day of the 10th on board the *Saale*. There was little to do and what there was did not tend to lift spirits. Reports came in that the British blockade had tightened and that departure from this area was not possible. Napoleon could still try to sneak off to the ships in the river or perhaps elsewhere, but that was more and more problematic and, besides, his dignity would not allow that to happen. The Bertrands had several times promoted the idea of going to England, and Napoleon seemed more and more resigned to that possibility. He decided to send Savary and Las Cases to the *Bellerophon* to sound out its captain as to the status of any passports as well as to see if he would consider allowing either French or neutral ships with the Emperor on board to pass unmolested in their journey to the United States. Las Cases spoke good English, but agreed to keep this to himself, so that he might possibly hear important side comments made by the captain to his staff.

At 7 a.m. on the 10th the two men boarded the *Bellerophon* and met with Captain Frederick Maitland, a 38-year-old Scotsman who commanded the ship. Maitland didn't know it yet, but he was about to go down in history in a way that he could not possibly have imagined.

Las Cases had a letter from Bertrand, which had actually been dictated by Napoleon, for the captain:

Rochefort, 9 July 1815

Monsieur l'Admiral:

The Emperor Napoleon, having abdicated from power and chosen the USA for a refuge, has embarked in the two frigates which are in the roads for the purpose of reaching his destination. He is awaiting the passport from the British Government of which he has been informed [*qu'on lui a annoncé*], which compels me to send you the present flag of truce to ask if you have any knowledge of the said passport, or if you think it may be the intention of the British Government to impede our passage to the USA. I should be extremely obliged if you would give me any news you may have. I have asked the bearer of this letter to tender you my thanks and my apologies for any trouble it may give you.

I have &c.

Le Grand Maréchal
Comte Bertrand[6]

Of course, Napoleon had not been informed that he would receive passports, but rather than an effort at deceit the comment was probably a reflection of the continuing

This period engraving shows Napoleon as he looked in exile on Elba, and is dedicated to Count Bertrand.

This gilt snuffbox, dated 20 March 1815, shows Napoleon, Marie Louise and their son the King of Rome. Of course, the Allies never allowed this reunification to take place.

This early nineteenth-century engraving shows Napoleon's triumphal return to the Tuileries Palace.

Nineteenth-century engraving of Marshal Emmanuel Grouchy, who is often blamed for Napoleon's loss of the Battle of Waterloo.

Marshal Ney, shown here in a rare nineteenth-century engraving by Martinet, was both dashing and foolish; this latter quality led to his execution.

This nineteenth-century engraving is after the painting by Steuben, and shows Napoleon as he leaves the field of Waterloo.

This mid-nineteenth-century porcelain statue shows the Marquis de La Fayette, who was manipulated into calling for Napoleon's abdication.

Marshal Joachim Murat was one of Napoleon's greatest soldiers, but his brashness may have doomed Napoleon's quest for peace.

King Louis XVIII, shown in this period engraving, was twice given power by the Allied forces.

LAFAYETTE

ancis II, seen here in an 1815 engraving, was apoleon's father-in-law, but that didn't mean much hen all of Europe declared war on Napoleon.

Nineteenth-century engraving of Field Marshal Blücher.

A period snuffbox showing the Duke of Wellington.

Joseph Fouché, seen here in
nineteenth-century engraving, serve
Napoleon well but himself better. *
the end, he betrayed the man who ha
given him everything he ha

Nineteenth-century
engraving of Marshal Louis
Nicolas Davout, one of
Napoleon's best marshals.

Nineteenth-century engraving of Charles Maurice
de Talleyrand-Périgord, who represented France at
the Congress of Vienna and helped rally the Allies
against Napoleon.

This period painting on ivory shows
Count Molé, whose memoirs are key to
understanding this period.

lle George was a beautiful and gifted ctress, whose charms Napoleon enjoyed uring the Hundred Days. This is a eriod painting on ivory.

Top Right: *Nineteenth-century engraving of Armand-Augustin-Louis Caulaincourt, Duke of Vicence.*

Centre: *A period miniature on ivory of General Henri Gratien Bertrand, one of Napoleon's most loyal companions.*

Bottom left: *Nineteenth-century engraving of Napoleon's stepdaughter, Queen Hortense, who offered Napoleon hospitality – and diamonds.*

Napoleon's home on the Île d'Aix (photo by the author).

The commemorative plaque on the monument where Napoleon left mainland France for the final time (photo by the author).

Napoleon's brother Joseph, seen here in a rare period engraving, was not always competent but he was loyal to the end.

This period engraving (detail) shows Baron General Charles Lallemand, who was denied permission to accompany Napoleon into exile and eventually tried to establish colonies of French veterans in Texas.

Count Emmanuel Las Cases, seen here in an 1824 engraving, accompanied Napoleon into exile and made his name by writing memoirs of his experiences on St Helena.

Count Charles Montholon who followed Napoleon to St Helena.

This 1825 engraving shows Napoleon leaving French soil for the last time.

Above: *Captain Frederick Maitland received Napoleon aboard his ship and gave the Emperor his last decent treatment by the British. Nineteenth-century engraving.*

Left: *This large period engraving shows Napoleon returning as Caesar, accompanied by Winged Victory and happy cherubs. Victory, however, eluded the Emperor on the field of Waterloo – and in Paris.*

delusion that pervaded Napoleon's thoughts on the matter. Maitland professed to know nothing about passports. This was a blatant lie, of course, as he knew full well that no passports were forthcoming. Indeed, he had been given orders to get Napoleon on his ship if at all possible and then to take him to Admiral Sir Henry Hotham. On 1 July the Secretary of the Admiralty had written to Admiral Lord Keith:

My Lord … a proposition reached HM Government last night from the present rulers of France demanding a passport and safe conduct for Bonaparte and his family to proceed to America. To this proposition HM Government have returned a negative answer; and it now seems more probable than ever that Bonaparte will endeavour to effect his escape, either to England, or what is much more likely to America.

Your Lordship will therefore repeat to all your cruisers the orders already given with further directions to them to make the strictest search of any vessel they may fall in with; and if they should be so fortunate as to intercept Bonaparte, the captain of HM ship should transfer him and his family to HM ship and there keeping him in careful custody should return to the nearest port of England with all possible expedition. He should not permit any communication whatsoever with the shore, and he will be held responsible for keeping the whole transaction a profound secret until their Lordships' further orders shall be received …[7]

A copy of these instructions arrived while Savary and Las Cases were still on board, thus putting even more pressure on Maitland. They had been brought by Captain Knight, commander of HMS *Falmouth*, which had just arrived on the scene. Captain Knight also brought word that no further ships of any significance would be forthcoming anytime soon.

Maitland, of course, said nothing of any of this to his guests. He felt that deception was necessary if he were to carry out his instructions and prevent Napoleon from escaping. Even so, the meeting was a friendly one. Maitland was courteous to his French guests, insisting that they have breakfast at his table. Savary and Las Cases told Maitland of Waterloo and of Napoleon's desire to retire to America and refrain from any further political involvement. They pointed out that Napoleon had many supporters in France and could have still been a major political and military factor, but that instead Napoleon preferred to retire quietly. Maitland reflected his government's skepticism when he questioned whether anyone could really believe that Napoleon would voluntarily retire from politics. To this, Savary responded:

When the Emperor first abdicated the throne of France, his removal was brought about by a faction, at the head of which was Talleyrand, and the sense of the nation was not consulted. But in the present instance he has voluntarily resigned the power. The influence he once had over the French people is past. A very considerable change has taken place in their sentiments towards him, since he went to Elba, and he could never regain the power he had over their minds; therefore, he would prefer retiring into obscurity, where he might end his days in peace and tranquility, and were he solicited to ascend the throne again, he would decline it.[8]

They discussed the various possibilities for Napoleon to leave, with Maitland making it clear that, as there was still a state of war between the two nations, any French ship would be fired upon and any neutral ship would be searched. Lieutenant John Bowerbank was present during some of the meeting between Maitland and the French and suggests that a request for passage 'was peremptorily refused by Captain Maitland, notwithstanding a *friendly hint* that such refusal would probably induce them *to force a passage!*'[9] Friendly hint or not, that option was clearly still a possibility, which was why Maitland was happy to stall for time as best he could. But it was Maitland, not the French, who was operating from strength. While Savary and Las Cases tried to put up a good front, anyone could see that Napoleon was becoming desperate. If not, why hadn't he simply availed himself of whatever opportunities he felt he had to leave?

Maitland also, it seems, tried to steer Savary and Las Cases towards the possibility of Napoleon's settling in England, where he claimed the climate was better than Napoleon might have imagined. He also tried to encourage the idea that he would be well treated in England. Napoleon's emissaries were not able to talk much about that possibility, but certainly reported Maitland's comments to Napoleon when they returned. Several in Napoleon's entourage had suggested the possibility, most notably Madame Bertrand, and Napoleon had acknowledged it as an option. But now it was a British officer who was making the suggestion, which would seem to suggest that Napoleon and his followers might be treated well were he to take that option. All in all, though, it was not a very hopeful meeting, as it served to reinforce the hopelessness of their situation.

Maitland, meanwhile, stalled for time. He told Las Cases and Savary that any final decision on whether Napoleon would be allowed to leave was really up to his superiors, namely Admiral Hotham, and that he would send an immediate request for clarification, an answer to which could be expected in two days. In the meanwhile, Napoleon would be welcome to come on board the *Bellerophon* whenever he might wish. As Maitland recalled in his memoirs:

> The bearers of the letter [Savary and Las Cases, with the letter from Bertrand] had instructions to demand of me whether I would prevent Buonaparte from proceeding in a neutral vessel, provided I could not permit the frigates to pass with him on board. Having received in my orders the strictest injunctions to secrecy, and feeling that the force on the coast at my disposal was insufficient to guard the different ports and passages from which an escape might be effected, particularly should the plan be adopted of putting to sea in a small vessel, I wrote the following reply to the above communication; hoping, by that means, to induce Napoleon to remain for the Admiral's answer, which would give time for the arrival of reinforcements.[10]

The letter from Maitland to Bertrand read as follows:

Maitland to Count Bertrand
  HMS *Bellerophon*, off Rochefort
  10 July 1815
  Sir, I have the honour to acknowledge your letter of yesterday's date addressed to the Admiral commanding the English cruisers before Rochefort, acquainting me that the Emperor Napoleon, having abdicated the throne of France, and chosen the USA as an asylum, is now embarked on board the frigates at Rochefort to proceed for that destination, now awaits a passport from the English Government, requesting to know if I have any knowledge of such a passport, and if I think it is the intention of the English Government to prevent the Emperor's voyage.

  In reply, I have the honour to acquaint you I cannot say what the intentions of my Government may be; but the two countries at present being in a state of war, I cannot allow any ships of war to put to sea from the port of Rochefort.

  As to the proposal made by the Duc de Rovigo and the Count de Las Cases of allowing the Emperor to proceed in a merchant vessel, it is out of my power, without the sanction of my commanding officer (Sir Henry Hotham, who is at present in Quiberon Bay and to whom I have forwarded your dispatch), to allow any vessel, under whatever flag she may be, to pass with a personage of such consequence.

  I have the honour to be,
  Sir,
  Your very humble servant

F. L. Maitland
Captain of HMS *Bellerophon*[11]

Chapter 14

The Last Dance

A Last Effort for Freedom

Back on the *Saale*, Napoleon could hardly have been encouraged by the results of Savary and Las Cases' visit to Maitland. Anyone could see that Maitland was stalling for time and now knew with virtual certainty that he had Napoleon pinned down on and around the Île d'Aix. It must have been completely clear to them by now that there would be no passports (Maitland cleverly didn't lie about his knowledge of their denial but simply didn't mention them at all), and that there would be no dignified trip to America with the blessings of the French and Allied governments. If Napoleon were to avoid the necessity of surrendering to the British, he would have to make a run for it.

There was still the possibility of a successful escape, however. Captain Ponée of the *Méduse* was prepared to join with the brig *L'Épervier* and attack the *Bellerophon*. While this would do great damage to the two ships, they might well overwhelm the British ship and allow the *Saale* to make good her escape. The idea took hold and Napoleon ordered preparations to be made during the afternoon and evening of the 10th. There was no doubt excitement in the air: finally, Napoleon was going to act to secure his freedom.

It was not to be. Savary, who actually says that Napoleon made the decision late in the evening and sent him to Captain Philibert with orders to leave immediately, ran up against an insurmountable obstacle:

> I was aware of the precise tendency of the instructions which he [Philibert] had received from the minister. I went in full confidence to give him the order to set sail; but great was my surprise when Captain Philibert informed me that he had secret orders; 'he was strictly forbidden to carry his mission into effect, if the vessels of the state ran any risk'! All this, therefore, I said to him, is mere deception: the only object intended by the commission of government was that the Emperor should be placed under the necessity of delivering himself up to the enemy. – 'I do not know,' replied the captain, 'but I have orders not to sail.'[1]

Without the cooperation of both of the French frigates, there was no hope of running the blockade. There were still other possibilities, of course, all of which had been considered before. General Lallemand had been sent to explore the possibilities still remaining at the mouth of the River Gironde. That mission was in itself dangerous, given what was going on in France, and Lallemand went disguised as a sailor. There he met with Baudin, who insisted that it was still possible for Napoleon to escape. If

Napoleon would quietly arrive, with only three men with him, it was still possible for him to make it to America.

Napoleon could still take off over land and seek a different port of departure. These possibilities were there, but they were far less viable than they had been even a few days earlier. The day went by with no further event of note, but Napoleon was increasingly aware that Captain Philibert was not to be trusted, that his loyalties lay with the government in Paris, not with his deposed Emperor. One can easily imagine how different things might have been had he boarded the *Méduse* instead of the *Saale*. The captain there was far more loyal to Napoleon and far more willing to run a risk to spring his Emperor free of the trap into which he had been driven.

On the other hand, recall the confidential orders presented by Minister of Marine Decrès (Appendix VII) that made it clear that Captain Philibert was to command whichever ship Napoleon used to make good his escape. Was that order designed to put the best captain in charge of Napoleon's fate, or to ensure that a captain more loyal to Fouché or Louis XVIII commanded Napoleon's ship? It is impossible to say, though given events of this period a healthy skepticism is probably in order.

Worse, word arrived on the 11th of Louis XVIII's triumphal entry into a now subdued Paris. The government had changed hands and at least some of Napoleon's followers – Lallemand, Savary, Gourgaud and Montholon come to mind – might well stand accused of treason. It was unclear what Louis's attitude towards Napoleon would be, but it was not likely to be favorable. Moreover, some of the Allies would still like to get their hands on Napoleon. Surrender to the British was one thing, but capture by the Prussians was quite another.

Given the potential problems to be encountered by staying on a ship captained by someone whose loyalty was clearly elsewhere, Napoleon decided to move to the Île d'Aix, which he did on 12 July. That same day, HMS *Cyrus* joined in the British blockade, and some other small ships were also now in the area. Meanwhile, spies had informed Maitland of many of the comings and goings and he had moved to tighten the noose:

> Tuesday, the 11th. – About noon, a small boat came off from the Island of Oleron, to where the ship was at anchor in Basque Roads, rowed by four men, in which sat two respectable-looking countrymen, who asked for the Captain; and upon my being pointed out to them, requested to speak with me in private. When showed into the cabin, where I went accompanied by Captain Gambier, of the *Myrmidon*, they acquainted me that a message had been sent from Isle d'Aix early in the morning for a man who was considered the best pilot on the island for the Mamusson passage, being the only person that had ever taken a frigate through; that a large sum of money had been offered to him to pilot a vessel to sea from that passage, and that it certainly was Buonaparte's intention to escape from thence; either in the corvette, which had moved down some days before, or in a Danish brig, which was then lying at anchor near the entrance.
>
> On receiving this information, I immediately got under weigh, and though the flood-tide had just made in, beat the ships out of the Pertuis d'Antioche

before it was dark, when I sent the *Myrmidon* off the Mamusson, with orders to anchor close in with the entrance, when the weather would admit of it, while I remained with the *Bellerophon* and *Slaney*, which rejoined me that evening, under weigh between the lighthouses.[2]

Napoleon took his quarters at the garrison commander's home, located towards one end of the island. It was a very pleasant two-storey home that had been built in 1808. Napoleon would be comfortable there, though it was hardly Malmaison. In 2005 it was a wonderful museum that featured the furniture Napoleon used as well as paintings, snuffboxes and other artifacts of the time. General Gourgaud had provided most of the objects found there, and it is well worth a visit by anyone interested in the history of this chapter of Napoleon's career.

Napoleon was still safe, as most of the people of the Île d'Aix hated the British, who years earlier had destroyed a French fleet with fire ships while they watched. They loved the Emperor, but he now had to begin to worry about events on the mainland. The white flag of the Bourbons could be seen hoisted in Rochefort from time to time. True, it was generally withdrawn in favor of the tricolor, but the tide was clearly turning. Napoleon's back was no longer safe. Soon, it would be treason for anyone to give him aid and comfort.

This also made it virtually impossible for Napoleon to return to the mainland and seek a different port. General Beker was in command of the military forces there and would probably have resisted any such effort. Even if Napoleon could have returned to the mainland by stealth or by seizing control of the local forces by force of his personality and popularity, he would encounter a France increasingly dominated by supporters of King Louis. It would have been almost impossible to get to another port undetected and, in any event, the British would probably have beat him there.

Capture by the Prussians and perhaps even the French would lead to his execution or, at best, imprisonment in some small cell somewhere. Capture by the British would make him a legitimate prisoner of war, at least until some treaty of peace was signed. Napoleon felt that *surrender* to the British, however, would put him in an entirely different, and more favorable, legal situation than surrender to the French.

But the decision to surrender to the British had not yet been made. His brother Joseph arrived on the Île d'Aix on the 13th and again urged Napoleon to flee to the mainland, possibly posing as Joseph, and make good his escape. Joseph had been making his arrangements and everything was ready. Napoleon declined and wished his brother well. Joseph left and the two would never see each other again.

General Lallemand returned and joined others in urging Napoleon to flee on a smaller boat that could perhaps make its way along the coast. Saint-Denis relates that Napoleon ordered the ship to be made ready, and had assembled several firearms and other materials for the journey. Captain Besson and his crew had come to get the material and stow it on board:

The persons who were to embark with His Majesty to go to America were the Duke of Rovigo, the Grand Marshal, and General Lallemand. I had been chosen to accompany the Emperor, as being the one who could best endure seasickness and fatigue. All was prepared; I was waiting, fully equipped, when I learned, about midnight, that in a family council and after mature deliberation it had been decided that the Emperor should surrender to the English.[3]

Thus, after weeks of indecision, Napoleon had made his final choice. He chose dignity and safety for himself and his companions over a greater choice of freedom in America. But Napoleon had not heeded the warnings of General Beker and others of what he might expect if he put himself in the hands of the British.

There were other, smaller, choices that Napoleon made now. Choosing the people to accompany him into what they hoped would eventually be exile in America had not been easy. Gourgaud had been especially incensed at being left out and argued a great deal with Napoleon over the matter. In the end, he was included.

Early in the morning of the 14th, Napoleon sent Count Las Cases and General Lallemand to visit Captain Maitland. They took the schooner *Mouche* under a flag of truce. As he had with Savary and Las Cases, Maitland welcomed the two men graciously. Lallemand had been a prisoner under Maitland's command in Egypt for several weeks and during that time he had also known Savary. The group sat down to breakfast and was soon joined by the quickly summoned captain of the *Slaney*.

The official purpose of the meeting was to determine whether Maitland had heard further news about the passports or of British willingness to see Napoleon retire to America. Of course, the answer to this question was already known, as Maitland had promised to send word of any response as soon as it was received. The real purpose clearly was to sound out Maitland as to Napoleon's reception should he seek asylum on the *Bellerophon*. It seems likely that all parties to the discussion fully realized what the real purpose for the meeting was. After some discussion of the possibility of going to America, with the expected negative response from Maitland, the conversation turned to the real task at hand:

> 14th. I returned to the *Bellerophon* at four in the morning, accompanied by General Lallemand, to ascertain whether any answer had been received. The Captain told us he expected it every moment; adding, that if the Emperor would embark immediately for England, he had instructions to convey him thither. He still farther declared it as his private opinion, and several captains who were present expressed themselves to the same effect, that there was not the least doubt of Napoleon's meeting with all possible respect and good treatment; that there, neither the King nor his ministers exercised the same arbitrary authority as those of the Continent: that the English people possessed a generosity of sentiment and liberality of opinion, far above sovereignty itself. I replied that I would return and communicate the Captain's offer to the Emperor, as well as the whole of his conversation. I added that I had sufficient knowledge of the Emperor Napoleon's character to induce a belief that he would not feel much hesitation in proceeding to England thus confidentially, so as to be able to continue his voyage to the United States.[4]

In Maitland's account of the meeting, he only says that Las Cases indicated he had 'little doubt that you will see the Emperor on board the *Bellerophon*'. There is no mention of that as being a first leg on a trip to America.[5] General Lallemand was especially concerned with his fate, as he would almost certainly be shot by the Bourbon government. Accordingly, he asked Maitland if he, Lallemand, was likely to be forcibly sent back to France. All three accounts of this meeting – Maitland's, Las Cases' and Lallemand's – agree that Maitland gave strong positive assurance that Lallemand should have no worries to that effect.

The meeting concluded, Las Cases and Lallemand left for the Île d'Aix, arriving there around eleven in the morning. They really had no news of great import, other than Maitland's assurance that Napoleon would be well received should he decide to go to England. This, backed up by the assurances given Lallemand, seemed to turn the tide. Savary, another man in deep trouble in France, was no doubt pleased with the assurance given Lallemand.

It was time to make a final decision. At around 2 p.m., Napoleon called a meeting of all his close advisers. Lallemand was the most outspoken, insisting that Napoleon could still take a ship from La Rochelle. He could pretend to be sick in bed, leaving Marchand to make excuses. That would work for at least twenty-four hours before Beker or someone else would demand to see the Emperor in person. Marchand writes that Las Cases, Savary and Bertrand (no doubt speaking for his wife as much as for himself) argued for going to England, while Lallemand, Montholon and Gourgaud thought Napoleon should make a run for it.[6] Montholon relates that it was only he and Gourgaud who argued against going to England:

General Gourgaud and myself alone were of a contrary and directly opposite opinion, which we endeavoured to enforce by showing that it would be a thousand times better to run all the risks enumerated in the frank and devoted reply of Captain Baudin, who said he would take upon himself the charge of conducting the Emperor to the extremity of the world. In fact, if it proved impossible to escape the English cruisers and to reach the American soil, going to England was a *pis-aller* [lesser evil], to which recourse might always be had. It was a complete illusion – we repeated it twenty times to the Emperor – a complete illusion to confound the intentions of the English ministry with the public feeling of the English nation; that sound and calm reason ought to dispel this illusion, and recall to his recollection that the policy of St. James's had always been guided by a hatred for his person; and that those ministers who had encouraged and sanctioned the incessant conspiracies of the royalists – from that of the infernal machine, and the attempt at assassination by Georges Cadoudal, down to the treasons of 1814 – could not, without being false to themselves and their convictions, receive the Emperor in England in any other way than as a trophy of Waterloo.[7]

Whether Montholon is recalling his participation in a self-serving way or not, his points about the difference between the British government and the British people, as well as the idea that they could always surrender to the British later, were well taken. But this point of view did ignore the clear dangers in making a run for it.

Napoleon considered all that was said, though it is extremely likely that his mind was already made up. In addition to making an escape, there was also still the possibility of returning to France and leading the many loyal units that were nearby. But Napoleon was having none of any of that, or of making a run for it.

'If it were a question,' said the Emperor, 'of marching to the conquest of an empire, or of saving one from ruin, I might attempt a repetition of the return from the island of Elba. But I only seek for repose, and if I should once more be the cause of a single shot being fired, malevolence would take advantage of the circumstance to asperse my character.

'I am offered a quiet retreat in England. I am not acquainted with the Prince Regent, but from all I have heard of him, I cannot avoid placing reliance on his noble character. My determination is taken. I am going to write to that prince, and tomorrow at daybreak we will repair on board the English cruiser.'

Everyone withdrew to make preparations for the departure.[8]

Napoleon had no doubt been keeping in mind the example of his brother Lucien. In 1811 Lucien had surrendered to the British and been kept in England as a prisoner. Some prisoner! He had purchased a country estate and entertained many of the country's elite nobility. On Elba Napoleon had entertained his share of visiting British nobility, and had been quite impressed. It is easy to see how Napoleon could see England as a reasonable alternative. All well and good, but the English nobles he entertained were not the British government, and Lucien was not Buonaparte the Usurper.

Storm Clouds in the East

Napoleon had plenty of reasons to get a move on. Back in Rochefort, on the 14th Bonnefoux received instructions from Count Jaucourt, Louis XVIII's Minister of Marine, to have Napoleon remain on the *Saale* and not to allow him to communicate with the British. Clearly Louis wanted Napoleon for himself, and Fouché and Talleyrand were doing their best to oblige. The Allies, looting museums, inflicting onerous billeting requirements on French citizens and making France understand as best they could just who had won at Waterloo, were anxious that Napoleon pay the price for his return. Orders were sent to prevent Napoleon's escape or surrender, calling for his arrest and rendition to Louis XVIII. Bonnefoux, who seems to have been trying to keep the Emperor from falling into the hands of the Bourbons, forestalled any action, giving Napoleon time to act. It was not easy, as there were royalist spies and supporters everywhere, but he was able to claim that bad tides and weather kept him from acting faster. That evening, he wrote to Captain Philibert:

Rochefort, 14 July 1815. 8 p.m.
    To Captain Philibert, in the roads at the Île d'Aix

Express service

Monsieur Le Commandant,

I am in tortures of anxiety. I do not know if the Emperor has gone, and I have received an order to arrest him if he is on land.

If he is on the Île d'Aix, please at once inform him, and him alone, of this cruel disposition, that he may determine immediately to depart. I am not permitted to exercise any influence upon the determination of this unfortunate Monarch, nevertheless, I now repeat with deep conviction that the best and only course that remains for him to take is to go on board the English ship. I insist the more upon this advice because one of my friends who left Paris on Tuesday evening reports to me that Lord Wellington has replied to the Commissioners charged with the arrangement of the armistice, that if Napoleon went to England he would be treated with all the regard that he has a right to expect from a great and generous nation.[9]

Early in the morning of the 15th, Philibert finally wrote to General Beker:

Saale, Aix Roads, 15th July 1815

General,

I have the honor to send to you the letter I have just received from the maritime Prefect. I beg you to communicate it immediately to the Emperor, that he may see how urgent it is that he should not lose a minute in embarking. I have given all the necessary orders for that purpose, both for the brig and for the boats which have been drawn up on the beach.

The Captain Commandant, Philibert

PS: I beg you to return to me, by the bearer, the letter of the Prefect.[10]

These orders notwithstanding, it is not entirely clear what Louis would do with Napoleon even if he caught him. The British, and perhaps all of the Allies save Prussia, understood that Napoleon still had a great following in much of the country. It is unlikely that the French people would have stood for Napoleon's execution or, perhaps, even imprisonment. The British, especially, understood this and Wellington had made it clear that he wanted no harm to come to Napoleon. A civil war led by Napoleon would have been a disaster for France; a general uprising against Louis resulting from Napoleon's execution would have been just as bad. Thus, the interests of Napoleon, the British and the Bourbons all converged into one: Napoleon should come under the control of the British.

All that notwithstanding, from Napoleon's perspective the risks were increasing by the hour. Clearly it was time to leave the country, as there were now specific orders to prevent Napoleon from escaping France. Napoleon sent Baron General Gourgaud and Las Cases to alert Maitland (who had requested the courtesy of such prior notification) that Napoleon would arrive the next day, the 15th. Gourgaud carried with him three documents of great importance. The first, of course, was the famous letter to the Prince Regent. The date of the letter is somewhat in question, shown as either the 13th or the 14th. Maitland and others sometimes use this to show that Napoleon had made up his mind a day earlier. Perhaps, but it is also likely that Napoleon had prepared a draft of the letter with the earlier date. In any event, Napoleon had clearly been moving in this direction, so this decision could not have been a surprise to anyone. Marchand and others fix the date of the letter as the 14th, and that is the date recorded in Napoleon's *Correspondance*.

Maitland read Napoleon's letter to the Prince Regent in the presence of Captains Gambier and Sartorius of the *Myrmidon* and *Slaney*, respectively. The letter was Napoleon at his finest, and all were duly impressed:

> Letter from Napoleon to the Prince Regent
> Île d'Aix, 14 July 1815
> Your Royal Highness, faced with the factions that divide my country and the enmity of the greatest powers in Europe, I have ended my political career. I come, like Themistocles, to sit by the hearth of the British people. I place myself under the protection of their laws, which I ask from Your Royal Highness, as the most powerful, the steadiest, and the most generous of my enemies.[11]

This letter has long been the subject of sometimes heated discussion. Did Napoleon feel that this appeal would send him in glory to England, or was it a desperate gamble? It is impossible to say. Perhaps Count Molé had it right when he commented, 'By the heroic tone of this letter Bonaparte concealed from himself the feebleness of this decision. It cannot be supposed that he expected it to have any result: the only effect was that he was sent to Saint Helena.'[12]

Gourgaud also had his instructions to share with the Prince Regent:

> My aide-de-camp, Gourgaud, will repair on board the English squadron with Count de Las Cases. He will take his departure in the vessel which the commander of that squadron will dispatch either to the admiral or to London. He will endeavour to obtain an audience of the Prince Regent and hand my letter to him. If there should not be found any inconvenience in the delivery of passports for the United States of America, it is my particular wish to proceed to that country, but I will not accept of passports for any other country. I shall take the name of Colonel Muiron, or of Duroc. If I must go to England, I should wish to reside in a country-house, at the distance of ten or twelve leagues from London, and to arrive there in the strictest *incognito*. I should require a dwelling-house sufficiently capacious to accommodate all my suite. I am particularly anxious to avoid London, and this wish must necessarily fall in with the views of the government. Should the ministry be desirous of placing a commissioner near my person, Gourgaud will see that this condition shall not seemingly have the effect of placing me under any kind of confinement, and that the person selected for the duty may, by his rank and character, remove all idea of an unfavourable or suspicious nature.
> If it be determined that Gourgaud should be sent to the admiral, it would be more expedient that the captain should keep him on board his ship, in order to

dispatch him in a corvette, and thereby make sure of his reaching London before us.

Napoleon
At the Île d'Aix, the 13th of July 1815.[13]

Finally, there was a letter to Maitland from Count Bertrand:

14 July 1815
Monsieur le Commandant:
Count de Las Cases has reported to the Emperor the conversation he had with you this morning. His majesty will repair on board your ship at four or five o'clock in the morning.

I send to you the Count de Las Cases, a councillor of state, performing the functions of Maréchal des logis [sergeant], with a list of the persons composing His Majesty's suite.

If the Admiral, in consequences of the demand you have addressed to him, should send you the passports requested for the United States, His Majesty will go there with great pleasure. In the absence of those passports, however, he will willingly go to England as a simple individual, to enjoy there the protection of your country's laws.

His Majesty has sent the Maréchal de Camp Baron Gourgaud to the Prince Regent with a letter of which I have the honour to send you a copy, requesting you will transmit it to the particular minister to whom you may think it right to refer to that general officer, in order that he may have the honour of delivering to the Prince Regent the letter confided to his charge.

I have the honor to be, Monsieur le Commandant, Your very humble and obedient servant,

The Grand Marshal
Count Bertrand[14]

The list of persons accompanying Napoleon was lengthy, to say the least.

Generals and Noblemen: Lieutenant-General Count Bertrand, Grand Marshal; Lieutenant-General the Duc de Rovigo [Savary]; Lieutenant-General Baron Lallemand, aide-de-camp; Brigadier-General Count de Montholon, aide-de-camp; Count de Las Cases, Councillor of State; General Gourgaud.
Ladies: Countess Bertrand; Countess de Montholon.
Children: Three children of Countess Bertrand [Napoleon, Hortense and Henri], one child [Charles] of Countess de Montholon.
Officers: Lieutenant-Colonel de Planat; Lieutenant-Colonel Resigny; Lieutenant-Colonel Schultz; Captain Autric; Captain Mesener; Captain Piontkowski; Lieutenant Rivière; Second-Lieutenant Sainte-Catherine; M. Maingault, surgeon to His Majesty; M. de Las Cases, Page [son to the Count].

Service of the chamber: M. Marchand, head valet; M. Gillis, valet; M. Saint-Denis, valet; M. Noverraz, valet; M. Denis, page of the wardrobe.

Livery: M. Archambaud, Olivier, footman; M. Gaudron, footman; M. Gentilini, footman; M. Archambaud, Achille, footman; M. Joseph, footman; M. Le Charron, footman; M. Lisiaux, pantry man; M. Orsini, footman; M. Fumeau, footman; M. Santini, usher; M. Chauvin, usher; M. Rousseau, lamplighter.

Food service: M. Fonaain, major-domo (or Totain); M. Cipriani [Franceschi], steward; M. Pierron, chef; M. La Fosse, cook; M. Le Page, cook.

Servants of persons accompanying His Majesty: Two Lady's-maids of Countess Bertrand; one Lady's maid of Countess de Montholon; one valet of the Duc de Rovigo; one valet of the Comte de Montholon; one footman of Count Bertrand.[15]

Las Cases and Gourgaud were graciously received by Captain Maitland, who immediately informed them that he would be honored to receive Napoleon aboard his ship. Maitland also promptly sent General Gourgaud to England aboard the *Slaney*, along with various dispatches explaining the situation to the Admiralty. Maitland told Gourgaud that it would not be possible for him to actually go to London unless the government authorized it, but that a copy of the letter would be sent by courier in prompt fashion.

Among the dispatches was this letter to the Admiralty:

Extract of a Letter from Captain Maitland, of His Majesty's ship *Bellerophon*, addressed to the Secretary of the Admiralty, dated in Basque Roads, 14th July, 1815.

For the information of the Lords commissioners of the Admiralty, I have to acquaint you that the Count Las Cases and General Lallemand this day came on board His Majesty's ship under my command with a proposal from Count Bertrand for me to receive on board Napoleon Buonaparte for the purpose of throwing himself on the generosity of the Prince Regent. Conceiving myself authorized by their Lordships' secret order, I have acceded to the proposal, and he is to embark on board this ship tomorrow morning. That no misunderstanding might arise, I have explicitly and clearly explained to Count Las Cases that I have no authority whatever for granting terms of any sort, but that all I can do is to carry him and his suite to England, to be received in such manner as his Royal Highness may deem expedient.

At Napoleon Buonaparte's request, and that their Lordships may be in possession of the transaction at as early a period as possible, I dispatch the *Slaney* (with General Gourgaud, his Aide de Camp), directing Captain Sartorius to put into the nearest port, and forward this letter by his first Lieutenant, and shall in compliance with their Lordship's orders proceed to Torbay to await such directions as the Admiralty may think proper to give.

Enclosed I transmit a copy of the letter with which General Gourgaud is charged, to his Royal Highness the Prince Regent, and request that you will acquaint their Lordships that the General informs me he is entrusted with further particulars, which he is anxious to communicate to his Royal Highness.[16]

Of course, there continues to be dispute as to whether or not Maitland more or less suggested that Napoleon would be allowed to retire to England (the French position, clearly denoted in Lallemand's account in Appendix X) or made it very clear that he could make no promises but simply convey the Emperor to England with his fate to be decided by others (Maitland's position expressed in his memoirs). The argument is largely pointless, as by the time Napoleon was willing to take decisive action, his realistic, safe options had been reduced to one.

Chapter 15

Surrender to the British

Out in the Nick of Time

Early on the morning of 15 July, Savary warned Napoleon that General Beker had told him of the move to arrest him. None of the local French officials wanted Napoleon arrested, but to prevent that he would have to act fast. They could only stall so long. Napoleon quickly dressed in the uniform of the Chasseurs of the Guard, the green coat so familiar to his subjects then and collectors of his image now, and set out to make his move to meet his fate. They made their way to the dock. In the town and on ships, Napoleon could see the white flag of the Bourbons being hoisted; the two French frigates held off doing that for a time, and *L'Épervier* continued to fly the tricolor.

Napoleon boarded the boat that would take him to *L'Épervier*. Marchand describes the scene with a special poignancy:

> Indeed, the next morning at 6 a.m., the brig *L'Épervier*, flying a truce flag, took the Emperor on board and conveyed him to the *Bellerophon*. The deepest sadness showed on every face, and when the British gig approached to take the Emperor on board, the most heartrending cries were heard: officers and sailors saw with despair His Majesty trust his fate to the generosity of a nation whose perfidy they well knew. Having said goodbye to the crew and cast a final look on this beautiful France whose destiny he was abdicating, the Emperor climbed into the gig. Cries of *Vive l'Empereur!* mixed with sobs accompanied him until he arrived on board the *Bellerophon*. Despair was so great among some that they pulled their hair out, while others trampled their hats with their feet, out of rage.
>
> It is regrettable that the Emperor did not board the *Méduse* rather than the *Saale*; the two captains did not have the same amount of vigor. The latter was a cold man who perhaps had orders to attempt nothing to save the Emperor; he had kept the fleurs-de-lis on the panes that separated the dining room from the salon, which could attest to his small measure of Bonapartism. The captain of the *Méduse* on the other hand was bursting with it. To save the Emperor or to die was his motto, and he envisioned that possibility by attacking the *Bellerophon* with both frigates while *L'Épervier* got through. That act of devotion was still possible on the day he went on board, but the next day the presence of Admiral Hotham made it impossible. Learning of the Emperor's

decision to surrender to the British, good Captain Ponée cried, 'Ah! Why did he not come on board my ship, rather than the *Saale*! I would have gotten him through in spite of the cruisers. In what hands is he placing himself? Who could have given him such vicious advice? That nation is nothing but perfidy! Poor Napoleon, you are lost, a terrible premonition tells me so!'[1]

It is interesting to note that the instructions given by the Minister of Marine specifically provided that Napoleon would go to the *Saale* and thus put his destiny in the hands of perhaps the captain least loyal to the Emperor. While the *Saale* was the newer and faster ship, it may be no coincidence that its captain was the least likely to promote Napoleon's swift departure. And, of course, that same captain was ordered to command whichever ship Napoleon chose.

When the boat reached the brig, General Beker offered to accompany Napoleon to the *Bellerophon*, but Napoleon relieved him of what would have been an onerous task with at least some danger to Beker. He told Beker that he did not want people to feel that he had delivered France's deposed Emperor to the British, an accusation that would do Beker no good. The two men embraced, and Napoleon went on board *L'Épervier*. Once on the ship, Napoleon inspected the crew and the ship and talked at some length with the captain, who tried one last time to get Napoleon to make a run for it (see Appendix XI). But Napoleon's mind was made up and he had sent officers to tell Maitland of his decision. Now his word of honor, and concern for his men, prevented any action other than to place his hopes in British honor. It would be misplaced hope, but he no longer had a choice.

The previous day, Captain Maitland had been informed that Napoleon had escaped to the mainland and was heading for another port. He confronted Las Cases with this information, and Las Cases assured him that this could not possibly have been the case. Maitland accepted his word, but was no doubt nervous as to what the situation really was.

Maitland also discussed arrangements for Napoleon's quarters while on board ship. Las Cases suggested that Napoleon would probably prefer the entire after-cabin to himself, thus affording him ample room to exercise. Maitland's response, and his comment on the matter in his memoirs, bears repeating here:

I answered, 'As it is my wish to treat him with every possible consideration while he is on board the ship I command, I shall make any arrangement you think will be most agreeable to him.'

This is the only conversation that ever passed on the subject of the cabin, and I am the more particular in stating it, as Buonaparte has been described, in some of the public Journals, as having taken possession of it in a most brutal way, saying, '*Tout ou rien pour moi:*' – all or nothing for me. I here therefore, once and for all, beg to state most distinctly, that from the time of his coming on board my ship to the period of his quitting her, his conduct was invariably that of a gentleman, and in no one instance do I recollect him to have made use of a rude expression, or to have been guilty of any kind of ill-breeding.[2]

Boarding the *Bellerophon*

At dawn on the 15th, Maitland saw *L'Épervier* sailing towards them under a flag of truce. Sir Henry Hotham's flagship, the *Superb*, was also seen approaching from another direction. Shortly thereafter, the wind shifted and *L'Épervier* was dead in the water. Maitland understood well the politics of the situation and wanted full credit for nabbing Napoleon. As he relates in his memoirs:

> By half-past five the ebb-tide failed, the wind was blowing right in, and the brig, which was within a mile of us, made no further progress, while the *Superb* was advancing with the wind and tide in her favour. Thus situated, and being most anxious to terminate the affair I had brought so near a conclusion previous to the Admiral's arrival, I sent off Mr. Mott, the First Lieutenant, in the barge, who returned soon after six o'clock, bringing Napoleon with him.[3]

By all accounts, the officers and sailors on *L'Épervier* were in tears at the loss of their Emperor. Virtually to a man they thought Napoleon was making a mistake and should have sought passage, however difficult, to America. The sound of their cheers rang in Napoleon's ears until they were out of hearing. Napoleon, himself in tears, dipped his hand three times in the water, throwing it on *L'Épervier* as a salute to their loyalty.

At shortly after six in the morning, the barge pulled alongside Maitland's ship. Its rowers appear to have been French prisoners, allowing Napoleon to arrive borne by French citizens rather than British sailors. When they arrived, the *Bellerophon*'s crew manned the yards and its marines were at attention on deck. It was a reception for a general, not an emperor, but it was understandable. Maitland was unclear just what honors, if any, he should afford the Emperor. He wanted to show him every courtesy, but felt that his superiors might not approve full honors. As it was not yet eight in the morning, he fell back on regulations that precluded the firing of a salute, but in all other ways treated Napoleon as well as could possibly be expected.

The barge secured, General Count Bertrand, in what must have been one of his most difficult moments, regardless of his feelings that the English option was the best available at the time, boarded the *Bellerophon* and announced that 'The Emperor is in the boat.'[4] Captain Maitland and all his officers stood by the gangway, and Napoleon made his entrance. Count Las Cases presented Captain Maitland to Napoleon, whose first words were, upon removing his hat, 'I come on board your ship to place myself under the protection of the laws of England.'[5] Maitland made no response to the statement, but gave Napoleon a low bow and then offered to show him to his cabin. Napoleon expressed great pleasure with the accommodations, and also commented on the youthful beauty of a portrait of Maitland's wife. Thus did the two men establish a friendly relationship. Napoleon, incidentally, did not speak English, but Maitland spoke reasonably good French, though it took him some effort to understand Napoleon's rapid speech.

Meanwhile, Captain Jourdan wanted official notice that the transfer had taken place, and sent a letter along with Napoleon asking for confirmation. No doubt understanding Jourdan's concern, Captain Maitland was happy to oblige (see

Appendix XI). On his way back, Jourdan encountered one of the boats bringing some of Napoleon's suite that was having difficulty making headway. He took it under tow to the *Bellerophon*, giving Napoleon and the sailors yet another opportunity to say farewell.

Napoleon then asked to have the officers introduced to him, which was done. One of the officers presented to Napoleon was the ship's surgeon, Barry O'Meara. Neither man knew it at the time, of course, but their two fates would soon become intertwined, and O'Meara would make a major contribution to the creation of what has become known as the Napoleonic Legend.

Napoleon was friendly, asking each one personal questions as to their service, place of birth, family, and so on. Napoleon had always been a man who could be very charming, and he was at his finest now. And why not? He still anticipated that his worst fate would be to live in a nice home in the English countryside, much like his brother Lucien had done. And the best-case scenario? British passage to America.

A short time later, Napoleon insisted on touring the ship, even though the men were in the process of doing their daily early-morning cleaning. He was quite impressed and complimented the men to their captain. Lieutenant Bowerbank describes him thus:

> Napoleon Buonaparte is about five feet seven inches high, rather corpulent, but remarkably well made. His hair is very black, cut close; whiskers shaved off; large eye brows; grey eyes, (the most piercing I ever saw); rather full face; dark, but peculiar, complexion; his nose and mouth proportionate; broad shoulders, and apparently strongly built. Upon the whole he is a good-looking man, and, when young, must have been handsome. He appears about forty-five or forty-six, his real age, and greatly resembles the different prints I have seen of him in London. His walk is a march, or (as far as a sailor may be allowed to judge) very like one; – and to complete the portrait, I must add that, in walking he generally carries his hands in the pockets of his pantaloons, or folded behind his back.[6]

At nine o'clock, Napoleon, Maitland and the officers sat down to breakfast. It was a typical English breakfast, and Napoleon found it less than agreeable. Maitland made arrangements that for all future meals Napoleon's staff should have access to the ship's oven and other facilities.

Sir Henry Hotham

Around 10.30 Sir Henry Hotham's flagship, the *Superb*, pulled up nearby, and Maitland immediately went over to see his superior officer. Maitland was, naturally enough, worried that his superiors might not agree with his actions, but Hotham was actually quite pleased. The fact that Maitland had not made any promises to Napoleon was a bonus, as far as he was concerned. Hotham offered to take Napoleon off of Maitland's hands, but the captain was more than willing to continue acting as Napoleon's 'host'.

Maitland returned to tell Napoleon that Hotham would visit him that afternoon. To follow protocol, Napoleon quickly sent Bertrand, accompanied by Captain Maitland, over to make contact with the admiral. No one objected to this little game, and when Hotham arrived with Captain Senhouse and his secretary Mr Irving later in the day, Napoleon played the gracious host. He clearly felt that the British were showing him proper honors, and now had even more reason to feel that he would be allowed to retire in England as a country gentleman. Napoleon showed the admiral his portable library, and they discussed any number of topics, many of which had to do with the British navy.

Around five o'clock they settled down to dinner. Napoleon was the host of the dinner, which was served with his imperial service, and had Admiral Hotham to his right and Madame Bertrand on his left. The conversation was friendly and everyone seemed in good spirits. Napoleon happily accepted Hotham's offer to join him on his ship for breakfast the following day. Strong coffee followed dinner. They then retired to the after-cabin, where Napoleon demonstrated his camp bed. The party finally over, Napoleon retired in the early evening. It had been an amazing day.

Early the next day, Napoleon prepared to visit the admiral. First, however, he reviewed the marine guard that had assembled in his honor. He asked many of the men about their history and asked to see them perform certain drills. The men were no doubt flattered by this attention and it must have caused them to question what they had been told about this 'ogre from Corsica'.

In boarding the barge to go to Hotham's ship, the *Superb*, Las Cases showed up in a navy officer's uniform. It was the first time Napoleon had seen that on him and he commented to that effect. Las Cases had been a navy lieutenant before the French Revolution and felt that it might now give him some additional status, given their position.

The time with Admiral Sir Henry Hotham went well. He had turned out the ship's company in honor of the Emperor (and there had been no problems ever expressed with Napoleon having that title), presented his officers and gave a tour of the ship. Breakfast was served in the captain's cabin. It was an English breakfast, so Napoleon ate very little. After breakfast, the admiral agreed to issue a passport for Napoleon's horses and carriages to be brought from Rochefort to the *Superb*, but nothing ever came of it.

By noon, the party had returned to the *Bellerophon*, where Napoleon was again met with the honor of having the crew manning the yards. Napoleon's first two days of captivity had been pleasant. He had been shown great honor and courtesy, and there was every reason for him to believe that Maitland had been right, that he would be received well by the British government and the British people. But the tide was about to turn. The *Myrmidon* was loaded with the rest of Napoleon's entourage and materials. They were soon joined by the *Mouche*, which contained sheep and vegetables from the French Commodore.

Some time on the afternoon of the 16th, the small fleet set sail for Torbay, England. Napoleon was optimistic, but he was sailing to a destiny far different from anything he had imagined.

Chapter 16

Epilogue

Napoleon arrived at Torbay, England, on the morning of 24 July. The journey had been pleasant, and he and Captain Maitland had enjoyed each other's company. Admiral Keith had received a letter that Maitland had sent to seek confirmation that the Admiralty approved of his actions (see Appendix XIII). Keith forwarded that to the Admiralty, and greeted Maitland with orders that were ominous for Napoleon and his entourage. They were to be treated well and given every consideration, but they were not to leave the ships and no one was to be allowed to come into communication with them. General Gourgaud was reunited with Napoleon, but the news was not good: he had been refused the opportunity to set foot on English soil. His letter to the Prince Regent had been taken from him and, allegedly, sent on to the government.

Lord Keith also asked Maitland to thank Napoleon on his behalf for his treatment of his nephew, Captain Elphinstone, at the Battle of Waterloo. Napoleon had seen to it that his wounds were properly dressed and he was sent to a small hut to recuperate. Without this attention, the lad would have surely died.

That nicety notwithstanding, the demeanor of the crew began to change, which acted as a belated warning signal to the French. The British government had been deliberating Napoleon's fate. They rejected sending him to Louis XVIII as too risky. They also rejected the possibility of allowing him to settle in England as a country gentleman, fearing that he would become the center of attention and a force to be reckoned with. In this they were certainly correct. Already, at Torbay, small ships were circling the *Bellerophon*, hoping for a glimpse of the great man.

There was a real possibility that he would be kept in Fort George in northern Scotland. The Commander's house there was quite large and luxurious, and Napoleon would have been comfortable in it (though not happy at being confined in a fort, however large it might have been). Indeed, Prince Metternich actually wrote to Napoleon's wife, Marie Louise, that this was where Napoleon was to go:

Metternich to the Empress Marie Louise
   Paris, July 1815
   Madame,
   I promised before my departure from Vienna to inform Your Imperial Majesty what was decided concerning the fate of Napoleon.
   You will see by the enclosed article, an extract from the *Moniteur*, that he has surrendered to the English vessel, the '*Bellerophon*,' after having vainly tried to escape the surveillance of the cruisers which had been placed before Rochefort.
   According to an arrangement made between the Powers he will be sent as a

prisoner to Fort George, in the North of Scotland, and placed under the surveillance of Austrian, Russian, French, and Prussian commissioners. He will be well treated there, and will have as much liberty as is compatible with the certainty that he cannot escape.

The persons most directly involved in the conspiracy of last March are mentioned in the same *Moniteur* of the 18th. They have left France, or are on their way to leave it. M. de la Bédoyère will be arrested unless he makes his escape. Ney is in Switzerland.

Madame Mère and Cardinal Fesch left yesterday for Tuscany. We do not know exactly where Joseph is. Lucien is in England under a false name, Jérôme in Switzerland, Louis at Rome. Queen Hortense has set out for Switzerland, whither General de Flahaut and his mother will follow her. Murat seems to be still at Toulon; this, however, is not certain.[1]

But, perhaps mindful of the long historic alliance between the Scots and the French, the government soon decided on St Helena as Napoleon's destiny. Word went forth on the 26th to sail to Plymouth. There, the crowds were incredible: hundreds of boats filled with spectators seeking a view of the fallen Emperor. Extra ships were brought in to serve as a shield. Napoleon showed himself, and the crew even put up signs telling spectators of his movements. But they had moved farther from London, a fact not unnoticed by Napoleon and his suite.

It soon became clear that Napoleon was to be considered a prisoner of war. Were that status derived from the war with France, he would have to be released when peace was signed. But the British government decided to say that the war was against Napoleon the *man* and that there would be no peace with him, and that therefore they could hold him forever. It was a dubious proposition at best, but there was no one to take up Napoleon's cause. Word immediately went forth that Napoleon was no longer to be treated as an emperor, but only as a general officer. By the 29th, newspapers were full of stories that Napoleon would be sent to St Helena.

On the 31st Admiral Lord Keith and Sir Henry Bunbury, Under-Secretary of State for the Colonies, visited Napoleon, with Bertrand in attendance. Keith read to Napoleon a letter from the First Lord of the Admiralty, Lord Melville, which informed Napoleon that he would be kept as a prisoner forever, sent to St Helena and treated as a general officer. Napoleon was outraged and made every possible argument against the decision. He pointed out that he had voluntarily gone to the British and that Captain Maitland assured him that he would be able to go to England. He also objected to being styled a general officer, pointing out that he had been recognized as First Consul of France before being made Emperor, and that he had also been Emperor of Elba. It was to no avail. When the British left, Napoleon dictated the following letter to be sent to Lord Keith:

Napoleon to Keith

Milord, I have carefully read the extract of the letter you have sent me. I have informed you of my protest: I am not a prisoner of war, but I am the guest of

England. I came to this country on the war vessel *Bellerophon*, after having informed its captain of the letter I was writing to the Prince Regent, and having received from him the assurance that his orders were to receive me on board and transport me to England with my retinue, if I so requested. Admiral Hotham has since reiterated the same assurances. From the moment I was freely received on the *Bellerophon*, I have found myself under the protection of your country's laws.

I prefer death to being taken to St. Helena, or shut up in any fortress. I wish to live in the interior of England, in the enjoyment of freedom, and under the protection and supervision of the law, and in agreement with all engagements and measures which might be deemed appropriate. I do not wish to have any correspondence with France, or to partake in any political affairs. Since my abdication, my intention has always been to reside in the United States or in England.

I flatter myself that you, Milord, and the undersecretary of your government shall make a faithful report of these facts. It is on the honor of the prince regent and the protection of your country's laws that I have, and place, my confidence.

31 July 1815

Napoleon[2]

It was no use. Nor would an effort to serve a writ of habeas corpus to force Napoleon to testify at a trial work. The *Bellerophon* was ordered to sail in circles in the open sea until the *Northumberland* arrived to take him into exile. On 4 August, Napoleon sent another protest to the British government:

At sea on board the *Bellerophon*, August 4, 1815

I hereby solemnly protest, before heaven and mankind, against the violence which is being done to me, and against the violation of my most sacred rights, in disposing by force of my person and my freedom. I came freely on board the *Bellerophon*, I am not a prisoner, I am the guest of England. I came here myself at the instigation of the captain who had orders from the government to receive me and take me to England with my retinue, if that were my desire; I presented myself in good faith, to come place myself under the protection of its laws. As soon as I set foot on board the *Bellerophon*, I was among the British people. If the government in giving orders to the captain of the *Bellerophon* to receive me and my retinue had only wanted to set a trap for me, an ambush, it has forfeited its honor and blemished its flag.

If this act is consummated, it will be in vain for the British in the future to speak to Europe of its loyalty, its laws, and its liberty; British faith would be lost with the hospitality of the *Bellerophon*.

I appeal to history; it shall say that an enemy who made war for twenty years against the British people came freely, in his misfortune, to seek shelter under their laws – and what greater proof could he give of his esteem and trust? But how did England reply to such magnanimity? She pretended to extend a hospitable hand to this enemy and, when he gave himself up in good faith, she slaughtered him.

Napoleon[3]

Napoleon's suite was to be greatly reduced, most notably by the absence of Lallemand and Savary. These two men objected strenuously to their exclusion, which they feared would lead to their execution in France. Captain Maitland put in a good word for them, but in the end, they were not allowed to join Napoleon on St Helena. (See Appendix X for Lallemand's story and Appendix XIV for Savary's protest.) The two men were ultimately sent to Malta, rather than France, and eventually released.

On the afternoon of 7 August, Napoleon said farewell to Savary, Lallemand and a few others who were not accompanying him to St Helena. He then boarded the *Northumberland*, was introduced to its crew and shown to his quarters. William Warden, the *Northumberland*'s surgeon describes the scene:

> As the boat approached, the figure of Napoleon was readily distinguished, from his apparent resemblance to the various prints of him which are displayed in the windows of shops. The Marines occupied the front of the poop, and the officers kept the quarter-deck. A universal silence prevailed when the Barge reached the side, and there was a grave but anxious aspect in all the spectators which, in the opinion of others as well as myself, was no small addition to the solemnity of the ceremonial. Count Bertrand ascended first, and having bowed, retired a few steps to give place to him whom he still considered as his Master, and in whose presence he appeared to feel that all his most respectful homage was still due. The whole ship's company seemed at this moment to be in breathless expectation. Lord Keith was the last who quitted the barge, and I cannot give you a more complete idea of the wrapped [sic] attention of all on board to the figure of Napoleon, than that his Lordship, high as he is in naval character, Admiral also of the Channel Fleet, to which we belonged, arrayed in the full uniform of his rank, and emblazoned with the decorations of his orders, did not seem to be noticed, nor scarcely even to be seen, among the group which was subject to him.
>
> With a slow step Buonaparte mounted the gangway, and, on feeling himself firm on the quarter-deck, he raised his hat, when the guard presented arms and the drum rolled. The officers of the *Northumberland*, who were uncovered, stood considerably in advance. Those he approached, and saluted with an air of the most affable politeness.[4]

After a long and generally uneventful voyage, the ship dropped anchor in the harbor of Jamestown, St Helena.

On the evening of the 17th, Napoleon I, Emperor of the French, now outrageously styled General Buonaparte by the British government, set foot on his last island and walked forward to meet his ultimate destiny.

Appendix I

Decree by Louis XVIII as he left France on 6 March 1815

Louis, by the grace of God, King of France and Navarre, salutations to all who read this.

Article 12 of the constitutional charter has charged us with making rules and ordinances regarding the security of the state. It would be severely compromised should we not take prompt measures to repress the venture just undertaken against our kingdom, and put an end to the plots and the attempts at inciting civil war and destroying the government.

Because of this, and on the report made to us by our beloved and faithful knight chancellor of France, Sir Dambray, commander of our orders, and on the advice of our council, we have ordered and order as follows:

Art. 1.—Napoleon Bonaparte is declared a traitor and rebel, for having entered the department of the Var under arms. All governors, military commanders, national guard, civilian authorities, and even simple citizens are enjoined to seek him out, arrest him, and promptly bring him before a court martial, which after identifying him shall pronounce against him the penalties provided under the law.

Art. 2.—Shall be likewise punished as guilty of the same crimes, all military and employees of all ranks who have accompanied or followed Bonaparte in his invasion of French territory, unless – within eight days following the publication of this ordinance – they surrender to our governors, commanders of military divisions, generals, or civil administrators.

Art. 3.—Shall also be sought out and punished as agitators and accomplices of rebellion and attempts to change the form of government and provoke a civil war, all civil and military administrators, heads and employees in said administrations, payers and collectors of public funds, and even ordinary citizens who would either directly or indirectly provide aid and assistance to Bonaparte.

Art. 4.—Shall be likewise punished, in accordance with article 102 of the penal code, those who – through speeches given in public places or meetings, posters, or printed writings – have taken part or encouraged citizens to take part in the revolt, or abstained from stopping it.

Our chancellor, our ministers, secretaries of state, and our director of the police, each as far as he is concerned, are charged with the execution of this ordinance that shall be inserted in the evening bulletin, and sent to all governors of military divisions, generals, commanders, prefects, sub-prefects and mayors of our kingdom, with orders to have it printed and posted in Paris as well as elsewhere and wherever needed.

Given in the Tuileries château on March 6, 1815, the twentieth year of our reign.

Signed: Louis
For the King: the Chancellor of France
Signed: Dambray[1]

Appendix II

The Additional Act to the Constitution

BULLETIN DES LOIS
No. 19.
(No. 112) ADDITIONAL BILL to the Constitutions of the Empire
At the Elysée Palace, 22 April 1815

NAPOLEON, by the grace of God and the constitutions, EMPEROR OF THE FRENCH, to all who are present and those to come, GREETINGS:

Since we were called fifteen years ago by the wishes of France to govern the State, we looked several times at how best to improve the constitutional forms, according to the need and wishes of the nation, and by taking advantage of the lessons learned through experience. The Empire's constitutions have thus been formed by a series of bills that have received the acceptance of the people. Our goal at the time, was to organize a great European federative system that we had adopted to reflect the spirit of the century, and favorable to the progress of civilization. In order to make it complete and to give it the scope and stability it required, we had postponed setting up several interior institutions especially designed to protect the people's liberty. Our goal, from now on, is to increase France's prosperity by strengthening public freedom.

It is with this in mind that we find the necessity to modify several important constitutions, senate decrees and other bills governing this Empire. TO THIS END, wanting on one side and on the other to make the constitutions of the Empire totally in accordance with the wishes and needs of the nation, as well as the state of peace that we desire to maintain with Europe, we have resolved to propose to the people a follow up of the measures striving to modify and improve the constitutional bills, to give all guarantees to the rights of the citizens, to give the representative system all possible expansion, to give the intermediary corps the consideration and power needed; in other words, to combine the highest point of political freedom and individual safety with the strength and centralization necessary to insure the respect by foreigners of the independence of the French people and the dignity of our crown. Consequently, the following articles forming a supplementary bill to the constitutions of the Empire will be submitted to the free and solemn acceptance of all the citizens in all of France.

TITLE 1
General measures

ART. 1. The Empire's constitutions, namely the constitutional act of 22 Frimaire year VIII [13 December 1799], the Senate Decree [*Sénatus-Consultes*] of 14 and 16 Thermidor year X [2 and 4 August 1802], and of 28 Floréal year XII [18 May 1804], will be modified by the following measures. All of their other measures are confirmed and maintained.

2. Legislative power is exercised by the Emperor and by the two Chambers.

3. The first Chamber, named Chamber of Peers [*Chambre des Pairs*], is hereditary.

4. The Emperor names its members, who are irrevocable, them and their male descendants, from the elder to the elder in a direct line. The number of Peers is unlimited. Adoption does not transmit the dignity of Peer to the person in question. Peers join session at twenty-one years of age but do not have a deliberative voice until the age of twenty-five.

5. The Chamber of Peers is presided over by the Grand-Chancellor of the Empire, or, in the case provided for in article 51 of the Senate Decree of 28 Floréal year XII, by one of the members of this chamber specially designated by the Emperor.

6. Members of the imperial family, in order of heredity, are Peers by right. They sit after the president. They join the session at eighteen years of age but do not have legislative voice until the age of twenty-one.

7. The second Chamber, called the Chamber of Representatives [*Chambre des Représentants*], is elected by the people.

8. There are six hundred twenty-nine members of this chamber. They must be at least twenty-five years old.

9. The president of the Chamber of Representatives is named by the Chamber at the first session. He keeps this position until the renewal of the Chamber. His nomination is submitted to the Emperor for his approval.

10. The Chamber of Representatives verifies the power of its members, and pronounces on the validity of contested elections.

11. Members of the Chamber of Representatives receive the indemnity decreed by the constituting Assembly for their travel expenses during the session.

12. They are indefinitely re-eligible.

13. The Chamber of Representatives is renewed by right and in full every five years.

14. No member of either Chambers can be arrested, except in the case of being caught red-handed, nor can they be pursued in criminal or correctional matters during the sessions, except through a resolution by the Chamber of which he is a member.

15. None can be arrested or held because of debts, from the time of their convocation, or forty days after the session.

16. Peers are judged by their Chamber in criminal and correctional matters, according to the rules of law.

17. The quality of peer and representative is compatible with all public functions, except that of accountant. However, prefects and sub-prefects cannot be elected by the

electoral college of the department or the district that they administer.

18. The Emperor sends to the Chambers some state ministers and state counselors, who have a seat there and take part in the discussions, but who have deliberative voice only in the case where they are a member of the Chamber as Peers or elected by the people.

19. Ministers who are members of the Chamber of Peers or the Chamber of Representatives, or who are seated as government representatives, give the Chambers explanations deemed necessary, as long as their publication does not compromise the interest of the State.

20. Sessions of the two Chambers are public. However, they can meet in a secret committee, upon the request of ten members for the Chamber of Peers, and the request of twenty-five members for the Chamber of Representatives. The Government can also request secret committees for communications to be arranged. In all cases, the deliberations and votes cannot take place except in a public session.

21. The Emperor can prorogue, adjourn and dissolve the Chamber of Representatives. The proclamation pronouncing the dissolution will convene the electoral colleges for a new election, and will recommend the meeting of the Representatives in not more than six months.

22. During the interval of the sessions of the Chamber of Representatives, or in the case of dissolution of this Chamber, the Chamber of Peers cannot assemble.

23. The Government has the preponderance of the law; the Chambers may propose amendments: if the amendments are not adopted by the Government, the Chambers must vote on the law as it has been offered.

24. The Chambers have the ability to invite the Government to propose a law on a particular subject, and to write what seems appropriate to insert in the law. This request can be made by either of the two Chambers.

25. When a draft resolution has been adopted in one of the two Chambers, it is taken to the other; if it is approved, it is then taken to the Emperor.

26. No written discourse, except the reports from the commissions, the minister's reports dealing with the laws that are presented, and the minutes that are taken, can be read in either of the Chambers.

TITLE II
Of the electoral colleges and of the mode of election

27. Electoral colleges of department and district are retained in accordance with the Senate Decree of 16 Thermidor year X [4 August 1802], except for the following modifications.

28. The county assemblies will fill all vacancies in the electoral colleges each year by annual elections.

29. Starting from year 1816, a member of the Chamber of Peers, designated by the Emperor, will be president for life and irremovable of each department electoral college.

30. Starting from the same epoch, the electoral college of each department will

name, from the members of each district college, the president and two vice-presidents. To this end, the assembly of the department college will precede by fifteen days the assembly of the district college.

31. The colleges of department and district will name the established number of representatives for each of them by the bill and the attached table, No. I.

32. The representatives can be chosen indiscriminately throughout France. Each department or district college that will choose a representative from outside of the department or of the district, will name a replacement who will have to be chosen from the department or district.

33. Industry and manufacturing and commercial property will have special representation. The election of commercial and manufacturing representatives will be done by the electoral college of the department, on a list of eligible persons, drawn up by the chambers of commerce and consultative chambers together, per the bill and table attached, No. II.

TITLE III
Of the Income Tax Law

34. The general direct tax, on either business or property, is voted for the duration of only one year; the indirect income taxes can be voted for the duration of several years. In case of the dissolution of the Chamber of Representatives, the taxes that were voted on during the preceding session are continued until the new meeting of the Chamber.

35. No direct or indirect tax in money or property can be collected, no loan can take place, no credit issued from the book of public debt, no estate can be alienated or exchanged, no drafting of men for the army can be ordered, no part of the territory can be exchanged, but for a law.

36. All proposition of income tax, loan, or drafting of men, can only be made to the Chamber of Representatives.

37. It is also to the Chamber of Representatives that the following is taken: 1st, the general State budget, showing the expected revenues and the proposition for the assignment of funds to each of the ministry's departments for the year; 2nd, the accounting of the revenues and expenses of the preceding year or years.

TITLE IV
Of the Ministers, and of Responsibility

38. All the bills of the Government must be counter-signed by a minister of a department.

39. Ministers are responsible for the bills of the Government signed by them, as well as the execution of the laws.

40. They can be accused by the Chamber of Representatives, and are judged by the Chamber of Peers.

41. Any minister, any commander of the army of land or sea, can be accused by the Chamber of Representatives and judged by the Chamber of Peers, if he has compromised safety or honor of the nation.

42. In this case, the Chamber of Peers has the discretionary power to characterize the offense, or inflict the penalty.

43. Prior to pronouncing the accusation of a minister, the Chamber of Representatives must declare that there is cause for examination of the proposal for accusation.

44. This declaration can only be done after the report from a commission of sixty members drawn in lots.

This commission will give its report no sooner than ten days after its nomination.

45. When the Chamber declares a need for an examination, it can call the minister to join them and give some explanations. This call can only be made ten days after the commission's report.

46. In any other case, ministers that have departments cannot be called or sent for by the Chambers.

47. When the Chamber of Representatives has declared that there is a need to examine a minister, a new commission is formed with sixty members drawn in lots, like the first one, and the commission makes a report analyzing the accusation. This commission does not do its report until ten days after its nomination.

48. The accusation can only be pronounced ten days after the reading and distribution of the report.

49. Once the accusation is pronounced, the Chamber of Representatives names five commissioners taken from within, to pursue the accusation in front of the Chamber of Peers.

50. Article 75 of title VIII of the constitutional bill of 22 Frimaire year VIII [13 December 1799], declaring that Government agents cannot be pursued except in virtue of a decision from the State Council, will be modified by a law.

TITLE V
Of Judicial Power

51. The Emperor names all the judges. They are irremovable and named for life as soon as they are nominated, except for the nomination of judges of the peace and commerce, which will remain the same as in the past. Current judges named by the Emperor, at the end of the decree of the senate of 12 October 1807, who will be deemed worthy of continuing on, will receive life term appointments before next January 1st.

52. The institution of jurors is continued.

53. Debates in criminal matters are public.

54. Military offenses alone are under the jurisdiction of military tribunals.

55. All other offenses, even if committed by military personnel, are under the competence of civil tribunals.

56. All crimes and offenses that were sent to the imperial high court and whose judgment is not reserved for the Chamber of Peers by this bill, will be carried in front of ordinary tribunals.

57. The Emperor has the right to pardon, even in correctional matters, and to give amnesty.

58. Interpretations of the laws, requested by the final court of appeals, will be given in the form of a law.

TITLE VI
Citizens Rights

59. The French people are equal before the law, either for the contribution to income taxes and public dues or for admission to public or military employment.

60. No one can, under any pretext, be separated from the judges assigned to him by the law.

61. No one can be pursued, arrested, held or exiled, except in the cases provided for by the law and according to the prescribed forms.

62. Freedom of worship is guaranteed for all people.

63. All properties owned or acquired by virtue of the laws, and all debts to the State, are inviolable.

64. Any citizen has the right to print and publish his thoughts, signing them, without being censored, except for any legal responsibility, after publication, by judgments of juries, even if it required only a correctional penalty.

65. The right of petition is assured to all citizens. Every petition is individual. These petitions may be addressed, either to the Government, or to both Chambers: however, they must bear the title, To His Majesty The Emperor. They will be presented to the Chambers under the guarantee of a member recommending the petition. They are read in public; and if the Chambers takes them under consideration, they are taken to the Emperor by the President.

66. No place, no part of the territory can be declared under a state of siege, except in the case of an invasion by a foreign force, or civil troubles. In the first instance, the declaration will be done by the Government. In the second instance, it can only be done by the law. However, if it should be the case that the Chambers are not yet assembled, the Government's action declaring a state of siege must be converted into a proposition of law during the first fifteen days of the meeting of the Chambers.

67. The people of France declare that, in the delegating it has done and is doing of its powers, they did not and do not wish to give the right to propose the reinstallation of the Bourbons or any prince of this family on the throne, even in the case of the extinction of the imperial dynasty, nor the right to reestablish the former feudal nobility, or the feudal and seigniorial rights, the tithes, no privileged or dominant cult, nor the possibility to bring any assault to the irrevocability of the sale of national domains; it strictly forbids the Government, the Chambers and the citizens, any proposition in this regard.

Given at Paris, 22 April 1815
Signed NAPOLEON.
By the Emperor:
The Minister Secretary of State, signed Duc de Bassano[2]

Appendix III

Treaty of the Allies against Napoleon

In the name of the Holy and Indivisible Trinity, His Majesty the Emperor of Austria, King of Hungary and Bohemia, and His Majesty the King of the United Kingdom of Great Britain and Ireland, having taken into consideration the consequences which the invasion of France by Napoleon Buonaparte and the actual position of that kingdom may have on the security of Europe, have by common consent, together with His Majesty the Emperor of all the Russias, and His Majesty the King of Prussia, resolved to apply to this important circumstance the principles laid down by the Treaty of Chaumont. In consequence of which they have agreed to renew by a solemn treaty, signed separately by each of these four powers with each of the other three, the undertaking to preserve, against all attempts to the contrary, the order of affairs so happily re-established in Europe, and to decide upon the most efficacious means of carrying this undertaking into effect and of giving it all the possible latitude so imperiously demanded by present circumstances. With this view His Majesty the Emperor of Austria, King of Hungary and Bohemia, has for the purpose of discussing, concluding, and signing the conditions of the present treaty with His Majesty the King of the United Kingdom of Great Britain and Ireland, named the Sieur — and His Britannic Majesty having on his side named the Sieur — the said plenipotentiaries after having exchanged their full powers and found them in proper and due form, have drawn up the following articles:

Art. I—The high contracting parties above named solemnly engage to combine in making every effort within their respective states, to maintain in all their integrity, the conditions of the treaty of peace concluded in Paris, May 30th, 1814, as well as the stipulations drawn up and signed at the Congress of Vienna, with the object of completing the arrangements of that treaty, and guarding them against all attacks, and particularly against the designs of Napoleon Buonaparte. For this purpose they engage themselves, if required, to direct together and with mutual consent in the spirit of the declaration of the 13th of March last, all their efforts against him and against all those who have joined his faction or may do so later, in order to compel him to desist from his projects and place him beyond the possibility of disturbing for the future, the tranquility and general peace under the protection of which, the rights, the liberty and the independence of the nations have just been established and assured.

Art. II—Although it is impossible to estimate the measures necessary to attain so great and beneficent a result, and although the high contracting parties are determined to devote to it all those which according to their respective positions they can command, they are nevertheless agreed to keep permanently in the field a total of one hundred and fifty thousand men each, at least one-tenth of which shall be cavalry and a proper proportion of artillery, without reckoning the garrisons, and to employ these actively and jointly against the common enemy.

Art. III—The high contracting parties reciprocally undertake not to lay down arms except by common consent and until the object of the war named in the first article of the present treaty has been attained, and so long as Buonaparte shall not have been placed absolutely beyond the possibility of raising fresh disturbances and renewing his attempts to seize the supreme power in France.

Art. IV—This treaty being solely applicable to present circumstances, the stipulations of the treaty of Chaumont, and particularly those contained in Article XVI, will again come into full force as soon as the actual end has been attained.

Art. V—All that which relates to the command of the allied armies, their maintenance ... will be regulated by a special convention.

Art. VI—The high contracting parties will have the power respectively of accrediting to the generals in command of the troops, certain officers who will be at liberty to correspond with their governments, and keep them informed of military events and everything relating to the operations of the armies.

Art. VII—The engagements entered into by the present treaty having for their aim the maintenance of universal peace, the high contracting parties have resolved between them to ask all the other powers of Europe to agree to them.

Art. VIII—The present treaty having been solely entered into for the purpose of supporting France or any other country that may be invaded, against the attempts of Buonaparte and his adherents, His most Christian Majesty will be specially asked to give his consent thereto, and to make known, in case he should require the forces named in Article II, what assistance circumstances will permit him to bring forward towards the object of the present treaty.

Art. IX—The present treaty shall be ratified, and the ratifications thereof shall be exchanged in two months, or sooner if necessary.

In witness whereof the respective plenipotentiaries have hereunto signed their names and set their seals.

Executed at Vienna, March 25th, in the year of our Lord, 1815.

> The Prince de Metternich
> The Baron de Wessenberg
> The Duke of Wellington

On the same day the same treaty was concluded between Russia and Great Britain, and likewise between Great Britain and Prussia.[3]

Appendix IV

Proclamations of King Louis XVIII upon his return to France

PROCLAMATION OF THE KING
Câteau-Cambresis, 25 June 1815

LOUIS, by the grace of God, King of France and of Navarre, to all those who will see these presents, GREETINGS.

Very early in the time when the most criminal enterprises, helped by the most inconceivable defection, forced us to momentarily leave our kingdom, we informed you of the dangers that were menacing you if you did not hastily shake off the yoke of the tyrant usurper. We did not wish to add our arms or those of our family to the tools used by Providence to punish treason.

But today, helped by the powerful efforts of our allies to dissipate the tyrant's henchmen, we hastily return to our States to reestablish the constitution that we had given to France, repair with all the means in our power the ills of the revolt and the ensuing war, reward the good people, carry out the existing laws against those who are guilty, finally to call to join us around our throne the huge majority of the French people whose loyalty, courage and devotion brought gentle solace to our heart.

Given at Câteau-Cambresis, the twenty-fifth day of the month of June in the year of grace 1815, and of our twenty-first year of Reign.

Signed LOUIS
By the King:
The minister Secretary of State of the war,
Signed Duc de Feltre[4]

PROCLAMATION OF THE KING
Cambrai, 28 June 1815

LOUIS, by the grace of God, King of France and of Navarre, to all our loyal subjects, GREETINGS.

The doors to my kingdom are finally open in front of me. I hurry to bring my lost subjects back to me, to soften the ills that I had tried to prevent, to place myself a second time between the allied armies and the French people, hoping that the respect that I receive may bring them peace: it is the only way that I could take part in the war. I did not permit that any prince of my family should appear in the ranks of foreigners, and I connected with the courage of those of my servants who gathered around me.

Back on the soil of the homeland, I am pleased to speak of confidence to my people. When I returned amongst them, I found their spirit agitated and excited by adverse passions; my eyes saw nothing but difficulties and obstacles everywhere: my Government must have made some mistakes; perhaps they did. There are times when the purest of intentions are not sufficient to govern, or sometimes they mislead. Experience alone could warn: it will not be lost. I want everything that will save France.

My subjects learned through some cruel episodes that the principle of the legitimacy of sovereigns is one of the fundamental bases of social order on which to establish a wise and organized liberty for all the people. This doctrine has just been declared for all of Europe. I had dedicated it in advance by my charter, and I desire to add to this charter all of the guarantees necessary to insure its benefit.

The unity of the ministry is the strongest that I can offer; I want it to continue so that the sincerity and confidence of my Council can guarantee all interests and calm all disquiet.

We have heard, lately, of the reinstatement of the Tithe and the feudal rights. This fable, made up by a common enemy, does not need to be refuted. We will never see the king of France lower himself to the point of refuting slander and lies. The treason's success has very much indicated its source. If the buyers of national domains have expressed some anxiety, the charter should have been sufficient to put their mind at rest. Did I not, myself, propose to the Chambers and ask them to sell some of these properties? This proof of my sincerity is without retort.

Lately, my subjects of all classes have given me equal proof of their love and loyalty. I want them to know how much it touched me, and it is among the French that I would like to choose those who will be close to me and to my family.

I only want to exclude from my presence those men whose fame is a subject of pain for France and of terror for Europe. In the plot they hatched I see many of my subjects lost and a few guilty.

I promise, I, who never promised in vain (all of Europe knows it), to forgive the French who have strayed, all that has happened since the day when I left Lille, in the midst of many tears, until the day I returned to Cambrai, in the midst of much acclamation.

But the blood of my children was shed by treason, the likes of which the world has no example: this treason called foreigners into the heart of France; each day I learn of some new disaster. Therefore, I must, for the dignity of my throne, for the interest of my peoples, for the peace of Europe, exclude from pardon the instigators and authors of this horrible plot. They will be subject to the revenge of the laws by the two Chambers that I will assemble shortly.

French people, these are the sentiments brought to you by the one that could not be changed by time, misfortune could not tire, and injustice could not destroy.

The King, whose fathers reigned over you for eight centuries, returns to devote the rest of his days to defending and comforting you.

Given at Cambrai, the twenty-eighth day of the month of June of the year of grace 1815, and of our twenty-first year of Reign.

Signed LOUIS
By the King:
The minister Secretary of State of foreign affairs,
Signed Le Prince de Talleyrand[5]

Appendix V

Proclamation to the French people from Prince Schwarzenberg

Frenchmen!

Twenty years of trouble and misfortune have crushed Europe. The insatiable thirst for power and conquest of one single man had depopulated and ruined France, had devastated the most remote countries, and the whole world was astonished to see in an enlightened century the disasters of the middle ages.

The whole of Europe arose; one cry of indignation was sufficient to rally all the nations. The Allied Powers in 1814 might have exercised on France the just vengeance so long provoked by her; but the great monarchs, united in one single and salutary object – the re-establishment of peace in Europe – will not confound the author of so much evil with the people of whom he made use to crush the world.

The allied Sovereigns declared, under the walls of Paris, that they would never make peace or truce with Napoleon Bonaparte. The capital itself arose against the oppressor of Europe; France, by a spontaneous movement, rallied round the principles which will restore and guarantee to herself liberty and peace. The allied armies entered Paris as friends. So many years of misfortune, so much spoliation of the country, the death of so many millions of brave men, fallen on the battlefield, or victims to the scourges inseparable from war, were all forgotten. Bonaparte solemnly abdicated a power which had brought nothing but evil on the world. Europe from that time had no enemy to fight.

Napoleon Bonaparte has re-appeared in France; he finds the whole of Europe under arms against him.

Frenchmen! It is for you to decide for peace or war. Europe wishes to be at peace with France, but she will make war against the usurper of the French throne. France, by admitting Napoleon Bonaparte, has overturned the first foundation on which rested her relations with the other Powers.

Europe does not wish to encroach on the rights of a great nation; but she will not allow France, under a chief recently proscribed by herself, to threaten again the repose of her neighbours.

Europe wishes to enjoy the first benefits of peace. She wishes to disarm, and this she cannot do as long as Napoleon Bonaparte is on the throne of France.

Europe, in short, wishes for peace, and because she wishes it she will never come to an agreement with one whom she regards as a perpetual obstacle to peace.

Already in the plains of Brabant Heaven has confounded his criminal enterprise. The allied armies have passed the frontiers of France. They will protect peaceable citizens; they will fight against the soldiers of Bonaparte; they will treat as friends the provinces which have declared against him, and they will recognize as enemies only those who maintain his cause.

From headquarters at Heidelberg, June 23, 1815. The General-in-Chief of the Austrian Imperial and Allied Armies on the Upper Rhine,

The Marshal de Schwarzenberg[6]

Appendix VI

Letter from Louis XVIII to Talleyrand

Ostend

26 March 1815

My Cousin,

I take advantage of an English courier who will probably arrive at Vienna before the letters written to you by the Count of Blacas, and the Count of Jaucourt. The total defection of the troops left me no choice as to what I must do. They say my life is necessary to France, I therefore deemed that its security might be risked if I waited some hours longer at Lille. Buonaparte has now all the armed force, but all the hearts belong to me; of this I have had ample proof all along my route. The powers cannot therefore be in any doubt this year as to the desires of France: there you have the text. I rely on you to enlarge upon it. I cannot too highly praise Marshal Macdonald and Marshal Mortier. The former behaved just in the same way as he did at Lyons, the latter, although he had received a telegraphic message to arrest me, insured my departure from Lille and my route as far as Menin. Whereupon I pray that God may have you, my cousin, in His safe and holy keeping.

Louis[7]

Appendix VII

Instructions given by the Minister of Marine to Captain Philibert, commanding the *Saale*, and Captain Poncé, commanding the *Méduse*

(Most Confidential)

The two frigates are destined to transport to the United States of America the individual who was recently our Emperor.

He will embark on board the *Saale*, with such persons of his suite as he may point out.

The rest will embark on board the *Méduse*.

The private baggage will be distributed on board the frigates in the manner he may desire.

If either before the departure or during the passage the *Méduse* should appear to be a much better sailor than the *Saale*, he would embark on board the *Méduse*, and Captains Philibert and Poncé would exchange commands.

The greatest secrecy must be observed with respect to the embarkation, which is to be effected under the special superintendence of the maritime prefect, as well as with respect to the individual on board.

Napoleon travels *incognito*, and he will himself make known the title and name which he may be desirous to assume.

Immediately after his embarkation, all communication with the shore must cease.

The commanders of the frigates, the officers and crews will find in the dictates of their hearts sufficient motives for treating the individual on board with all the consideration and respect which is due to his situation, and to the crown which once encircled his brow.

The utmost honours shall be paid to him on board, unless he should decline them. He will dispose of the interior of the frigates for his accommodation in the manner best suited to his wishes, without interfering with their means of defence. His table and personal service shall be attended to according to his own directions.

He will dispose of whatever may contribute to the accommodation of his voyage, without any attention to expense, and the maritime prefect has received instruction to that effect.

The prefect shall send on board as much provisions for himself and his suite as is consistent with the impenetrable secrecy to be observed respecting his abode and his embarkation.

Napoleon being once embarked, the frigates shall put to sea within twenty-four hours at latest, if the wind should permit, and if the enemy's cruisers should not obstruct their departure.

They will remain twenty-four hours in the roads after Napoleon's embarkation, only in case he should desire it, for it is important that they should set sail as soon as possible.

The frigates will proceed with the utmost rapidity to the United States of America, and land Napoleon and his suite at Philadelphia or Boston, or any other port of the United States which they might find it easiest to reach within a shorter delay.

The commanders of the two frigates are forbidden to enter any roads from which they might find it equally difficult and attended with delay to extricate themselves. They are only authorized to do so in case it might become necessary for the safety of the ships.

They will avoid every ship of war they may fall in with. If compelled to fight against superior forces, the frigate on board of which Napoleon shall not be embarked will sacrifice itself to draw off the enemy, and to give the one who conveys him the means of effecting its escape.

I have no occasion to remind the commanders that the Chambers and the Government have placed the person of Napoleon under the safeguard of French loyalty.

Once arrived in the United States, the landing is to be effected with every possible dispatch, and unless the frigates should be prevented by superior forces, they are not to remain there, under any pretence whatever, for a longer time than twenty-four hours, but must immediately return to France.

The laws and regulations respecting the police of ships at sea, and the military subordination of persons embarked as passengers, with reference to the commanders of those vessels, are to be observed in all their rigour.

I recommend to the inward sense which the captains entertain of their duties, and to their delicacy of feeling, every object that might not have been foreseen by these instructions.

I have nothing to add to what I have above stated, that the person of Napoleon is placed under the safeguard of the loyalty of the French people, and this deposit is specially confided in the present circumstance to the captains of the *Saale* and of the *Méduse*, as well as to the officers and crews of both ships.

Such are the orders which the Commission of Government has directed me to transmit to Captains Philibert and Poncé.

The Duke Decrès[8]

Appendix VIII

Convention agreed to by the French and Allied military commanders around Paris, 3 July 1815

Article I

There shall be a suspension of hostilities between the allied armies commanded by his highness Prince Blücher, his Excellency the Duke of Wellington and the French army under the walls of Paris.

Article II

Tomorrow the French army shall commence its march, to retire behind the Loire. The total evacuation of Paris shall be effected in three days, and its movement of retiring behind the Loire shall be finished in eight days.

Article III

The French army shall take with it its stores, field artillery, military convoys, horses, and property of the regiments, without any exception. This shall equally apply to what belongs to [*le personnel des*] the depots, and the different branches of administration belonging to the army.

Article IV

The sick and wounded, as well as the medical officers, whom it may be necessary to leave with them, are under the particular protection of MM. the commissaries in chief of the English and Prussian armies.

Article V

The military and non-military persons mentioned in the preceding article may rejoin the corps to which they belong as soon as they are recovered.

Article VI

The women and children of all persons belonging to the French army shall be at liberty to remain in Paris.

These women shall meet with no obstruction to their quitting Paris to rejoin the army or to taking with them their own property or that of their husbands.

Article VII

The officers of the line employed with the federates, or with the sharpshooters of the national guard, may either rejoin the army or return to their place of residence, or to the place where they were born.

Article VIII

Tomorrow, July the 4th, at noon, St. Denis, St. Ouen, Clichy and Neuilly shall be delivered up; the next day, July the 5th, at the same hour, Montmartre shall be delivered; and on the 3rd day, July 6, all the barriers shall be delivered.

Article IX

The interior duty of Paris shall continue to be performed by the National Guard, and by the corps of municipal gendarmerie.

Article X

The commanders in chief of the English and Prussian armies *engage to respect, and to make those under them respect, the present authorities, as long as they subsist.*

Article XI

Public property, except what relates to war, whether it belongs to the government or depends on the municipal authority, *shall be respected*, and the allied powers will not interfere in any manner in its management, or in its conduct.

Article XII

The persons and property of individuals shall be equally respected: the inhabitants, and all persons in general, who happen to be in the capital, shall continue to enjoy their rights and liberties, *without being molested, or any inquiry being made into the functions they occupy or may have occupied, their conduct, or their political opinions.*

Article XIII

The foreign troops shall oppose no obstacle to the supply of the capital with provision; and on the contrary shall protect the arrival and free circulations of articles intended for it.

Article XIV

The present convention shall be observed, and serve as a rule for the mutual conduct of the parties, until a peace is concluded.

In case of a rupture, it shall be announced in the usual forms at least ten days beforehand.

Article XV

If any difficulties arise respecting the execution of some of the articles of the present convention, *the interpretation shall be in favour of the French army*, and the city of Paris.

Article XVI

The present convention is declared common to all the allied armies, saving the ratification of the powers to which those armies belong.

Article XVII

The ratifications shall be exchanged tomorrow, at six o'clock in the morning, at the bridge of Neuilly.

Article XVIII

Commissioners shall be named by the respective parties to superintend the execution of the present convention.

Done and signed at St. Cloud, in triplicate, by the commissioners under named, the day and year abovementioned,

[Signed] Baron Bignon
Count Guilleminot
Count de Bondy
Barron de Muffling
F. B. Hervey, Colonel

Approved and ratified,
[Signed] Blücher
Wellington
Marshal Prince Eckmühl[9]

Appendix IX

Proclamation from the Committee of Government to the French

5 July 1815

Frenchmen,

Under the difficult circumstances in which the reins of government were entrusted to us, it was not in our power to master the course of events and repel every danger: but it was our duty to protect the interests of the people, and of the army, equally compromised in the cause of a prince abandoned by fortune and by the national will.

It was our duty *to preserve* to our country the precious remains of those brave legions whose courage is superior to misfortune, and who have been the victims of a devotion, which their country now claims.

It was our duty to save the capital from the horrors of a siege, or the chances of a battle; to maintain the public tranquility amid the tumults and agitations of war, *to support the hopes of the friends of liberty* amid the fears and anxieties of a suspicious foresight. It was above all our duty to stop the useless effusion of blood. We had to choose *between a secure national existence* or run the risk of exposing our country and its citizens to a general convulsion that would leave behind it neither hope nor a future.

None of these means of defence that time and our resources permitted, nothing that the service of the camps or of the city required, have we neglected.

While the pacification of the West was concluding, plenipotentiaries went to meet the allied powers, and all the papers relative to this negotiation have been laid before our representatives.

The fate of the capital is regulated by a convention: its inhabitants, whose firmness, courage and perseverance are above all praise, will retain the guarding of it. *The declarations of the sovereigns of Europe must inspire too great confidence, their promises have been too solemn, for us to entertain any fears of our liberties, and of our dearest interests being sacrificed to victory.*

At length we shall receive guarantees that will prevent the alternate and transient triumphs of the factions by which we have been agitated these five and twenty years; that will terminate our revolutions and *melt down under one common protection* all the parties to which they have given rise, and all those against which they have contended.

Those guarantees, which have hitherto existed only in our principles and in our courage, *we shall find* in our laws, in our constitution, in our representative system.

For whatever may be the intelligence, the virtues, the personal qualities of a monarch, these can never suffice to render the people secure against the oppressions of power, the prejudices of pride, the injustice of courts and the ambition of courtiers.

Frenchmen, peace is necessary to your commerce, to your arts, to the improvement of your morals, to the development of the resources remaining to you. Be united, *and you are at the end of your calamities*. The repose of Europe is inseparable from yours. Europe is interested in your tranquility and in your happiness.

Given at Paris, July the 5th, 1815

[Signed] The president of the Committee, the Duke of Otranto[10]

Appendix X

General Lallemand's account of Napoleon's departure

Napoléon Refuses to Go To America
Excerpt of the journal of General Charles-Frédéric-Antoine Lallemand, July–August 1856

Having left Paris on the 30th of June, around 8 o'clock at night, with the intention of rejoining the Emperor, I reached him at Niort in the middle of the night on the 2nd of July. Around three o'clock in the morning, on the 3rd, he arrived at Rochefort where I arrived two hours later.

He had crossed France, followed by several cars, almost always going without escort, and refusing the one offered to him at Niort. He was told that the Vendée region did not offer as much security, he only accepted a few men and he was not troubled on the way. Everywhere he was given proof of devotion and respect. From everywhere you could hear people expressing regrets and sending him wishes: he received the same welcome at Rochefort, on board the frigates and at the Île d'Aix. He was invited to return to command the army; he was asked to reunite the troops which were in Bordeaux, Rochefort, La Rochelle and in all of the south of France; he would have been joined by many partisans from all departments. But the favorable time for France would have been lost. Napoléon would have been accused of instigating civil war without a favorable end for the public. He judged this role to be unworthy of him and rejected these propositions.

During these days of misfortune the Emperor received many tokens of devotion. A crowd of sailors distinguished themselves by the most eulogizing zeal. Preparations were made for the departure: several plans offered favorable chances. It was especially in the plans that were being made at the mouth of the Gironde, that you could hope for an assured success.

Napoléon left Rochefort on 8 July to reach and board the frigate *La Saale* in the harbor of the Île d'Aix. From there, it would be easier for him to make a decision, according to the circumstances, and seize the most favorable moment to put it into motion as soon as the last decisions had been taken. There, several well experienced sailors were still talking of the project of embarkation at the mouth of the Gironde and went about demonstrating that this plan was, quite evidently, the one they should follow.

But several of the officers who accompanied the Emperor, particularly those who had long ago gained his confidence and therefore had easier access and more influence upon him, were not in favor of this plan, saw only obstacles in the plans that were proposed and managed to slow down the decision making, causing a deadly delay in decisions which, at the time, required rapidity. The coolness with which they received the plans, the irresolution they caused incessantly was principally derived from a desire that they had since before leaving Paris, to see the Emperor choose to go to England.

One is overwhelmed by disbelief and pain at the same time, to see men whose judgment should have been clear from much experience, men who give the Emperor all kinds of proof of their sincere devotion, and now act in the same way as the enemies who have plotted his demise, – these men who would shed their blood for him, with the same pride, who have arduously wished for the honor to share his misfortune, who would be ashamed at trying to escape the situation are now incapable of voluntarily separating themselves from him.

This, however, is the secret of the destiny imposed on the Emperor; these are the causes that rapidly sent him in a tomb while still alive. He could have kept his freedom and reached a hospitable land.

Moreover, unfortunately as there was no high political interest any longer and nothing more to be done for glory, the Emperor became much too indifferent as to his personal consideration and left everything up to the men who were with him to take care of the situation. He could not have left this in more loyal hands, but guided by less clear-sightedness.

My only consolation, if there could be one applied to this misfortune, would be that I did not share the common error.

Struck with wonder by the realities demonstrated to me by the sailors with whom I had spoken regarding the best way to insure the safe departure of the Emperor, I alone insisted, but I strongly insisted on the plan to have the Emperor leave by the mouth of the Gironde, and on the necessity for taking care of it urgently. I tried everything to advance this proposition but it was in vain. The only answers I received were objections as to the execution of the plan, and doubts on the certainty of the means by which it could be accomplished. The only thing that I was able to convey was that we should not neglect lightly a project that might save the Emperor. All that I was able to obtain was to go by myself and check out the realities in the area itself.

I traveled there by way of Royan and it became easy to convince myself that the project was solid. I made sure it would be easy to pass through if leaving from the designated point. The wisest dispositions had been taken; everything had been ready for several days. The ships designated for the Emperor had gone out and several had made their trip without being visited by the English even though they had not really tried to bypass them or taken any of the precautions or measures that would have been taken to insure the safety of the Emperor, had he chosen to take this option.

Meanwhile, General Savary and M. de Las Cases had been sent as parliamentarians, from the 10th to the 11th, to the English cruising fleet comprised of the vessel *Bellerophon* and the corvette *Myrmidon*. They carried with them a letter from General Bertrand for the station commander. Captain Maitland, commander of the *Bellerophon*, received them. After having read the letter, in response to the question regarding whether or not he had received the requested passports for the Emperor, he replied that he had been advised of nothing in regards to passports and therefore did not have a solution for the request that was the object of the message; he added that he would surely know more about it because a corvette that was approaching had signaled that it was coming from England and had messages for him. He invited General Savary and M. de Las Cases to have lunch saying that during this time they would maneuver to be able to communicate quicker with the corvette. Captain Maitland was not aware of the Waterloo battle and knew nothing of the Emperor's abdication, or his arrival at Rochefort. Soon, the corvette's captain entered. It was the corvette *Fallmouth* that was arriving from England, had come thru the Quiberon bay, and had given the messages to Admiral Hotham. After he had read the letters, Captain Maitland said to General Savary and M. de Las Cases, 'There is still nothing relative to the message you have brought. I also see that at the time the corvette left England, no one knew about what you have just told me.'

The two English captains began conversing in their own language, the one from the corvette said that he had learned, on board from Admiral Hotham, that Napoléon had just arrived in Nantes and was causing trouble. 'I see that they don't know the truth there any better than anywhere else,' said Captain Maitland, laughing, 'the Emperor is at Rochefort; these men are officers who came here on his behalf.'

After we were done with lunch, the conference started up again. Captain Maitland repeated that he could not satisfy the request having to do with the passports, that he would immediately address his report and the letter from General Bertrand to his admiral who was in the bay of Quiberon, that the admiral would surely give him a response right away, and that we could have his answer the next day or the day after that, and that without a doubt the admiral would find it all important enough to come out himself. Then, taking the initiative on a question that had not yet been discussed, M. Maitland said 'But why doesn't the Emperor come to England?'

'We do not have any order permitting us to discuss this question, but we assume that he worries about the climate.'

'There are counties in England where the weather is as mild as it is in France.'

'We think as well that having always been at war with England, he might fear meeting with prejudices and resentment.'

'He is mistaken; it would indeed be a way of extinguishing all resentment. The Emperor, coming of his own accord to England would be sheltered from all the efforts of his enemies, the best possible position in which he might find himself.'

MM. Savary and de Las Cases repeated that this proposition was not part of their mission; they would inform the Emperor and asked if the Emperor could depend on the English vessel to take him to England if he decided to accept this proposition. M. Maitland answered that he did not have any orders in this regard, but that if the Emperor declared his intention they would certainly accept. He gave a written answer to General Bertrand's letter and said that his vessel would be anchored in the Basques harbor the next day, then we left.

The Emperor received this report on the 11th, on board the frigate *La Saale*, and went ashore the next day at the Île d'Aix. It was in this circumstance that I arrived quickly in the Gironde. It soon became apparent that the project of going to England was prevailing in the mind of most of the people around the Emperor; they spoke only of Captain Maitland's proposition and presented it in the most favorable way, as thoughtless and frivolous as it was, they were happy to give it a lot of weight, attaching to it the most seductive illusions.

However, the Emperor did not find all these explanations sufficient to bring him to the decision they were trying to help him make. He decided that, while waiting for the passports he had requested or a positive response from the admiral commanding the station, he would get prepared to use the means still available to take him to the United States. But time was passing and we had lost some most precious days. The means available for salvation were disappearing constantly. Far from making the situation better for the Emperor with the message taken to the English vessel, we had made it more difficult by letting them know of his presence, which they had not been aware of, and causing them to more actively observe what was happening.

We decided to go out to sea as soon as the decision would be definitively taken: for the Emperor, we adopted the plan of his departure on a small Danish ship. Some small French ships were to carry the officers who would accompany him. Some had already set sail and were out of the channels, when, in the evening of the 12th, as the *Bellerophon* was anchored in the Basques harbor we thought we could see a signal announcing the desire to communicate. It was late so we waited until the next morning to send someone there.

On the 14th of July, at daybreak, I was sent to the *Bellerophon* with M. de Las Cases. We asked Captain Maitland if he had received the passports for the Emperor or a response to the letter we had given to him a few days earlier. Captain Maitland answered that he had not received any passports, he was waiting for the admiral's response at any moment, and that contrary winds had slowed him down.

'But,' he added, 'I have received some dispatches from my government, and I am authorized to make the offer to the Emperor to be received on board so that he can be taken to England, if he so desires, along with all the people who accompany him.'

'Captain, you are authorized by your government to make this proposition?'

'Yes I have the authorization of my government.'

'Although the Emperor has not positively made a decision, if the dispositions of the English government have ceased to be hostile towards him, we think it is possible that he may decide to accept the offer that is made to him. We are very aware of the high esteem he has for the English nation, and believe that he may not be averse to going to England, in the hope that he might find there the rest that he would like to enjoy, with the intention of finding a way to continue his travels to America if his time in England became contrary to his well being. But if it is permissible to believe that there could be abuse of the advantages obtained from him, it is a certainty that he would follow thru with the chances he still has in his favor, rather than let himself be subject to procedure unworthy of him.'

'He must not worry about that; it is most certainly not to expose him to mistreatment that we proposed that he come to England if he desires to come. I have not been told what kind of existence he will lead. My instructions only authorize me to accept him on board to take him to England if he so desires. That is saying enough. There is no doubt that he will receive only honorable treatment. The English nation enjoys, more than any other, generosity of sentiments and liberty of opinions.'

'If the Emperor accepts your proposition, if he freely comes to England, it is obvious that he must continue to have his liberty.'

'I have already told you that I am not aware of what his existence might be in England, but it is certain that coming of his own accord he should find himself in a respectable position. He must be aware of how his brother Lucien has been treated. It is probable that someone will be placed close to him, just as there has been an English colonel placed near his brother; but it will be as much for his own tranquility as for any other reason. We could not do otherwise. The government is not a referee and the laws and opinions are quite liberal.'

During this conference, lunch had been served and we were seating at the table when Captain Sartorius, from the corvette *Slaney*, came in immediately after lunch. Captain Maitland went into the parlor with General Lallemand, M. de Las Cases and Captain Sartorius who was present during the last part of the discussion. We restarted the conference pertaining to the Emperor but in a more overall nature. Overall we only did a summary of what had already been said. What did get particularly repeated was the comment made by Captain Maitland relative to the Emperor's brother. 'It is probable that someone will be placed close to him, just as there has been an English colonel placed near his brother; but it will be as much for his own tranquility as for any other reason. He can expect, he added, to receive the same courtesy and more satisfying procedures.' Captain Maitland again seized this occasion to speak in strong terms of the generosity of the sentiment, the liberty of the laws and opinions in England, and of the well-earned confidence in the British flag.

After having discussed that which concerned the Emperor, I informed Captain Maitland that since I had been actively engaged in the latest events that had taken place in France, I desired the assurance that neither I nor any of those who might find themselves in the same circumstance, could be pursued because of the cause we had defended.

'You have nothing to fear,' answered Captain Maitland, 'all of this is foreign to the English government. You are coming to England of your own accord; no authority can pursue you there.'

'I ignore,' I observed, 'what the Emperor will decide, but if he comes to England and if I accompany him, I do not want to be exposed to persecutions just because I am a particular case that had not been provided for, and that I should have known. I never had any intention of going to England; nothing is forcing me to go, and I declare to you that I will not come there, not only if there is the slightest chance that I might be sent back to France, but also if there was the slightest risk of seeing my liberty taken from me, or to be pursued in any fashion.'

'That is impossible,' said Captain Maitland warmly. 'In England the government is not despotic, it must conform to the laws and the opinion. You are under the protection of English laws as soon as you are under the British flag.'

At the time of our departure, Captain Maitland told us that if the Emperor decided to come on board his vessel to go to England, he wanted to be aware of it before his arrival and receive as soon as possible the list of persons who would accompany the Emperor, so that the necessary preparations could be made in order to welcome each person with the least possible problems.

We came back in the morning to give an account of our mission.

The Emperor having received the report concerning our conference with Captain Maitland, and being a long way from suspecting any kind of treachery, decided rather easily to accept the proposition that had been offered to him, especially in view of the fact that most of the people around him had most likely prepared him to choose this plan.

However, because he did not want to entirely dispose of the destiny of the men who had remained loyal to him without their agreement, he called upon the officers who were there. The others had already embarked and had passed the pertuis (strait), awaiting his orders to continue on.

The officers who gathered at the Emperor's place were Generals Bertrand, Savary, Lallemand, Montholon, and Gourgaud and Mr. De Las Cases. After having informed them of the propositions given by Captain Maitland as well as all that had taken place during the conference with him, the Emperor asked each of these officers to state their opinion.

Five of these officers declared without hesitation that they thought it was suitable to accept this proposition as it offered the characteristic of loyalty. Alone, I maintained an opposite opinion and alleged that he should not let himself be fooled by the offers we had received, that there was no liberty for the Emperor except on the soil of the United States, that the Emperor could still hope to reach it and retain his independence, that he still had some chances in his favor and that we should hurry to take advantage of them, and further, that if these chances were lost, we at least would have attempted everything for the well-being of the Emperor, that in any case he could not have a more unfortunate fate than to go on an English vessel where he would be dependent on a ministry in which it was imprudent to place any confidence.

This opinion was cause for amazement. 'You reported yourself,' said the Emperor, 'the propositions and the words of Captain Maitland. You are the only one here who had the occasion to know of this earlier, and you spoke of him as being an honorable man. Have you doubts, then, of his truthfulness in this circumstance?'

'No, Sire, I do not doubt that; when I met Captain Maitland, at the time of the war in Egypt, I saw in him the honest character of a military man and a sailor. I have confidence in him, but I have none in the English ministry. We have never seen it being generous when it could oppress with impunity. Captain Maitland, in spite of himself, will be made the instrument for treachery, and will be disavowed if it becomes necessary.'

Everyone fought this opinion, they all claimed it could not be proven and that the propositions made by Captain Maitland offered the character of loyalty and that they were equally honorable for the Emperor and for the English government. 'This motive, however right it may seem, is not the determining factor for me,' I said, 'the English government has too often and strongly declared its enmity against the Emperor for anyone to believe that it will not be its only principle. An implacable hate, this is the principle on which we must judge its behavior. If, when the parliament is assembled, the Emperor happened to be in the middle of England and the truth was known, of course, we could believe that magnanimity could direct them; but when we are placed on a war vessel how will the ministry react? Do we know the facts? I repeat, nothing can bring me to have any faith in the English government.'

Then the subject went back to the solicitations the Emperor had received asking him to come back and command the troops; he pushed aside, without hesitation, this project and any idea of civil war. 'It would be to combat only for personal interests,' he shouted, 'I do not want to cause a cannon to fire.'

I have shortened this conference but I have given its account honestly. I remained alone in my judgment and the Emperor stopped all discussions, saying: 'If it was a question of giving liberty to a nation, I could attempt a return to the Island of Elba. I look only for some rest, it is offered to me in England. I accept it. I do not know the Prince Regent, but I must have confidence in his character. I will write to him tomorrow; at daybreak, we will go and board the English vessel.'

A few hours after this conference I went to the Emperor's quarters and asked permission to submit a few new observations to him. Three or four of the above named officers were present.

'Sire, as we left Paris, I was thinking that it could be useful to have near you a few men desirous to assure the respect towards you that you deserve, in the different situations you may encounter. The decision you have taken to go to England does not give me the opportunity to be of service to you if I accompany you. I ask that you permit me to go in a direction that may give me the opportunity to be of bigger service to you.'

'You want to leave me?'

'I think of leaving you only momentarily, Sire, and with the intention of being more useful to you.'

'Explain yourself; I cannot guess what you mean.'

'I persist in the opinion that I have already given. My distrust continues to grow as I consider how the English ministry has always conducted itself. I am convinced that Your Majesty's trust will be betrayed if the truth is not told. I believe it is of the utmost importance that one of the men with you, especially one of those who spoke with Captain Maitland, be able to keep all his liberty. The means that were at the disposition of Your Majesty to go to America, I can use them to go to England. I will arrive totally unknown, and if the government does not act with loyalty, I will publish what happened on board the *Bellerophon*. The opinion may not permit me to violate the hospitality that has been offered to you. If Your Majesty approves, I believe that I can be of real help if I go to England alone.'

'No,' said the Emperor, 'there cannot be a trap; your mistrust is not well founded. Come to England with me, you will enjoy the rest we all deserve.'

'I cannot share the confidence Your Majesty shows and let myself believe in the hopes that you have the goodness to give me.'

'Are you worried that you could be delivered to the French government? You cannot think that. The assurances given to you by Captain Maitland should make you tranquil.'

'In spite of Captain Maitland's assurances, I believe it is very possible that I could be transferred to the French government. That seems even very probable if they can surround us with so much mystery as to do it with impunity. But I am above fear. The question Your Majesty just posed to me does not permit me any reflection. If Your Majesty thinks that I may be useful, I am ready to accompany you.'

'Yes, you will be useful to me,' said the Emperor with goodness, 'I would be sad to see you go away.'

'I have no more thinking to do, I told Your Majesty, I will come.'

In relating this short version of the details, I have no other intention except to tell what happened, to show the principal lines that drew the Emperor's position, characterize his trust and the opinion that directed him.

On the same day, 14 July, General Gourgaud and M. de Las Cases were sent to the *Bellerophon*. M. de Las Cases was in charge of letting Captain Maitland know that, as had been discussed, the Emperor would come aboard the next day, and to give him the list of the persons that would accompany him.

General Gourgaud carried the letter of the Emperor expressing his wish that this general officer be sent to England immediately in order that he be able to go to London to present the letter to the Prince Regent. He was told that he could leave right away and that there was no objection to his going directly to London to finish his mission. He departed, in fact, on the corvette *Slaney*, commanded as we have already mentioned, by Captain Sartorius.

Also the same day, M. de Las Cases wrote from the *Bellerophon* to tell the Emperor that General Gourgaud had left, and that preparations were made to welcome him and that Captain Maitland continued to confirm everything he had said during the conference that had taken place the very same morning.

At daybreak the next day, 15 July, the Emperor boarded a French war ship flying the tricolor flag and a parliamentary flag, to go to the *Bellerophon*. The departure of the French ship had been delayed because the tide had left it outside the harbor of the Île d'Aix, and the wind had become contrary. Captain Maitland sent his dinghy to the Emperor and he accepted it.

The moment he left the ship was a time of most fiery regrets.

You could see the emotion on all the faces, painful expressions on the lips of people and, why would I not say it, tears were flowing from everyone's eyes when we saw the Emperor getting in the English dinghy.

These tears did not come from shameful weakness; they were the tears of courage quivering at having become so helpless. They find the heart of a warrior from where they are torn by the misfortune of an illustrious chief that it can no longer defend or cover with its blood.

The dinghy left and the thousands of repeated cries of *Vive l'Empereur*, following him all the way to the *Bellerophon*, are the last good-byes that he received; these adieus, these regrets, these acclamations that were not dictated by adulation, but are inspired by devotion, as Napoléon sheds all of his power, these are the ones that will have the most impact in his heart.

Painful transition! The Emperor is now on an English vessel. There, he will also find nothing but consideration and signs of respect.

Eight or ten officers and other persons of the Emperor's following did not arrive on the *Bellerophon* until late in the day. They had embarked on two small ships that had been prepared to sail to America before the Emperor had decided to accept the proposition of the English. When they were called up, after his decision, they were out of the *Pertuis* and out of sight from the cruisers.

Admiral Hotham arrived that same day, the 15th. He was bringing the vessel *Superb*, and came to anchor next to the *Bellerophon*. The admiral soon came to visit the Emperor and invited him to go and see his vessel the next day. That invitation was accepted. On board the *Superb*, the Emperor also received many tokens of respect. The admiral offered his vessel to take him to England. The Emperor did not take advantage of this offer, he would not have wanted to be disagreeable toward Captain Maitland and not recognize his respect and consideration. Admiral Hotham and Captain Maitland were sincere, without a doubt, but their procedures probably hid the irons prepared by the ministers.

The *Bellerophon* set sail on the 16th from the Basques harbor, immediately after the Emperor returned from the vessel *Superb*, and left for England with the corvette *Myrmidon*.

During the trip, Captain Maitland's comments continued to be the same as they had been during the conference of the 14th, still inspiring total confidence. But on July 24, when they arrived at Torbay, the comments began to contradict the facts. The strict measures taken to prevent all communications were difficult to explain. It became even more difficult to justify what we heard about the mission of General Gourgaud.

On the 14th, before the Emperor had come on board the *Bellerophon*, it had been necessary to give him some confidence; it had been promised that General Gourgaud would be put on land when he arrived in England and would go to London immediately. When he arrived, he was not permitted to disembark. The captain of the *Slaney* jumps in his dinghy right away, and without any explanation, hurries to get on land and leaves for London. General Gourgaud is held on board the *Slaney* with the Emperor's letter. This left no more doubts, it was evident that we were unworthily misled. They wanted the Emperor to be a prisoner, so they had to keep the letter from being taken by General Gourgaud to the Prince Regent, so that this letter as well as the audience given to General Gourgaud should not irrevocably establish Napoléon's sacred rights to the hospitality of the English people.

However, at the news of his arrival, the local people came running and the local boats surrounded the *Bellerophon* during the two days we spent at Torbay.

On the 26th, we went to Plymouth. There, the measures taken to prevent all communications became stricter each day. There also, as it had been at Torbay, the eagerness of the people became more remarkable each day.

Soon, the public newspapers and other reports were in agreement, saying that the Emperor was to be transferred to St Helena.

'That is impossible,' was his response. 'I was not brought here by force of arms; I received an offer to come to England; I came to place myself under the protection of English laws; I asked for the sacred right to hospitality and the Prince Regent, who exercises sovereignty over the English people, cannot refuse me.'

The news, however, continued to spread and with more credibility each day. It did not take long for people on the *Bellerophon* and other war ships, where several following officers were placed, to realize that at the same time as the Emperor would leave for St Helena, General Savary and I would be taken back to France.

The positive answers given to us in this regard by English officers having confirmed the suspicions that were gaining more consistency, we decided to write to Lord Melritte and Lord Bathurst. We did not expect results from these letters; we asked to be able to communicate with a lawyer; they refused. In spite of the strict supervision conducted around us, other letters were able to reach some English citizens whom we made aware of our situation, of the assurances we had been given by Captain Maitland, of our rights under the English nation and of our complaints addressed to the ministers.

After a few days of uncertainty, Lord Keith and Sir Henry Bunbury came to tell the Emperor that a decision by the English government was sending him to St Helena. He voiced his opposition coming only from the strength of his soul, and protested with as much power as calm and dignity against this violation of his trust. Lord Keith and Sir Henry Bunbury answered that their order was only to inform him of the government's decision and that they would give it his speech.

The note that was given to the Emperor mentioned that three of the officers who accompanied him could follow him to St Helena. One article made an exception which specifically and expressly named General Savary and me from the number of those who were permitted to go. Immediately after the departure of Lord Keith and Sir Henry Bunbury, the Emperor said to me: 'You are mentioned in the note that is being translated; you will be able to read it shortly.' M. de Las Cases was translating. The Emperor walked about and spoke calmly. He did not have the strength to speak of the frame-up that was menacing us. When the note was translated, he read it with great attention then handed it to me with a sign of pain, unable to utter a word.

'I can see, Sire, what this exception means,' I said to him, after having read it; 'I did all I had to do, I have nothing to be sorry for; I have regrets only for my country and for Your Majesty who is more mistreated than I.' Hoping to give me the confidence he was not feeling himself, he told me that this decision could not be carried out, that it was too odious and too dishonorable.

We finally set sail to go and meet up with the *Northumberland* and the Emperor was transferred to this vessel on the 6th of August. I went on board the vessel with him where I received his good-byes, after having spoken with him in the room that had been designated for him. I left him only when the vessel started to go and I had to leave.

The Emperor was showing much sensitivity regarding the situation in which he was leaving General Savary and me. 'I am anxious,' he said, 'to learn that the fears you have will not be realized. I cannot rest until I am certain that your days are secure. It is too painful for me to see them compromised, but I still hope. No matter how disloyal the conduct of the English government is towards me, I cannot believe that it indulges in such revolting barbaric treatment towards General Savary and you.'

The impression that I retain of this last conversation is still in its entirety in my soul; it will never be erased from it.

The Emperor was calm, I have never seen him more superior to destiny, greater and more worthy of himself. He seemed to totally forget about himself and think only of his companions of misfortune, his family, and France. He spoke of his mother and his sadness. His heart was agitated at the thought of his son and of the Empress. He spoke of them with tenderness. The expression of compassion had preserved all of the strength of his soul. His thoughts were raised enthusiastically toward France. 'The schemers lost her; corrupt men made a mockery of her glory and independence; but I do not complain about the nation, she never ceased to be valiant and magnanimous.'[11]

Appendix XI

Account by M. Jourdan de la Passardière, commanding the sailing ship
L'Épervier

(Olivier Jourdan de la Passardière, born in Granville in 1783, oldest brother of François Jourdan de la Passardière, who had already made himself known by his success in the naval battle at Arromanches in 1811 – he got his start in the marine as a ship-boy at the age of 12. Midshipman in 1799, then ensign of vessel on board the *Formidable* on which he witnessed the battle of Trafalgar, he was taken by the English on November 4th and remained their prisoner for four years. Having escaped, he joined the French navy, assisted in the campaigns of Java and of the Spanish coasts, and was released from duty after the events of Rochefort in 1815, which is the reason it took until 1827 before he was nominated captain of frigate. He was in command of *Le Superb* during the Alger expedition, in 1830, and retired as vessel captain at Cherbourg, where he died in 1862.)

The services that I had rendered in accomplishing the special missions with which I had been entrusted and my recent successes against the English off the coast of Spain, had given me the hope to be named captain of a frigate during the year 1815.

While awaiting a promotion, I took command of the sailing ship *L'Épervier*, which was in armament at Bayonne (11 January 1815). I was still in this port when the Emperor returned to France.

We resumed flying the tricolor flag.

The English were starting to block our ports. When I pulled up sail to go to Rochefort, the Commissary General wrote to suggest I should sail under a white flag in order to be less likely to be taken by the English. I responded that I would have no honor if I flew any other flag than that of my nation, and that I would not fly any other during my trip unless he gave me formal and precise orders to do so. I entered Rochefort without being harassed.

At the start of July, *L'Épervier* was anchored in the harbor of the Bris, waiting for a favorable moment to go and enter the river of Bordeaux. *L'Épervier* was to replace *La Bayadère* that was stationed there under the orders of Commandant Baudin.

(Ch. Baudin, son of the Conventional of the same name, had resigned his post in 1815, rejoined the service in 1830 and became admiral in 1854.)

In the evening of 3 July the Emperor arrived at Rochefort.

On 4 July, one of his aides-de-camp, General Lallemand, came aboard and handed me an urgent order from the maritime prefect M. Bonnefoux, who instructed me to go back to the anchorage of the Île d'Aix. It was thru this aide-de-camp that I learned of the arrival of the Emperor.

The calm water and the winds kept me from following the order of the prefect before 6 July.

Upon my arrival on 6 July, Commandant Philibert, who was in command of the frigate *La Saale* (*L'Amphitrite*) and the anchorage, gave me the order to anchor at the port of the Basques and to quickly go and receive the instructions of the maritime prefect M. Bonnefoux.

M. Bonnefoux confirmed to me the presence of the Emperor and instructed me only not to leave my ship.

At twelve midnight on 8 July, a policeman brought me an order from the prefect, instructing me to go to the harbor at l'Île d'Aix. That same day, the embarkations of the sailing ship had been sent to Fouras to collect the baggage of the people traveling with the Emperor and take them on board *La Saale*.

On the 11th of July, at midnight, Commandant Philibert sent a dinghy to pick me up and gave me the official order to be ready to sail and fight at about five o'clock in the morning. I made my preparations accordingly.

At 3 o'clock in the morning, he sent for me again and ordered me to place the firearms of the ship in the hold and to send all the small arms and powders onboard his frigate.

On July 12, the Emperor came to the Île d'Aix with his following.

M. Besson, the vessel ensign, married to the daughter of a ship-owner of Altona, had proposed to the Emperor that he should leave France using a smack owned by his father-in-law.

The smack had come to Rochefort to unload, and was anchored at this moment at St-Martin (Île de Rhé). The Emperor would have been taken to board this ship using two tugboats from La Rochelle, attended by 4 navy officers.

(One of these officers, M. Doret, vessel ensign, and second of Commandant Baudin, was suspended. Later, he became vessel captain, governor of the Réunion, and a senator under the Second Empire.)

M. Besson had come to the Île d'Aix on 12 July to direct the embarkation; either there was a miscommunication, or the commandant of the Île d'Aix had some secret instructions, but when the embarkations that had stayed at large from the island approached the coast during the night of the 12th, the sentries fired several shots and started the alarm, pretending that some English barges were trying to bring some people on land. The garrison took to arms, which probably stopped the execution of the plan.

On the same day, 12 July, I received the order to go and anchor away from the Île d'Aix, accompanied by the schooner *La Sophie*, which was a ship servicing the port.

During the night, the gunshots that had been fired at the Île d'Aix caused several armed embarkations of the English division that were anchored at the dock of the Basques to start moving; these embarkations approached us. The captain of *La Sophie*, afraid of being taken by the English, cut the cables and returned to the harbor of the isle.

On the 13th of July, I gave an account of what had happened to Commandant Philibert. He ordered me to return and dock.

On the night of 14 July, he informed me that my ship was intended to sail in a parliamentary function to the English station; attached to his letter dated the 12th, was an instruction and a decree from the provisional government concerning the transportation of the Emperor.

At midnight, he instructed me to prepare for sailing, and told me that the Emperor was going to arrive on board the ship at two o'clock in the morning, in order to be taken for transport on the English cruiser.

Monsieur Jourdan, vessel lieutenant in command of the ship *L'Épervier*.

Saale (harbor at the Île d'Aix), 14 July 1815.

Monsieur le commandant, in accordance with the request that I have transmitted to you from Lieutenant General Beker, and per the orders and instructions of His Excellency the Minister of the Navy, and the Maritime Prefect, we ask that you get ready to welcome on board at 2 o'clock in the morning, the Emperor Napoleon 1st, with his entourage, and transport them on board the English cruiser at the harbor of the Basques; it is not necessary, Commandant, to remind you of the respect that should be shown to this illustrious person.

Sincerely,

Vessel captain, commandant of the harbor division of the Île d'Aix.

H. PHILIBERT

At the indicated time on 15 July, His Majesty arrived aboard my ship, accompanied by generals Bertrand, Savary, de Montholon and Lallemand, M. de Las Cases, ladies de Montholon and Bertrand, as well as General Beker.

The Emperor was welcomed with extraordinary enthusiasm and indescribable emotion on board *L'Épervier*. My crew was made up of young sailors, some of whom had been part of the contingent that we had sent to Paris for the Champ de Mai, and I could rely on them.

As for General Beker, who had been especially charged with accompanying the Emperor all the way to the English cruiser and to keep me under his orders, he left my ship before the casting off at the Île d'Aix. I then found myself alone in charge of this delicate mission.

I took the orders of the Emperor who inspected my crew, then set sail.

M. Borgnis-Desbordes, lieutenant of vessel, parent of Commandant Philibert and on board his frigate, had been sent on board the ship; this officer came to tell me in secret, during the cast off, to be very careful because the Emperor could very well be arrested on board my ship. I answered him that His Majesty would never be arrested while on board *L'Épervier*, at least not as long as I was alive to prevent it.

However, I heeded his advice: I quickly cast off, leaving one of my anchors. We headed toward the harbor of the Basques: the winds were to the N.W., almost calm.

While on the way, the Emperor had come up to where I was; aware that I had been a prisoner in England for four years, he questioned me as to the character of the English, and asked me if I had an opinion on the decision he had taken to go to England.

(Jourdan was in a much better position to inform the Emperor regarding the English, since not only himself but also his two uncles, MM. de Basprey and de Grancourt, had been prisoners on the pontoons.)

I answered His Majesty that his question put me in an embarrassing position but that, since he asked me to respond to him truthfully, my thought was that it would have been better to go to the United States.

His Majesty responded that people thought this passage was impossible, according to some competent people, due to the presence of English cruisers.

I agreed that, in fact, there were risks and I added that at this point my opinion was that we should try to force the English cruiser upon the frigate *La Méduse* or on the ship *L'Épervier*, both of which had a faster pace and that if it happened that the enemy caught up with us, His Majesty would be considered a prisoner of war, and that I believed he would be treated as such on board the *Bellerophon*; also, that I would prefer to use the way that offered the best chances.

After a moment of reflection, the Emperor said to me, 'It is too late, I have sent one of my general officers on board the English cruiser; they are expecting me, and I will go.'

He then went back down and rejoined generals Bertrand and de Montholon, to whom he recounted our conversation. These officers shrugged their shoulders and called me a 'young man'.

Around 8 o'clock in the morning, His Majesty drank some coffee on the capstan of the ship. He spilled a few drops of his coffee, and the crew carefully attended to the stains that remained for as long as I was in command.

At 9 o'clock in the morning, the calm and the tide delayed our journey.

The first lieutenant of the *Bellerophon*, traveling in a dinghy came on board *L'Épervier*. The Emperor used it to go to the English vessel; he was given the honors when he boarded the *Bellerophon*.

(As the vessel of Admiral Hotham approached, Captain Maitland, commandant of the *Bellerophon*, tried to keep his superior from taking from him the honor of 'terminating an affair he had brought so close to its end' (see his *Memoirs*), and as quickly as he could, he sent his dinghy to the ship to take Napoléon.)

I wrote to Captain Maitland to let him know of the mission I was charged with; the content of this letter was communicated to General Bertrand by my second in command; he found no reason not to send it. Captain Maitland acknowledged receiving the letter.

To the commandant of the English war vessel *Bellerophon*.
Ship *L'Épervier*, 15 July 1815.
Mr. le Commandant, I am in charge of the important mission of transporting

from the ship *L'Épervier*, which I command, to the English cruiser, the Emperor Napoléon. I have the honor of advising you, that His Majesty seized upon the occasion of the arrival of one of your dinghies, to leave my ship. I ask that you let me know if it is on board your vessel that His Majesty went.

O. JOURDAN, vessel lieutenant

To Monsieur Jourdin (sic), commander of the *Épervier*, French man of war brig.

His Majesty's ship *Bellerophon*, Basque roads, 15 July 1815

Sir,

Napoleon Bonaparte, late Emperor of the French, has this day embarked on board His Majesty's ship under my command, from the *Épervier*, French man of war brig, commanded by monsieur Jordin.

J. Maitland, Captain of HM ship *Bellerophon*

The calm continued and the tide sent me drifting towards land. I let go of the anchor.

I then boarded the *Bellerophon* to take the last orders of His Majesty, and to hurry the unloading of the schooner *La Sophie*, which carried the baggage of his following.

When I arrived, the Emperor was resting. When he awoke, he inspected the crew at the combat posts; then, His Majesty invited me to have lunch.

Before my departure, MM. Bertrand, de Montholon and de Las Cases came to discuss the opinion I had given to the Emperor, in regards to how he might be treated by the English.

As for themselves, they were convinced that they would be well received in England, that everything would get better in France, and they even entertained the thought of returning. I gave them my answer restating my doubts and that I hoped that their wishes would come true.

However, General de Montholon seemed troubled by my misgivings, and he would come to remember this when we saw each other again, after the death of the Emperor. General Bertrand had not forgotten this conversation either when, much later, he came and spent some time at Cherbourg; and during the whole time he lived in that town, there was hardly a day that he did not come to spend some great hours with me or my family.

At one o'clock, I left His Majesty in order to return to the anchorage at the Île d'Aix.

During this move, I met a port embarkation that carried several persons of the Emperor's following. This embarkation was missing her rudder and had difficulty maneuvering; I took it in tow to the *Bellerophon*.

As I was passing by the stern of this vessel, the Emperor came into the stern-gallery; the crew had come up in the yards to salute him; he waved at us in a sign of adieu and we soon lost sight of him.

At 3 o'clock in the afternoon, I returned to my regular anchorage and went to give an account of my mission.

After these events, I was relieved of my command, and did not rejoin the service until 1817 ...[12]

Appendix XII

Additional accounts of Napoleon's departure

Account by M. Bonnau, accountant on board the *L'Épervier*

On 15 July 1815, at four o'clock in the morning, His Majesty the Emperor Napoléon 1st arrived on board *L'Épervier* that was armed as parliamentary. As soon as all of the persons who accompanied him had arrived on board *L'Épervier*, it set sail in great silence in respect for the hero who was attracting the attention of the whole crew gathered on the bridge. The ship, under sail, tacked to reach the Basques harbor where the English ships were. The Emperor seemed very preoccupied, his eyes looked towards the Île d'Aix and other places on the coast from which he was moving away, never to see them again. The great tricolor flag fluttered above his head, and from the many points on the shore appeared rags of white cloth that must have affected him greatly.

At eight o'clock, the Emperor, never leaving the bridge, asked for coffee: it was served to him in a small vermeil cup that was placed on the head of the capstan. This was his favorite drink, and appeared to calm him. He let himself be drawn into a conversation, and asked how many crewmen were on the ship: 'ninety', said the Captain.

'The one on which I passed from the isle of Elba to France does not seem to be any bigger than this one and it had one hundred and twenty crewmen, and what is more, I had four hundred troops ... where was this one built?'

'At Bayonne.'

'How much water does it pull?'

'Thirteen feet.'

'We have often asked that the frigates be built at Bayonne,' said the Emperor, 'and it was always said that the pass of the helm was not deep enough for ships of this strength. However, it seems to me that we could have let a frigate pulling thirteen feet of water get it out of the port, without running too many risks, since totally loaded and armed she only pulls seventeen to eighteen feet of water, and especially since we have very close by as a place for release, the passage of Saint-Andre-Bilbao ... Is the dyke of Bayonne finished?'

'No, Sire,' answered the Captain.

'So many things were ordered that were never executed!' the Emperor responded.

Going on to the quarterdeck, his attention fell upon a sail called brigantine. The rigging of this sail was falling a long way under the yard, called baume, the Emperor observed, and he was right, that this sail should have been in the shape of a circle, made by a notch, from one point to the other (from the tack to the clew). We told him that his observation was correct, but that this could only be done after the canvas of this sail had sustained the first effects of wind and rain, in order to cut only what was still hanging after the canvas had tightened. He found this observation very judicious.

Meanwhile, *L'Épervier* still tacked about to reach the English division. Upon reaching within gunshot range of the *Bellerophon*, it settled down to anchor, and as soon as this maneuver was done, the commandant of the English vessel, who probably worried that at the last moment the Emperor would escape him, sent one of his embarkations to *L'Épervier*. Upon seeing this English dinghy, officers and sailors were seized with horror, having to witness from so close, the moment when the Emperor would be taken by his most cruel enemies and the enemies of France. When the embarkation arrived on board, the English officer went up to the bridge.

The Emperor with his elbow resting on the capstan, asked to see Madame Bertrand so she could be his interpreter, and he said to her, 'Ask this man how much time it takes to go to England with these winds (they were north-west).'

'It takes eight days,' answered the English officer.

'And what if we had good wind?' asked the Emperor.

'It would take forty-eight hours.'

After this last response, the Emperor winced; he ordered his following to get in the English dinghy, where the sailors were waiting for him while rubbing their hands together, happily chanting: 'Bonni, bonni, bonni ...!'

The Emperor was the last person to get on board the English dinghy, and as soon as he was placed on the bench that offered him only perpetual exile, the dinghy left as all of the crew of *L'Épervier*, gathered on the same side of the bridge (portside), were weeping and shouting: 'Vive l'Empereur!' The Emperor responded to these painful cries with very expressive signals, and his last gesture was to throw some water that he took with his hand to bless the French who were seeing him for the last time, on the shallow water that runs along the coasts of the beloved homeland he will never see again.

Notes of M. Pelletreau, vessel ensign

During his stay on board the frigate *La Saale*, a small parliamentary schooner was sent to the *Bellerophon* to make plans for his passage on this vessel. As soon as the plans were made, the ship *L'Épervier*, under the command of lieutenant of vessel M. Jourdan, was armed as parliamentary the day before its departure. At two o'clock in the morning the next day, wearing the national guard uniform and a green fitted coat, the Emperor came with his following to ask for passage to take him to board the English vessel anchored in the Basques harbor. His following consisted of Mr. and Mrs. Bertrand and their children, Mr. and Mrs. de Montholon, General Lallemand and a few domestics.

The Emperor had stayed on the bridge with his followers during the whole trip; being distracted, he had put a finger in the hose of the binnacle lamp, and had blackened his finger. He was rubbing it on his coat. Unable to remove this black spot, he turned and asked for some water. At that time I was next to him and I called for a pilotin, as is the custom on board ships, when generals Bertrand and Montholon arrived to ask me what the Emperor wanted. I told them that His Majesty wanted some water. They both hurried to the officers' quarters and asked for water, and they both came back, one with a basin and a pitcher full of water, and the other with a towel. I have to admit that I found myself embarrassed about this, and I have always been upset at myself for not having taken care of it before they did.

General Lallemand stayed in the officers' quarters; he seemed very troubled.

The Emperor walked about on the bridge and was pleased to talk with some old cannoniers and a few sailors who had been taken prisoners in England. At times, he would get up on the arms chest and, with his small opera glasses he would look at the white flags fluttering at Oléron and La Rochelle. The winds were contrary and we had to skid. He ordered the Captain not to get so close to land: we answered him that the winds were not favorable and we had to continue to hug the coast.

He examined the 'brick', and told us that the ship did not have good bearing. He asked about the power of the 'brick' and was told eighteen cannons, and that there were none built bigger in France. He told us that the 'brick' that had brought him back from Elba carried twenty-two pieces and six hundred men on board. The Captain told him that it was impossible, on such a small ship, to have more crew than we had; we were ninety-five men. Then he said: 'I believe that Decrès has deceived me like the others.'

The Emperor took his coffee at seven o'clock in the morning on the capstan of the ship, a small distance from the vessel *Bellerophon*. There was still no wind, so the English commodore sent to us his embarkations armed with French sailors, all former prisoners. Our crew recognized some of them: in one of these embarkations was the second in command of the *Bellerophon*.

At the time when these embarkations came on board, the Emperor had his elbow resting on the binnacle and was holding his head in his hand. Someone announced that the English barges were alongside the ship. He shuddered again, perhaps in a sign of disapproval; he turned to Mesdames Bertrand and de Montholon who were at the back of the ship and said to them: 'Mesdames, have you the strength to go on board the English vessel?' Madame Bertrand answered, 'Yes, sire.' He said to them: 'Go ahead and board, Mesdames!' The captain of the English frigate offered his arm to Madame Bertrand, and the rest of the people followed. The Emperor was the last to board, and before he left, he invited our captain to have lunch with him on the English vessel. At ten o'clock His Majesty left us, and as he was leaving told us that he would remember the ship *L'Épervier* and its crew for a long time. As he was passing by the ship, the Emperor three different times took water with his hand and threw it at us in a sign of adieu. Upon arriving on board the *Bellerophon*, he received the greeting appropriate to his rank.

Gédéon Henri Pelletreau,
Ensign of vessel, embarked on board *L'Épervier*[13]

Appendix XIII

Letter from Captain Maitland to Admiral Keith

18 July 1815

My Lord,

Having received directions from Sir Henry Hotham to forward the accompanying dispatch to your Lordship by an officer, I avail myself of the opportunity to explain the circumstances under which I was placed when induced to receive Napoleon Bonaparte into the ship.

After the first communication was made to me by Count Bertrand that Bonaparte was at the Île d'Aix, and actually embarked on board the frigates for the purpose of proceeding to the United States of America, my duty became peculiarly harassing and anxious, owing to the numerous reports that were daily brought from all quarters, of his intention to escape in vessels of various descriptions and from different situations on the coast, of which the limited means I possessed, together with the length of time requisite to communicate with Sir Henry Hotham at Quiberon Bay, rendered the success at least possible, and even probable.

Thus situated, the enemy having two frigates and a brig, while the force under my command consisted of the *Bellerophon* and *Slaney*, (having detached the *Myrmidon* to reinforce the *Daphne* off the Mamusson Passage, where the force was considerably superior to her, and whence one of the reports stated Bonaparte meant to sail,) another flag of truce was sent out, for the ostensible reason of enquiring whether I had received an answer to the former [Bertrand's letter, forwarded by Maitland to Hotham], but I soon ascertained the real one to be a proposal from Bonaparte to embark for England in this ship.

Taking into consideration all the circumstances of the probability of the escape being effected if the trial was made either in the frigates, or clandestinely in a small vessel, as had this ship been disabled in action there was no other with me that could produce any effect on a frigate, and from the experience I have had in blockading the ports of the bay, knowing the impossibility of preventing small vessels from getting to sea, and looking upon it as of the greatest importance to get possession of the person of Bonaparte, I was induced, without hesitation, to accede to the proposal, as far as taking him on board, and proceeding with him to England, but at the same time stating in the most clear and positive terms that I had no authority to make any sort of stipulation as to the reception he was to meet with. Under the circumstances, I am happy to say that the measures I have adopted have met with the approbation of Sir

Henry Hotham, and will, I trust and hope, receive that of your Lordship, as well as of His Majesty's Government.

I have &c,

F. W. Maitland[14]

Appendix XIV

General Savary's protest

Duc de Rovigo to Keith

Bellerophon, July 31, 1815

Monsieur l'Amiral. The Emperor has just informed me of what refers to me in the notification you have made to him. I cannot tell you how troubled I am at the exception which has been made in my case. I beg your Excellency to refer without delay to the British Government the statement which I have the honour of addressing to you. It was not my intention to go to St. Helena. That resolution was taken in view of the duties I owe to my large family. But, sir, it cannot follow that the exception which was made on account of my refusal must separate me forever from my children, whom I wish to rejoin.

I went on board an English vessel voluntarily and resigned every employment I had in France. My intention was to reside in England as much to avoid the troubles in France. I placed myself with confidence under the protection of the hospitable laws of England and I was far from suspecting the trap into which I put myself in all innocence. The news from France informs me that I am cited to appear before a military tribunal. I do not fear to appear before it, but only when things have become calmer and the demand for private vengeance, always prominent at the beginning of a revolution, will be extinguished, because my conscience tells me that it is not that which I have to fear.

Whatever may be the political relations between England and France I cannot think that they will be of a nature which would refuse refuge to hunted men who have come here in good faith and even at the invitation of those to whom they surrendered.

I appeal to your sense of justice: you are a father and a husband and you will understand my situation. If England rejects me I demand my liberty and permission to do what is necessary to leave. If your Excellency cannot reassure me on the point of the inconceivable exception made in my case, I beg that you will have the kindness to allow me to communicate with a lawyer in order that I may take the necessary steps regarding my family which is now on the road from Paris to London.

I have &c.

Le Duc de Rovigo[15]

Notes

Notes to Chapter 1: The End Game at Waterloo

1. Louis-Joseph Marchand. *In Napoleon's Shadow. Being the First English Language Edition of the complete Memoirs of Louis-Joseph Marchand, Valet and Friend of The Emperor 1811–1821*. Produced by Proctor Jones. Original notes of Jean Bourguignon and Henry Lachouque. Preface by Jean Tulard (San Francisco: Proctor Jones, 1998), 168.

2. Henri Houssaye. *The Return of Napoleon* (trans. T. C. Macaulay). Preface by Sir Fabian Ware (London: Longmans, Green and Co., 1934), 146.

3. David Chandler. *Waterloo: The Hundred Days* (London: Osprey, 1987), 19.

4. Baron Paul Charles François Adrien Henri Dieudonné Thiébault. *The Memoirs of Baron Thiébault (Late Lieutenant-General in the French Army)* (trans. Arthur John Butler). 2 vols (New York: Macmillan, 1896), II, 417–18.

5. Daniel Resnick. *The White Terror and the Political Reaction After Waterloo* (Cambridge, Mass.: Harvard University Press, 1966), 2.

6. Resnick. *The White Terror*, 2–3. General Gilly's generosity didn't do him much good. He was later condemned to death, but was only held prisoner until granted amnesty in 1820. On the other hand, his name is on the Arc de Triomphe in Paris.

7. John G. Gallaher. *The Iron Marshal: A Biography of Louis N. Davout* (Carbondale and Edwardsville: Southern Illinois University Press, 1976), 309. Gallaher is the leading authority on Davout.

8. Quoted in Marchand. *In Napoleon's Shadow*, 181–2.

9. Everett Thomas Dague. *Napoleon and the First Empire's Ministries of War and Military Administration: The Construction of a Military Bureaucracy* (Lewiston, NY: Edwin Mellen Press, 2007), 187.

10. Gallaher. *The Iron Marshal*, 310–11.

11. Count Mathieu Louis Molé. *The Life and Memoirs of Count Molé*. Edited by the Marquis de Noailles. 2 vols, illustrated (London: Hutchinson, 1923), I, 243–4.

12. Enno E. Kraehe. *Metternich's German Policy*, vol. II: *The Congress of Vienna 1814–1815* (Princeton: Princeton University Press, 1983), 355.

13. Marchand. *In Napoleon's Shadow*, 213. Molé later tried to promote the return of Louis XVIII in an address to the municipal council of Paris, and was lucky to get out alive.

14. No. 39. Talleyrand (from Vienna) to Louis XVIII. Charles Maurice de Talleyrand-Périgord, Prince de Bénévent. *The Correspondence of Prince Talleyrand and King Louis XVIII During the Congress of Vienna (Hitherto Unpublished). From the Manuscripts preserved in the archives of the ministry of foreign affairs at Paris, with a preface, observations and notes by M. G. Pallain.* Authorized American Edition with a portrait and descriptive index (New York: Charles Scribner's Sons, 1881), 414. Also in Talleyrand, *Memoirs of the Prince de Talleyrand.* Edited by the Duc de Broglie. Translated by Raphaël Ledos de Beaufort. With an introduction by Whitelaw Reid (New York and London: Anglo-American Publishing Company, n.d. [1896]), III, 80–1.

15. Kraehe. *Metternich's German Policy*, II, 329–30.

16. Ibid., 330.

17. Joseph Fouché. *The Memoirs of Joseph Fouché, Duke of Otranto, Minister of the General Police of France.* 2 vols (London: Charles Knight, 1825), II, 290–1.

18. Thiébault. *Memoirs*, II, 419.

19. Edith Saunders. *Napoleon and Mademoiselle George* (New York: E. P. Dutton and Co., 1959), 164–8. George was seldom without male companionship, and her lovers are said to have included Tsar Alexander of Russia. But her life ended sadly. She became enormously heavy and died destitute in 1867, at the age of 79.

Notes to Chapter 2: A Chaotic Return

1. Baron General Gaspard Gourgaud. *The Campaign of MDCCCXV; OR, A Narrative of the Military Operations which Took Place in France and Belgium During the Hundred Days* (London: James Ridgway, 1818), 133–4.

2. Louis Étienne Saint-Denis. *Napoleon from the Tuileries to St. Helena; personal recollections of the emperor's second mameluke and valet, Louis Etienne St. Denis (known as Ali).* Translated from the French and Notes by Frank Hunter Potter. With an Introduction by Professor G. Michaut, of the Sorbonne. With maps (New York and London: Harper and Brothers, 1922), 132–3.

3. Henri Houssaye. *1815 Waterloo* (trans. Arthur Émile Mann) (London: Adam and Charles Black, 1900), 246–7.

4. Henry Lachouque. *The Last Days of Napoleon's Empire: From Waterloo to St. Helena* (trans. Lovett F. Edwards) (New York: Orion Press, 1967), 28–9.

5. Houssaye. *1815 Waterloo*, 242.

6. Saint-Denis. *Napoleon*, 134.

7. Baron Pierre Alexandre Édouard Fleury de Chaboulon. *Memoirs of the Private Life, Return, and Reign of Napoleon in 1815* 2 vols (London: John Murray, 1820), 203. De Chaboulon was Secretary of the Emperor and of his Cabinets, Master of Requests to the Council of State, Baron, Officer of the Legion of Honour, and Knight of the Order of Reunion. His memoirs are not without fault, but the descriptions I use in this book are supported elsewhere as well.

8. These were militantly pro-Napoleon groups, mostly in cities in regions where the peasantry was largely royalist, who received some leadership from the central government. They were, in effect, an auxiliary homeland army of sorts.

9. Napoleon I, Emperor of the French. *Lettres Inédites de Napoléon Ier (An VIII–1815)*. Published by Léon Lecestre. 2 vols (Paris: Librairie Plon, 1897), II, no. 1225, 357–8. Translation mine.

10. Gourgaud. *The Campaign of MDCCCXV*, 137.

11. Marchand. *In Napoleon's Shadow*, 248.

12. Ibid., 246.

13. Fleury de Chaboulon. *Memoirs of Napoleon*, 200.

14. W. Hyde Kelly. *The Battle of Wavre and Grouchy's Retreat*. Facsimile of the 1905 edition (Felling: Worley, 1993), 123–4.

15. Comte de Grouchy. *Observations sur la Relation de la Campagne de 1815, Publiée par le Général Gourgaud, et Réfutation de Quelques-unes des Assertations d'Autres Écruts Relatifs à la Bataille de Waterloo*. (Paris: Chez Chaumerot, 1819), 93–6.

16. Gourgaud. *The Campaign of MDCCCXV*, 143–9.

17. Fleury de Chaboulon. *Memoirs of Napoleon*, 206–8.

18. Marchand. *In Napoleon's Shadow*, 248.

19. Fleury de Chaboulon. *Memoirs of Napoleon*, 210–11.

20. Marchand. *In Napoleon's Shadow*, 248.

21. Houssaye. *1815 Waterloo*, 251. See also his lengthy footnote 61 on p. 442, wherein he cites numerous sources from St Helena.

22. Gourgaud. *The Campaign of MDCCCXV*, 138–9.

Notes to Chapter 3: Paris and the Politics of Disaster

1. Fouché. *Memoirs*, II, 292.

2. Metternich to Fouché. 9 April 1815, no. 196. Prince Clemens Lothar Wenzel, Fürst von Metternich-Winneburg. *Memoirs of Prince Metternich 1773–1815.* Edited by Prince Richard Metternich. Papers classified and arranged by M. A. de Klinkowström. Translated by Mrs Alexander Napier. 2 vols (New York: Charles Scribner's Sons, 1880), II, 602.

3. Metternich to Talleyrand. 24 June 1815, no. 199. Written in Mannheim. *Memoirs,* II, 605–6. Also in Talleyrand, *Memoirs,* III, 154. Talleyrand was in Mons, Belgium, when he received this letter.

4. Chancellor Étienne-Denis Pasquier. *A History of My Time: Memoirs of Chancellor Pasquier.* Edited by the Duc D'Audiffret, Pasquier. Translated by Charles Roche. 3 vols (London: T. Fisher Unwin, 1893 [vol. I]; 1894 [vols II and III]), III, 259–60.

5. Fouché. *Memoirs,* II, 293.

6. Gilbert Martineau. *Napoleon Surrenders.* Translated from the French by Frances Partridge (London: John Murray, 1971), 4.

7. General Anne Jean Marie René Savary (Duke of Rovigo). *Memoirs of the Duke of Rovigo (M. Savary) Written by Himself: Illustrative of the History of the Emperor Napoleon.* 4 vols (London: Henry Colburn, 1828), IV (ii), 96.

8. Charles Jean Tristan, Marquis de Montholon. *History of the Captivity of Napoleon at St. Helena.* 4 vols (London: Henry Colburn, 1846), I, 5. Montholon's memoirs are often quite suspect, but it is certainly hard to argue with this comment, which reflects an opinion held by many, including me.

Notes to Chapter 4: Napoleon's Return to Parisian Politics

1. General Armand-Augustin-Louis, Marquis de Caulaincourt, Duc de Vicence. *Napoleon and His Times.* 2 vols (Philadelphia: E. L. Carey & A. Hart, 1838), II, 157.

2. Marie Joseph Emmanuel Auguste Dieudonné, Comte de Las Cases. *Mémorial de Sainte Hélène. Journal of the Private Life and Conversations of the Emperor Napoleon at Saint Helena.* 4 vols (Boston: Wells and Lilly, 1823), I (i), 13.

3. Fleury de Chaboulon. *Memoirs of Napoleon,* II, 218–19; a slightly different translation in Caulaincourt, *Napoleon and His Times,* II, 160–1.

4. Count Antoine Marie Chamant Lavalette. *Memoirs of Count Lavallette, Written by Himself.* 2nd edn, 2 vols (London: Henry Colburn and Richard Bentley, 1831), II, 192. Lavalette was a devoted loyalist to Napoleon. He was condemned to death but managed to escape.

5. Baron Claude-François de Méneval. *Memoirs of Napoleon Bonaparte, the Court of the First Empire, by Baron C.-F. De Méneval, His Private Secretary.* 3 vols (New York: P. F. Collier and Son, 1910), III, 1223.

6. Marchand. *In Napoleon's Shadow*, 250.

7. Lachouque. *The Last Days of Napoleon's Empire*, 54.

8. Savary. *Memoirs*, IV (ii), 98.

9. Gallaher. *The Iron Marshal*, 312.

10. Fleury de Chaboulon. *Memoirs of Napoleon*, II, 222.

11. Caulaincourt. *Napoleon and His Times*, II, 166–7.

12. Gourgaud. *The Campaign of MDCCCXV*, 151–2.

13. Thiébault. *Memoirs*, 422.

14. Lachouque. *The Last Days of Napoleon's Empire*, 66–7.

15. Las Cases. *Mémorial de Sainte Hélène*, II (iv), 75.

16. Lavalette. *Memoirs*, II, 193–4.

17. Hortense, Queen Consort of Louis, King of Holland. *The Memoirs of Queen Hortense*. Published by arrangement with Prince Napoleon. Edited by Jean Hanoteau. Translated by Arthur K. Griggs. 2 vols (New York: Cosmopolitan Book Corporation, 1927), II, 231.

18. Caulaincourt. *Napoleon and His Times*, II, 168.

19. Fleury de Chaboulon. *Memoirs of Napoleon*, II, 225.

20. Hortense. *Memoirs*, II, 232.

21. Marchand. *In Napoleon's Shadow*, 253.

22. Napoleon I, Emperor of the French. *Correspondance de Napoléon Ier; Publiée par ordre de l'empereur Napoléon III*. 32 vols (Paris: Imprimerie Impériale, 1858–69), XXVIII, no. 22062.

23. Fleury de Chaboulon. *Memoirs of Napoleon*, II, 229–30.

24. Ibid., 231.

25. Martineau. *Napoleon Surrenders*, 27.

26. Savary. *Memoirs*, IV (ii), 101.

27. George R. Russell. *The Hundred Days: 1815* (n.p., n.d., [*c.* 1870]), 61.

Notes to Chapter 5: Day of Decision

1. Gallaher. *The Iron Marshal*, 315.

2. Gourgaud. *The Campaign of MDCCCXV*, 159.

3. Las Cases. *Mémorial de Sainte Hélène*, II (i), 16.

4. Caulaincourt. *Napoleon and His Times*, II, 169.

5. Napoleon. *Correspondance*, XXVIII, no. 22063; *Bulletin des Lois, VI Série*, No. 37 (No. 274), 'Déclaration au Peuple Français' (Paris: Imprimerie Impériale, 22 Juin 1815); also *Itinéraire de Buonaparte de l'Ile d'Elbe à l'Ile Sainte-Hélène, ou, Mémoires Pour Servir à l'Histoire de la Seconde Usurpation. Avec le Recueil des Principales Pièces Officielles de Cette Époque. Deuxième Édition considérablement augmentée.* 2 vols (Paris: 1817), II, 286–7.

6. Martineau. *Napoleon Surrenders*, 35.

7. Fouché. *Memoirs*, II, 295–6.

8. Pasquier. *A History of My Time*, III, 263.

9. *Bulletin des Lois, VI Série*, No. 19 (No. 112), 22 Avril 1815, 140; Napoleon, *Correspondance*, XXVIII, no. 21839.

10. Pasquier. *A History of My Time*, III, 267–8.

11. Fleury de Chaboulon. *Memoirs of Napoleon*, II, 243.

12. A. Hilliard Atteridge. *The Bravest of the Brave: Michel Ney, Marshal of France, Duke of Elchingen, Prince of the Moskowa, 1769–1815* (London: Methuen & Co., 1912), 331. A similar description and translation is in Harold Kurtz, *The Trial of Marshal Ney* (New York: Alfred A. Knopf, 1957), 186–7.

13. Pasquier. *A History of My Time*, III, 259.

14. Ibid., 265.

15. *Bulletin des Lois, VI Série*, No. 38 (No. 275), 25 Juin 1815. Note that Fouché has the title of Duke of Otranto.

16. Ray Ellsworth Cubberly. *The Role of Fouché During the Hundred Days* (Madison: The State Historical Society of Wisconsin, 1969), 93.

17. Colonel Francis Maceroni [Macirone]. *Memoirs of the Life and Adventures of Colonel Maceroni, Late Aide-de-Camp to Joachim Murat, King of Naples – Knight of the Legion of Honour, and of St. George of the Two Sicilies – Ex-General of Brigade, In the Service of the Republic of Colombia, &c., &c., &c..* 2 vols (London: John Macrone, 1838), II, 238.

18. Marchand. *In Napoleon's Shadow*, 257.

Notes to Chapter 6: Napoleon II, Emperor of the French

1. Pasquier. *A History of My Time*, III, 269.

2. *Bulletin des Lois, VI Série*, No. 38 (No 279).

3. Lachouque. *The Last Days of Napoleon's Empire*, 97.

4. *Bulletin des Lois, VI Série*, No. 40 (No. 291), 26 Juin 1815.

5. *Bulletin des Lois, VI Série*, No. 41 (No. 304 and after), 28 Juin 1815.

6. Hortense. *Memoirs*, II, 233.

7. Maceroni [Macirone]. *Memoirs*, II, 238.

8. Caulaincourt. *Napoleon and His Times*, II, 173–4.

9. Pasquier. *A History of My Time*, III, 279.

10. Caulaincourt. *Napoleon and His Times*, II, 186.

11. Guillaume de Bertier de Sauvigny. *The Bourbon Restoration* (trans. Lynn M. Case) (Philadelphia: University of Pennsylvania Press, 1966), 106.

Notes to Chapter 7: The King Returns

1. Gourgaud. *The Campaign of MDCCCXV*, 161.

2. Lachouque. *The Last Days of Napoleon's Empire*, 105–6.

3. Gallaher. *The Iron Marshal*, 325–6. Gallaher gives a far more detailed account of this period than is possible here. He and I disagree on whether or not Davout should have been more aggressive against the Prussians.

4. Gourgaud. *The Campaign of MDCCCXV*, 165.

5. Fouché. *Memoirs*, II, 324. Fouché claims the exchange was through notes, others relate that it was in person.

6. Resnick. *The White Terror*, 5–14.

7. Ibid., 14–19. Resnick gives an excellent and detailed account of the White Terror throughout France.

8. François Auguste René, Vicomte de Chateaubriand. *Portrait of Bonaparte; being a view of his administration. Together with An Ode to Napoleon* (New York: Eastburn, Kirk & Co., 1814), 57.

9. Sauvigny. *The Bourbon Restoration*, 120.

10. Peter Hofschröer. *Waterloo 1814: Wavre, Plancenoit and the Race to Paris* (Barnsley: Pen & Sword, 2006), 80.

11. Ibid., 87–8.

12. Quoted in Norwood Young. *Napoleon in Exile: St. Helena (1815–1821)*. With two coloured frontispieces and one hundred illustrations mainly from the collection of A. M. Broadley. 2 vols (Philadelphia: John C. Winston, 1915), I, 23. He cites Castlereagh's Letters, 3rd series, V.ii, 386.

13. Gregor Dallas. *The Final Act: The Roads to Waterloo* (New York: Henry Holt, 1996), 392–4.

14. Kevin D. McCranie. *Admiral Lord Keith and the Naval War Against Napoleon* (Gainesville: University Press of Florida, 2006), 168. McCranie's book is by far the best account of Lord Keith's career that I have seen.

15. Pasquier. *A History of My Time*, III, 273.

16. Lachouque. *The Last Days of Napoleon's Empire*, 142.

17. Sauvigny. *The Bourbon Restoration*, 102–5.

Notes to Chapter 8: The Allies Take Command

1. Fleury de Chaboulon. *Memoirs of Napoleon*, II, 323.

2. Ibid., 349.

3. Cubberly. *The Role of Fouché*, 105–6.

4. Colonel Francis Maceroni [Macirone]. *Interesting Facts Relating to the Fall and Death of Joachim Murat, King of Naples; the Capitulation of Paris in 1815; and the Second Restoration of the Bourbons; Original letters from King Joachim to the Author; with some account of the Author and his persecution by the French Government. By Francis Macirone, Late Aide-de-Camp to King Joachim; Knight of the Order of the Two Sicilies*, 3rd edn, with additions (London: Ridgways, 1817), 41–2.

5. Ibid., 43–4.

6. Jacques Étienne Joseph Alexandre Macdonald, Duc de Tarente. *Recollections of Marshal Macdonald, Duke of Tarentum*. Edited by Camille Rousset. Translated by Stephen Louis Simeon (London: Richard Bentley and Son, 1892), II, 331.

7. Molé. *Life and Memoirs*, I, 276.

8. Maceroni [Macirone]. *The Fall and Death of Joachim Murat*, 47.

9. Quoted in Sauvigny, *The Bourbon Restoration*, 110.

10. Fouché. *Memoirs*, II, 317.

11. Ibid., 110.

12. Molé. *Life and Memoirs*, II, 31.

13. Las Cases. *Mémorial de Sainte Hélène*, I (i), 15.

14. Russell. *The Hundred Days*, 69–70. The reference is to a fable by Aesop where King Log was the inanimate king of the frogs, who despaired of his sluggishness. In response to their requests, Jupiter sent them King Stork who was much more active but proceeded to eat all the frogs.

Notes to Chapter 9: Napoleon's Farewell to Paris

1. Fleury de Chaboulon. *Memoirs of Napoleon*, II, 263–4. The 18th Brumaire reference is to Napoleon's initial taking of power in 1799.

2. Pasquier. *A History of My Time*, III, 281.

3. Fleury de Chaboulon. *Memoirs of Napoleon*, II, 265.

4. Marchand. *In Napoleon's Shadow*, 255.

5. Savary. *Memoirs*, IV, pt 2, 112–13.

6. Hotham to Keith, June 3, 1815. Admiral Viscount George Keith. *The Keith Papers. Selected from the Papers of Admiral Viscount Keith and Edited by Christopher Lloyd* (Aldwich: Navy Records Society, 1926 [vol. I]; 1950 [vol. II]; 1955 [vol. III]), III, 344 (2). This seems to have been in response to the existence of French frigates in that area.

7. Napoleon. *Correspondance*, XXVIII, 22065. Also, Marchand, *In Napoleon's Shadow*, 255–66; Gourgaud, *The Campaign of MDCCCXV*, 225–6; Fleury de Chaboulon, *Memoirs of Napoleon*, II, 269–70.

8. Napoleon. *Correspondance*, XXVIII, 22064. Barbier had been Napoleon's librarian, as well as librarian to the Directory and the Council of State. He was a favorite of Napoleon's, and helped establish major libraries in the Louvre and elsewhere.

9. Caulaincourt. *Napoleon and His Times*, II, 185.

10. Montholon. *History of the Captivity of Napoleon*, I, 26.

11. Marchand. *In Napoleon's Shadow*, 258–9.

Notes to Chapter 10: Malmaison

1. Hortense. *Memoirs*, II, 236.

2. Marchand. *In Napoleon's Shadow*, 263.

3. Gallaher. *The Iron Marshal*, 318–19.

4. Montholon. *History of the Captivity of Napoleon*, I, 31–2.

5. Caulaincourt. *Napoleon and His Times*, 186.

6. Marchand. *In Napoleon's Shadow*, 263.

7. Christine Sutherland. *Marie Walewska: Napoleon's Great Love* (New York and Paris: Vendôme Press, 1979), 236–7.

8. Hortense. *Memoirs*, II, 242.

9. Caulaincourt. *Napoleon and His Times*, 187.

10. Marie Joseph Emmanuel Auguste Dieudonné, Comte de Las Cases. *Memoirs of Emanuel Augustus Dieudonné Count de Las Casas [sic], Communicated by Himself. Comprising a Letter from Count de Las Casas [sic] at St. Helena to Lucien Bonaparte, Giving a Faithful Account of the Voyage of Napoleon to St. Helena, His Residence, Manner of Living, and Treatment on that Island. Also A Letter Addressed by Count de Las Casas [sic] to Lord Bathurst* (London: Henry Colburn, 1818), 99–100n.

11. Savary. *Memoirs*, IV (ii), 115.

12. Ibid., 117–18. Caulaincourt does not mention this conversation in his memoirs of the period.

13. Marchand. *In Napoleon's Shadow*, 264. Montholon, *History of the Captivity of Napoleon*, I, 36 presents the same list with a detailed description of the maps.

14. Savary. *Memoirs*, IV (ii), 125.

15. Las Cases. *Mémorial de Sainte Hélène*, I (i), 16.

16. Savary. *Memoirs*, IV (ii), 126.

17. Quoted in Frédéric Masson. *Napoleon at St. Helena 1815–1821*. Translated by Louis B. Frewer (Oxford: Pen In Hand, 1949), 6.

18. Savary. *Memoirs*, IV (ii), 126–7; Montholon, *History of the Captivity of Napoleon*, 38–9.

19. Savary. *Memoirs*, IV (ii), 127.

20. Montholon. *History of the Captivity of Napoleon*, I, 36–7. Las Cases, *Mémorial de Sainte Hélène*, I (i), 18–19n, also reproduces the letter in a slightly different translation and claims that Davout refused to actually sign it and that it might not have been sent.

21. Lavalette. *Memoirs*, 201–02.

22. Young. *Napoleon in Exile*, 33.

23. Montholon. *History of the Captivity of Napoleon*, I, 44.

Notes to Chapter 11: Heading South

1. Montholon. *History of the Captivity of Napoleon*, I, 41.

2. Marchand. *In Napoleon's Shadow*, 267–8.

3. Thiébault. *Memoirs*, 423–4.

4. Marchand. *In Napoleon's Shadow*, 268.

5. Montholon. *History of the Captivity of Napoleon*, I, 47–8; Marchand, *In Napoleon's Shadow*, 269.

6. Savary. *Memoirs*, IV (ii), 129.

7. Montholon. *History of the Captivity of Napoleon*, I, 49–50.

8. Napoleon I, Emperor of the French. *A Selection from the Letters and Despatches of the First Napoleon, with Explanatory Notes*. Compiled by Captain the Hon. D. A. Bingham. 3 vols (London: Chapman and Hall, 1884), III, 413.

9. Marchand. *In Napoleon's Shadow*, 270; Montholon, *History of the Captivity of Napoleon*, I, 52.

10. Montholon. *History of the Captivity of Napoleon*, I, 54.

11. Caulaincourt. *Napoleon and His Times*, II, 191–2.

12. Marchand. *In Napoleon's Shadow*, 270–1.

13. Montholon. *History of the Captivity of Napoleon*, I, 55–6.

14. Saint-Denis. *Napoleon*, 139.

15. Marchand. *In Napoleon's Shadow*, 272. Marchand gets much of his information from later conversations with Saint-Denis and has a few details that Saint-Denis did not put in his memoirs.

16. Saint-Denis. *Napoleon*, 145.

17. Marchand. *In Napoleon's Shadow*, 274.

18. Lachouque. *The Last Days of Napoleon's Empire*, 149.

19. Savary. *Memoirs*, IV (ii), 137.

20. Saint-Denis. *Napoleon*, 149; Marchand, *In Napoleon's Shadow*, 277.

21. Marchand. *In Napoleon's Shadow*, 279.

Notes to Chapter 12: Parisian Follies

1. Fleury de Chaboulon. *Memoirs of Napoleon*, II, 410n. Emphasis in original.

2. Ibid., 405–8.

3. Savary. *Memoirs*, IV (ii), 138–9. The italics are those of General Savary.

4. Montholon. *History of the Captivity of Napoleon*, I, 61.

5. Marchand. *In Napoleon's Shadow*, 278.

6. Savary. *Memoirs*, IV (ii), 148.

7. Marchand. *In Napoleon's Shadow*, 280.

8. Montholon. *History of the Captivity of Napoleon*, I, 67–8.

9. Savary. *Memoirs*, IV (ii), 137.

10. Marchand. *In Napoleon's Shadow*, 283.

11. Las Cases. *Memoirs*, 104.

Notes to Chapter 13: Inching Towards Departure

1. Savary. *Memoirs*, IV (ii), 165–6.

2. Montholon. *History of the Captivity of Napoleon*, I, 72–4.

3. Ibid., 77–8.

4. Saint-Denis. *Napoleon*, 152–3.

5. Montholon. *History of the Captivity of Napoleon*, 74–6.

6. *Keith Papers*, III, 350; also in Captain Frederick Lewis Maitland, *Narrative of the Surrender of Buonaparte and of His Residence on Board H.M.S. Bellerophon; with a Detail of the Principal Events that Occurred in that Ship, Between the 24th of May and the 8th of August, 1815* (London: Henry Colburn, 1826), 27–9.

7. Secretary of Admiralty to Keith, *Keith Papers*, III, 347–8.

8. Maitland. *Narrative*, 34–5.

9. Lieutenant John Bowerbank, RN. *An Extract from a Journal, Kept on Board H.M.S. Bellerophon, Captain F. L. Maitland, from Saturday, July 15, to Monday, August 7, 1815; Being the Period During Which Napoleon Buonaparte Was On Board That Ship. ... To which Is Added, An Appendix of Official and Other Documents* (London: Whittingham and Arliss, 1815), 10. Italics his. This is one of the rarest of all memoirs of this period.

10. Maitland. *Narrative*, 29–30.

11. *Keith Papers*, III, 350–1; Maitland, *Narrative*, 30–2.

Notes to Chapter 14: The Last Dance

1. Savary. *Memoirs*, IV (ii), 158–9.

2. Maitland. *Narrative*, 36–8.

3. Saint-Denis. *Napoleon*, 153–4.

4. Las Cases. *Mémorial de Sainte Hélène*, I (i), 22–3.

5. Maitland. *Narrative*, 45.

6. Marchand. *In Napoleon's Shadow*, 283.

7. Montholon. *History of the Captivity of Napoleon*, I, 87.

8. Savary. *Memoirs*, IV (ii), 161.

9. Quoted in Young, *Napoleon in Exile*, 48. Young says this letter is in the Earl of Crawford's collection.

10. Ibid., 48–9. This letter is also said to be in the Earl of Crawford's collection.

11. Napoleon. *Correspondance*, XXVIII, 22066; Marchand, *In Napoleon's Shadow*, 285.

12. Molé. *Life and Memoirs*, I, 309.

13. Savary. *Memoirs*, IV (ii), 162–3.

14. Ibid., 163; Maitland, *Narrative*, 49–55 (includes the original French and a list of all accompanying Napoleon).

15. Martineau. *Napoleon Surrenders*, 120n.

16. Maitland. *Narrative*, 60–1.

Notes to Chapter 15: Surrender to the British

1. Marchand. *In Napoleon's Shadow*, 285–6; Saint-Denis, *Napoleon*, 154–5.

2. Maitland. *Narrative*, 62–3.

3. Ibid., 68–9.

4. Ibid., 71.

5. Las Cases. *Mémorial de Sainte Hélène*, I (i), 25. Some accounts say that Napoleon threw himself on the protection of the Prince Regent as well as upon British law.

6. Bowerbank. *Extract from a Journal*, 13.

Notes to Chapter 16: Epilogue

1. Metternich. *Memoirs*, II, nos 203, 613.

2. *Keith Papers*, III, 386 (French text). Marchand, *In Napoleon's Shadow*, 318 and Savary, *Memoirs*, IV (ii), 173–4, have slightly different translations than the one provided here.

3. Napoleon. *Correspondance*, XXVIII, 22067; Marchand, *In Napoleon's Shadow*, 323; *Keith Papers*, III, 390 (French text).

4. William Warden. *Letters Written on Board His Majesty's Ship The Northumberland, and at Saint Helena; In Which the Conduct and Conversations of Napoleon Buonaparte, and His Suite, During the Voyage, and*

the First Months of His Residence in That Island, Are Faithfully Described and Related (London: published for the author by R. Ackermann, 1817), 8–9.

Notes to Appendices

1. Marchand. *In Napoleon's Shadow*, 181–2.

2. *Bulletin des Lois, VI Série*, No. 19 (No. 112).

3. Talleyrand. *Memoirs*, III, 91–2.

4. *Bulletin des Lois, VII Série*, No. I (No. 1) (Paris: De L'Imprimerie Royale, 12 Juillet 1815), 1–2.

5. Ibid., (No. 2), 2–4.

6. Metternich. *Memoirs*, II, 606–8.

7. No. 27, King Louis XVIII to the Prince de Talleyrand. Talleyrand, *Memoirs*, III, 87–8. Marshals Macdonald and Mortier had remained loyal to Louis during the Hundred Days. Macdonald had vainly attempted to rally the army to the Bourbon cause at Lyons when Napoleon was making his way to Paris along what is now known as the Route Napoléon.

8. Savary. *Memoirs*, IV, (ii), 276–8. Savary does not provide a date for this obviously important document, but it was probably written on or about 27 June 1815.

9. Fleury de Chaboulon. *Memoirs of Napoleon*, II, 388–392; Gourgaud, *The Campaign of MDCCCXV*, 227–31. Emphasis in original.

10. Fleury de Chaboulon. *Memoirs of Napoleon*, II, 395–7. De Chaboulon uses the term 'Committee', though it is usually 'Commission' elsewhere. Emphasis in original.

11. *The French American Review*, April–June 1949, No. 2, 63–80. Lallemand wrote this in July of 1816.

12. *Nouvelle Review Retrospective*, July–Dec. 1897, 241–51.

13. Ibid., 420–6.

14. *Keith Papers*, III, 357–8; Maitland, *Narrative*, 102–5.

15. *Keith Papers*, III, 382–3.

Selected Bibliography

Atteridge, A. Hilliard. *The Bravest of the Brave: Michel Ney, Marshal of France, Duke of Elchingen, Prince of the Moskowa, 1769–1815* (London: Methuen & Co., 1912).

Bowerbank, Lieutenant John, RN. *An Extract from a Journal, Kept on Board H.M.S. Bellerophon, Captain F. L. Maitland, from Saturday, July 15, to Monday, August 7, 1815; Being the Period During Which Napoleon Buonaparte Was On Board That Ship. ... To which Is Added, An Appendix of Official and Other Documents* (London: Whittingham and Arliss, 1815).

Bulletin des Lois, VI Série, Nos 1–42 (Paris: Imprimerie Impériale, 20 Mars – 2 Juillet 1815).

Bulletin des Lois, VII Série, No. I (Nos 1–2) (Paris: De L'Imprimerie Royale, 12 Juillet 1815).

Caulaincourt, General Armand-Augustin-Louis, Marquis de, Duc de Vicence. *Napoleon and His Times*. 2 vols (Philadelphia: E. L. Carey & A. Hart, 1838).

Chaboulon, Pierre Alexandre Édouard Fleury de, Baron. *Memoirs of the Private Life, Return, and Reign of Napoleon in 1815* 2 vols (London: John Murray, 1820).

Chandler, David. *Waterloo: The Hundred Days* (London: Osprey, 1980, 1987).

Chateaubriand, François Auguste René, vicomte de. *Portrait of Bonaparte; being a view of his administration. Together with An Ode to Napoleon* (New York: Eastburn, Kirk & Co., 1814).

Cubberly, Ray Ellsworth. *The Role of Fouché During the Hundred Days* (Madison: The State Historical Society of Wisconsin, 1969).

Dague, Everett Thomas. *Napoleon and the First Empire's Ministries of War and Military Administration: The Construction of a Military Bureaucracy* (Lewiston, NY: Edwin Mellen Press, 2007).

Dallas, Gregor. *The Final Act: The Roads to Waterloo* (New York: Henry Holt, 1996).

Fouché, Joseph. *The Memoirs of Joseph Fouché, Duke of Otranto, Minister of the General Police of France*. 2 vols (London: Charles Knight, 1825).

Gallaher, John G. *The Iron Marshal: A Biography of Louis N. Davout* (Carbondale and Edwardsville: Southern Illinois University Press, 1976).

Gourgaud, Gaspard, Baron General. *The Campaign of MDCCCXV; OR, A Narrative of the Military Operations which Took Place in France and Belgium During the Hundred Days* (London: James Ridgway, 1818).

Grouchy, Comte de. *Observations sur la Relation de la Campagne de 1815, Publiée par le Général Gourgaud, et Réfutation de Quelques-unes des Assertations d'Autres Écruts Relatifs à la Bataille de Waterloo*. (Paris: Chez Chaumerot, 1819).

Hofschröer, Peter. *Waterloo 1814: Wavre, Plancenoit and the Race to Paris* (Barnsley: Pen & Sword, 2006).

Hortense, Queen Consort of Louis, King of Holland. *The Memoirs of Queen Hortense*. Published by arrangement with Prince Napoleon. Edited by Jean Hanoteau. Translated by Arthur K. Griggs. 2 vols (New York: Cosmopolitan Book Corporation, 1927).

Houssaye, Henry. *The Return of Napoleon* (trans. T. C. Macaulay). Preface by Sir Fabian Ware (London: Longmans, Green and Co., 1934).

——. *1815 Waterloo* (trans. Arthur Émile Mann) (London: Adam and Charles Black, 1900).

Itinéraire de Buonaparte de l'Ile d'Elbe à l'Ile Sainte-Hélène, ou, Mémoires Pour Servir à l'Histoire de la Seconde Usurpation. Avec le Recueil des Principales Pièces Officielles de Cette Époque. Deuxième Édition considérablement augmentée. 2 vols (Paris: 1817).

Keith, Admiral Viscount George. *The Keith Papers. Selected from the Papers of Admiral Viscount Keith and Edited by Christopher Lloyd* (Aldwich: Navy Records Society, 1926 [vol. I]; 1950 [vol. II]; 1955 [vol. III]).

Kelly, W. Hyde. *The Battle of Wavre and Grouchy's Retreat*. Facsimile of the 1905 edition (Felling: Worley, 1993).

Kraehe, Enno E. *Metternich's German Policy*, vol. II: *The Congress of Vienna 1814–1815* (Princeton: Princeton University Press, 1983).

Kurtz, Harold. *The Trial of Marshal Ney* (New York: Alfred A. Knopf, 1957).

Lachouque, Henry. *The Last Days of Napoleon's Empire: From Waterloo to St. Helena* (trans. Lovett F. Edwards) (New York: Orion Press, 1967).

Las Cases, Marie Joseph Emmanuel Auguste Dieudonné, Comte de. *Memoirs of Emanuel Augustus Dieudonné Count de Las Casas [sic], Communicated by Himself. Comprising a Letter from Count de Las Casas [sic] at St. Helena to Lucien Bonaparte, Giving a Faithful Account of the Voyage of Napoleon to St. Helena, His Residence, Manner of Living, and Treatment on that Island. Also A Letter Addressed by Count de Las Casas [sic] to Lord Bathurst* (London: Henry Colburn, 1818).

——. *Mémorial de Sainte Hélène. Journal of the Private Life and Conversations of the Emperor Napoleon at Saint Helena.* 4 vols (Boston: Wells and Lilly, 1823).

Lavalette, Antoine Marie Chamant, Count. *Memoirs of Count Lavallette, Written by Himself.* 2nd edn, 2 vols (London: Henry Colburn and Richard Bentley, 1831).

Macdonald, Jacques Étienne Joseph Alexandre, duc de Tarente. *Recollections of Marshal Macdonald, Duke of Tarentum.* Edited by Camille Rousset. Translated by Stephen Louis Simeon (London: Richard Bentley and Son, 1892).

Maceroni [Macirone], Colonel Francis. *Memoirs of the Life and Adventures of Colonel Maceroni, Late Aide-de-Camp to Joachim Murat, King of Naples – Knight of the Legion of Honour, and of St. George of the Two Sicilies – Ex-General of Brigade, In the Service of the Republic of Colombia, &c., &c., &c..* 2 vols (London: John Macrone, 1838).

——, Colonel Francis. *Interesting Facts Relating to the Fall and Death of Joachim Murat, King of Naples; the Capitulation of Paris in 1815; and the Second Restoration of the Bourbons; Original letters from King Joachim to the Author; with some account of the Author and his persecution by the French Government. By Francis Macirone, Late Aide-de-Camp to King Joachim; Knight of the Order of the Two Sicilies*, 3rd edn, with additions (London: Ridgways, 1817).

Maitland, Captain Frederick Lewis. *Narrative of the Surrender of Buonaparte and of His Residence on Board H.M.S. Bellerophon; with a Detail of the Principal Events that Occurred in that Ship, Between the 24th of May and the 8th of August, 1815* (London: Henry Colburn, 1826).

Marchand, Louis-Joseph. *In Napoleon's Shadow. Being the First English Language Edition of the complete Memoirs of Louis-Joseph Marchand, Valet and Friend of The Emperor 1811–1821.* Produced by Proctor Jones. Original notes of Jean Bourguignon and Henry Lachouque. Preface by Jean Tulard (San Francisco: Proctor Jones, 1998).

Martineau, Gilbert. *Napoleon Surrenders.* Translated from the French by Frances Partridge (London: John Murray, 1971).

Masson, Frédéric. *Napoleon at St. Helena 1815–1821.* Translated by Louis B. Frewer (Oxford: Pen In Hand, 1949).

McCranie, Kevin D. *Admiral Lord Keith and the Naval War Against Napoleon* (Gainesville: University Press of Florida, 2006).

Méneval, Claude-François de, Baron. *Memoirs of Napoleon Bonaparte, the Court of the First Empire, by Baron C.-F. De Méneval, His Private Secretary.* 3 vols (New York: P. F. Collier and Son, 1910).

Metternich-Winneburg, Clemens Lothar Wenzel, Fürst von, Prince. *Memoirs of Prince Metternich 1773–1815.* Edited by Prince Richard Metternich. Papers classified and arranged by M. A. de Klinkowström. Translated by Mrs Alexander Napier. 2 vols (New York: Charles Scribner's Sons, 1880).

Montholon, Charles Jean Tristan, Marquis de. *History of the Captivity of Napoleon at St. Helena.* 4 vols (London: Henry Colburn, 1846).

Napoleon I, Emperor of the French. *Correspondance de Napoléon Ier; Publiée par ordre de l'empereur Napoléon III.* 32 vols (Paris: Imprimerie Impériale, 1858–69).

——. *Lettres Inédites de Napoléon Ier (An VIII-1815).* Published by Léon Lecestre. 2 vols (Paris: Librairie Plon, 1897).

——. *A Selection from the Letters and Despatches of the First Napoleon, with Explanatory Notes.* Compiled by Captain the Hon. D. A. Bingham. 3 vols (London: Chapman and Hall, 1884).

Pasquier, Chancellor Étienne-Denis. *A History of My Time: Memoirs of Chancellor Pasquier.* Edited by the Duc D'Audiffret, Pasquier. Translated by Charles Roche. 3 vols (London: T. Fisher Unwin, 1893 [vol. I]; 1894 [vols II and III]).

Resnick, Daniel. *The White Terror and the Political Reaction After Waterloo* (Cambridge, Mass.: Harvard University Press, 1966).

Russell, George R. *The Hundred Days: 1815* (n.p., n.d., [c. 1870]).

Saint-Denis, Louis Étienne. *Napoleon from the Tuileries to St. Helena; personal recollections of the emperor's second mameluke and valet, Louis Etienne St. Denis (known as Ali).* Translated from the French and Notes by Frank Hunter Potter. With an Introduction by Professor G. Michaut, of the Sorbonne. With maps (New York and London: Harper and Brothers, 1922).

Saunders, Edith. *Napoleon and Mademoiselle George* (New York: E. P. Dutton and Co., 1959).

Sauvigny, Guillaume de Bertier de. *The Bourbon Restoration* (trans. Lynn M. Case) (Philadelphia: University of Pennsylvania Press, 1966).

Savary, General Anne Jean Marie René (Duke of Rovigo). *Memoirs of the Duke of Rovigo (M. Savary) Written by Himself: Illustrative of the History of the Emperor Napoleon.* 4 vols (London: Henry Colburn, 1828).

Sutherland, Christine. *Marie Walewska: Napoleon's Great Love* (New York and Paris: Vendôme Press, 1979).

Talleyrand-Périgord, Charles Maurice de, Prince de Bénévent. *Memoirs of the Prince de Talleyrand.* Edited by the Duc de Broglie. Translated by Raphaël Ledos de Beaufort. With an introduction by Whitelaw Reid (New York and London: Anglo-American Publishing Company, n.d. [1896]).

——. *The Correspondence of Prince Talleyrand and King Louis XVIII During the*

Congress of Vienna (Hitherto Unpublished). From the Manuscripts preserved in the archives of the ministry of foreign affairs at Paris, with a preface, observations and notes by M. G. Pallain. Authorized American Edition with a portrait and descriptive index (New York: Charles Scribner's Sons, 1881).

Thiébault, Paul Charles François Adrien Henri Dieudonné, Baron. *The Memoirs of Baron Thiébault (Late Lieutenant-General in the French Army)* (trans. Arthur John Butler). 2 vols (New York: Macmillan, 1896).

Warden, William. *Letters Written on Board His Majesty's Ship The Northumberland, and at Saint Helena; In Which the Conduct and Conversations of Napoleon Buonaparte, and His Suite, During the Voyage, and the First Months of His Residence in That Island, Are Faithfully Described and Related* (London: published for the author by R. Ackermann, 1817).

Young, Norwood. *Napoleon in Exile: St. Helena (1815–1821).* With two coloured frontispieces and one hundred illustrations mainly from the collection of A. M. Broadley. 2 vols (Philadelphia: John C. Winston, 1915).

Index